THE ROUGH GUIDE TO

Westerns

ROUGH GUIDES

www.roughguides.com

Credits

The Rough Guide to Westerns

Editor: Ruth Tidball
Layout: Pradeep Thapliyal, Anita Singh
Picture research: Ruth Tidball
Proofreading: Susannah Wight
Production: Julia Bovis & Katherine Owers

Rough Guides Reference

Series editor: Mark Ellingham
Editors: Peter Buckley, Duncan Clark,
Matthew Milton, Ruth Tidball, Tracy Hopkins,
Joe Staines, Sean Mahoney
Director: Andrew Lockett

Publishing Information

This first edition published September 2006 by
Rough Guides Ltd, 80 Strand, London WC2R 0RL
345 Hudson St, 4th Floor, New York 10014, USA
Email: mail@roughguides.com

Distributed by the Penguin Group:
Penguin Books Ltd, 80 Strand, London WC2R 0RL
Penguin Putnam, Inc., 375 Hudson Street, NY 10014, USA
Penguin Group (Australia), 250 Camberwell Road, Camberwell,
Victoria 3124, Australia
Penguin Books Canada Ltd, 90 Eglinton Avenue East, Toronto,
Ontario, Canada M4P 2YE
Penguin Group (New Zealand), 67 Apollo Drive, Mairongi Bay,
Auckland 1310, New Zealand

Printed in Italy by LegoPrint S.p.A

Typeset in Bembo and Helvetica Neue to an original design by
Henry Iles

A catalogue record for this book is available from the British
Library

ISBN 13: 978-1-84353-649-9
ISBN 10: 1-84353-649-8

1 3 5 7 9 8 6 4 2

THE ROUGH GUIDE TO

Westerns

by
Paul Simpson

Contents

The Icons:
Western legends

The Stock Company:
Western archetypes

Western Country:
iconic locations

Way Out West:
Westerns around the world

Over The Horizon:
the wider picture

Introduction

Like Joey, I've been waiting for Shane to come back for most of my life. Actually, he did come back, in a way, in Clint Eastwood's *Pale Rider* (1985), but it wasn't the same. Clint's a phenomenally gifted filmmaker but he doesn't have George Stevens' knack of negotiating that thin line between pathos and bathos. When Joey shouts "Come back Shane! Mother wants you! I know she does!", it's still ridiculously moving on the umpteenth viewing.

Westerns move us in mysterious ways. When trying to define their appeal, I always end up quoting Robert Redford's gambler in *Havana* (1990), who, while making a fried-egg sandwich, tells Lena Olin: "I like Westerns. I don't know what they have to do with anything but I like them."

For a start, what is a Western? It's a simple question but, like most apparently easy questions, it's a trick one. Forget the geographical implications in the genre's name. A Western is usually set out West but, as John Ford showed with *Drums Along The Mohawk* (1939), a Western can happen anywhere there are frontiers to be tamed, pioneers to be celebrated and dangers to be faced. That's often been Monument Valley but, arguably, it has also been Kentucky, the Australian outback, or even the hills of Yugoslavia and the steppes of Soviet central Asia.

The Western has something to do with history. The genre is, as American historian Arthur Schlesinger noted, "America's distinctive contribution to the film" and wouldn't exist without America's distinctive history – especially that period from 1865 to 1890 when half a continent was explored, conquered, tamed and settled. That said, the greatest Westerns have so spun that history as to make it often unrecognizable.

In the beginning, the Western was as contemporary as paranoid thrillers about 9/11 are today. In 1903, the year in which the release of *Kit Carson* and *The Great Train Robbery* marked the birth of the genre, the hired killer Tom Horn was executed in Wyoming and Kid Curry, a member of the Wild Bunch, committed suicide. Pat Garrett still had five years to live before his murder.

The classic Western took the messy, awkward, violent history of the American West and turned it into a glorious, shiny, nation-unifying myth. Since the 1970s, with that history receding beyond living memory, the Western has struggled to find a formula that makes it feel contemporary, not nostalgic. The optimism that fuelled the Western – the sense that, as George Peppard says in *How The West Was Won* (1962), "there's always greener grass over the next hill" – has evaporated too – and not just in America.

It's easy to see why the Western appealed to Americans – their story is immortalized in the visual poetry of John Ford, their larger-than-life heroes are played by John Wayne, Gary Cooper and Clint Eastwood. It's harder to explain why, right from the start, the rest of the world was so interested.

For Sergio Leone, there was no mystery. "For me, the greatest screenwriter of Western films was Homer. Achilles, Ajax, Hector and the others are the archetypes of Western characters." The Argentinian writer Jorge Luis Borges echoed Leone, saying: "The epic has been saved for us, strangely enough, by the Western."

The great Westerns have always been more than the sum of their parts. You can list their essential ingredients – a lone gunfighter, revenge plots, cowboys, horses, cattle, a good girl, a bad girl (often a prostitute or a saloon girl), gunfights, an epic landscape, a hero, a villain – but not come close to explaining the stirring power of, say, that moment in *Stagecoach* (1939) when John Wayne kills three men with a carbine, while falling to the dusty street. By mythologizing its heroes, the genre created a powerful fantasy of a clear-cut world where the individual could make a difference. Filmmakers have spent thirty years whittling those heroes down to size – Clint Eastwood did a fine deconstruction job in *Unforgiven* (1992) – but they are still with us.

The genre has been spoofed, reinvented, rediscovered and declared irrelevant, yet it lives on. If a tombstone was erected every time a critic came along and declared the Western was dead, we'd fill more graveyards than the Man With No Name.

The Western has – as French critics in the *Cahiers du cinéma* crowd recognized back in the 1950s – the genius of simplicity. That simplicity meant that filmmakers could, in the guise of a shoot-'em-up, touch on all manner of themes and issues – racism, sexism, incest, homosexuality (yup, even before *Brokeback Mountain*), political intolerance, war, professionalism, existentialism – that cynics wouldn't expect to find in a genre wrongly pigeonholed as stereotypical, repetitive and conservative.

This book exists for one simple reason: to increase your enjoyment of the Western. To that end, *The Rough Guide To Westerns* shows you how the genre emerged from its historic and literary roots, explores the Western's evolution over eleven decades, introduces you to the actors, directors – and one composer – who have been the most influential and, controversially, lists fifty essential movies. I say controversially because with such a massive genre, it was no easy choice – but you will find smaller reviews of many of the 8000 or so Westerns that weren't included in that list dotted around the book.

Hopefully the book will help you discover – as I realized, watching movies again for this book – that, although the Western will always be associated with a few unforgettable images, the individual films yield surprising subtleties, unexpected depths and intriguing ambiguities. For example, there is a counter-theory that Shane didn't survive the final glorious shootout but one of the evil Ryker brothers did. True or not, the theory is plausible enough to make the film even more enjoyable. Just don't tell Joey.

Acknowledgements

Additional writing: Shaun Campbell, Angie Errigo, Helen Rodiss.
Thanks to: Simon Jamieson, Kim Newman, Jack Simpson, Lesley Simpson, Denis Turner.

Once Upon A Time In The West:
the origins

Foes and co-stars: Sitting Bull and Buffalo
Bill pose to publicize Bill's Wild West show.

Once Upon A Time In The West:

the origins

William S. Hart, the Western's greatest silent star, said "The truth of the West mattered more to me than a job." But many Western filmmakers since – including Hart himself – have preferred legends to facts.

Muddied by over a century's worth of serious myth-making, the American West's true history starts 16,000 years ago when the first humans crossed over from Siberia. The continent was later "discovered" by Europeans but, for our purposes, the history of the West should start in 1763, when the British authorities, to defuse tension with Indian tribes, decreed that white settlers in its American colony would stay east of the Appalachian mountains – a pledge ignored, after 1783, by the independent USA. By 1807, explorers had reached Colorado. In the 1840s, with a trail to Oregon established, nation-building – and

westward expansion – became, many American leaders declared, their "manifest destiny". By the 1850s, such significant states as Texas, Florida, Louisiana and California had joined the Union. The mood of unshakeable faith in the rightness of this cause is caught perfectly in John Ford's underrated trail Western *Wagon Master* (1950).

The Indians' role, historian Frederick Jackson Turner indicated in his famous 1893 thesis on the importance of the frontier in American history, was to get out of the way. In 1838, the bloody repercussions of America's mission were highlighted by the Trail of Tears, a forced relocation West

Mr Choo-Choo comes to town

East and west America were united, by railroad, in 1869, a giant step towards national unity. But the railroad owners were depicted in early Western literature as "robber barons" who fleeced "widows and orphans", built poorly made tracks across huge tracts of land donated by the government and overcharged everybody. Some railroads, notably Southern Pacific, which hired guns to get its way, were so ruthless they fuelled this evil stereotype.

In early Western movies the railroad was a nation-building, civilizing force (see **John Ford**'s *The Iron Horse*, 1924, and **Cecil B. DeMille**'s *Union Pacific*, 1939). But **Henry King**'s *Jesse James* (1939), invoking sympathy for its outlaw hero who fought the "ever-growing ogre" of the railroad, changed that. In *The Wild Bunch* (1969) **Sam Peckinpah** depicted the railroad as destroying the Old West. He was half right. The railroad made Western cities like Dallas, Los Angeles and Denver economically viable.

The Mussel Slough shootings, condemned by Frank Norris in his novel *The Octopus* (1901), obviously influenced **Sergio Leone**'s *Once Upon A Time In The West* (1968), in which "Mr Choo-Choo", the crooked railroad boss dreaming of spreading the railroad across America, dies crawling for water, in an exit a slug might consider undignified.

🎬 Union Pacific
dir Cecil B. DeMille, 1939, US, 135m, b/w

Westward ho with Cecil B. DeMille, engineer Joel McCrea and Barbara Stanwyck as the fiery postmistress with a dodgy Oirish accent! For Cecil, the first transcontinental railroad is a heartwarming, patriotic enterprise only a fool or a knave would oppose. The plot is simplistic, the story unhistoric, but the movie – like the railroad – has momentum. Best of all, DeMille knew how to wreck trains.

The Iron Horse: most railway Westerns that followed would run on similar lines to John Ford's classic.

of 15,000 Cherokee that killed 4000 of them on the journey. Turner's thesis gave an uplifting, intellectual gloss to the ruthless, brutal, if sometimes heroic, business of conquering the West.

In this period, the preconditions for the Wild West were established. Guns were perfected, the telegraph was invented and, in 1858, an overland stage route was set up. But the Civil War proved a bloody distraction. It took a certain myopic arrogance for a nation that had killed a million of its own people to portray its westward progress as a civilizing process, and the war between the states has proved difficult for Western directors. In *Escape From Fort Bravo* (1953), John Sturges alludes to it mainly to suggest that the West could bind the conflict's lingering wounds – which, after some blood-letting and outlawry, is roughly what happened.

The vast majority of Westerns are set after the Civil War ended in 1865 – when the US government's hunger for ore and waves of migrants' hunger for land and opportunity sent the cavalry and covered wagons ever further afield – and before the 1890s, when cowboys first appeared in moving pictures. The West was the place where America was being made and, in a fantasy that continues to draw thousands to Hollywood today, unsatisfactory lives could be remade.

In 1865, **Wild Bill Hickok** staged the classic Western gunfight. By the end of the 1860s, Jesse James had robbed his first bank, the transcontinental railroad had been completed and thousands of cattle were being driven along the Chisholm Trail to Kansas to be sold at significant profit. History in the making soon became show business. In the 1870s, Hickok turned actor, touring in the play *Scouts Of The Prairie*. In 1883 former scout and Indian fighter **Buffalo Bill Cody** turned showman, assembling a sensational rootin'-tootin' show that confused theatrical, historical and mythological themes to market a romanticized Wild West.

The Wild West's heroic heyday lasted less than thirty years. In 1890, the US Census Bureau declared that the frontier officially no longer existed. But it lived on in the hearts and minds of writers and filmmakers who perpetuated, expanded and reshaped the legend of the West, enhancing America's self-image of resilience, resourcefulness and courage. They were preoccupied by what was then recent history: the rise of the cattle empires, the quest for law and order, conflicts over ranges and railroads. Real mundane hardships were soon augmented by the dangers of cardsharps, claim jumpers, confidence men, quickdraw killers and wild Indians.

The American West was one of the most armed societies in history. In English law, a person had to flee a dispute that threatened to turn violent. Yet, as Ohio's top court declared in 1876, "a true man was not obligated to fly". If you met an opponent face to face, you could legitimately kill him as long as you shot from the front. But the incidence of showdowns and violent death has been greatly exaggerated – initially by those involved in the mayhem (Hickok, for example, claimed to have killed a hundred men, not seven as research suggests). Between 1870 and 1885 only 45 fatal shootings were recorded in the notorious cattle towns, including Abilene and Dodge City.

Vigilantism – citizens taking the law into their own hands – was much more common in the West than in Westerns. There were over 200 vigilante movements west of the Mississippi, often organized by capitalists, cattle kings and politicians. In Montana, over 150 people were killed in two outbreaks of vigilante justice between 1864 and 1881. In many Westerns such summary justice is portrayed as un-American, yet lynching was first used by Virginia planter **Charles Lynch** against those collaborating with the British.

The typical Western gunfight is a standalone clash between good and evil. Yet Richard Maxwell Brown, in *The Oxford History Of The American West*, argues that these disputes – certainly the career of the James gang, the OK Corral shoot-out and the Lincoln County War in which Billy the Kid died – were usually skirmishes in what he calls the Western Civil War of Incorporation. In this war, the West was opened up, initially by the forced removal of Native Americans and other minorities, and carved up by a wealthy, powerful elite, allied to the northern industrialist Republican party, that tried to force settlers off valuable land and dominate the West's economy. In 1936, William Wellman's rare socially conscious Western *Robin Hood Of El Dorado* explored this "heroic" rapacious opening up of the West.

Sometimes settlers had to be forced to see "reason" by hired guns like Hickok, **Wyatt Earp** and Walter J. Crow. In 1880, in the Wild West's deadliest civilian gunfight, Crow, hired by the Southern Pacific railroad, killed five settlers at Mussel Slough, California. This classically Marxist tale – Karl Marx followed the conflict closely from London – doesn't suit Western mythology so even though Crow killed more men in one gunfight than Hickok, the Kid or Earp, his tale remains largely untold.

In such a context, it is easy to see how outlaws like **Jesse James** and **Billy the Kid** became heroes to those who lost out as, across the West, big business took over. In the 1870s, many bestselling dime novels presented the outlaws as latter-day Robin Hoods, influencing Hollywood and the criminals themselves. In 1897, Frank James called the James gang's crimes shots in a war "between capital and labour, greed and manhood". By the end of the 1880s, however, many of the most famous outlaws had been killed in a deadly settling of accounts.

The declaration that the frontier no longer existed was made the same year, 1890, that the Indian wars ended with the 7th Cavalry's massacre of Sioux at Wounded Knee – terrible, belated, revenge for the Sioux's defeat of **General Custer** at Little Bighorn in 1876.

Art imitated life in handing Indians the worst deal from Western cinema, their tragic victimization in systematic slaughter, exile, starvation and disease twisted in countless tales of torture-loving savages repelled by the march of civilization. Ralph and Natasha Friar, in their study *The Only Good Indian*, found in Westerns filmed between 1909 and 1964 72 attacks on wagon trains (in 1860, 18 pioneers were famously killed in such a charge by Shoshone Indians), 32 attacks on stagecoaches, 45 on forts and 14 on railroads. The hardline approach to the Native American – probably reflecting real frontier attitudes – is epitomized in Charles Marquis Warren's *Arrowhead* (1953) and countered by Robert Aldrich's *Apache* (1954).

In 1901, **Butch Cassidy** and **Sundance** fled America to Bolivia – virtually official proof that the outlaw age was over. Two years later, the first Westerns were filmed. But history and genre would prove to be closer chronologically than – for all William S. Hart's good intentions – they ever were in reality.

🎬 The Robin Hood Of El Dorado
dir William Wellman, 1936, US, 86m, b/w

One of a handful of socially conscious 1930s Westerns, William Wellman's movie gives rare screen time to Joaquin Murrieta (Warner Baxter), a farmer who reacted to the death of his wife by terrorizing the land-grabbers who were displacing the Hispanic population of California so white settlers could move in. This self-important tale of lynching, prejudice and murder is that rare thing: a B Western with a fair degree of political consciousness and no happy ending.

Wagon Master
dir John Ford, 1950, US, 86m, b/w

The Mormon role in the West's exploration is often overlooked – possibly because they massacred 120 unarmed men, women and children in 1857, in a dispute with the government over the settling of Utah. But Ford was impressed by the work, dancing and faith of Mormon extras on *She Wore A Yellow Ribbon* and made this stirring wagon train movie in their honour. In a private joke, Ford cast Ward Bond, avid persecutor of Hollywood "lefties", as a Mormon elder persecuted for his religious beliefs.

Arrowhead
dir Charles Marquis Warren, 1953, US, 105m

"Apaches don't like horses, they ride 'em until they drop, kill 'em, eat 'em and steal some more", says heroic, psychotic scout Charlton Heston who strangles Jack Palance's Apache chief with his bare hands, in a denouement we are obviously supposed to applaud.

Escape From Fort Bravo
dir John Sturges, 1953, US, 98m

This tense, underrated Western is distinguished by the best use of arrows on screen since *Henry V* and let down by some dodgy studio interior shots. Ignore those and there's much to enjoy, with William Holden as the tough Army captain in charge of Confederate prisoners, embroiled in a romantic triangle with lovely Eleanor Parker and dull John Forsythe, whose thoughts turn to duty when his charges are surrounded by angry Indians.

Apache
dir Robert Aldrich, 1954, US, 87m

Apache is a brutal, intelligent, lively Western compromised by a studio-dictated happy ending. The scenes where the onrush of Western "civilization" is seen through Apache eyes are so good they overshadow the rest of the film. Burt Lancaster is in fine acrobatic form as the renegade Apache warrior who fights a one-man war against the troopers who swarm forward to kill him. John McIntire is superb as Army scout Al Sieber.

Heroes and villains

Billy the Kid

Something like fifty films have been made alleging some connection with the young Henry McCarty (1859–81), aka William Bonney, aka Billy the Kid. But that includes *Billy The Kid Vs Dracula* (1966). Most are best-forgotten B-flicks, with Billy portrayed by actors who are far too old as a nice young man who's on the wrong side of the law through some silly misunderstanding. The facts behind the adolescent hitman who achieved

notoriety during a New Mexico land dispute usually get lost – although, to be fair, historians still argue about them.

The cliché that Billy was a misunderstood kid can – just – be supported by the facts. The small bucktoothed outlaw killed first in 1877, at 18, shooting a blacksmith who had slapped him in the face. Only when **John Tunstall**, his friend, mentor and ranch boss, was killed almost before his eyes did Billy begin the spree that would make him a legend. He swore vengeance and, in

Billie the Kid, a copy from a very old tin-type.

Seventy years before James Dean mumbled his way to stardom, Henry McCarty, aka Billy the Kid, was a rebel without a cause.

the Lincoln County War, killed three, aided the killing of five more, and staged a daring jail break before being shot dead, without warning, at 22 by sheriff **Pat Garrett**. The sheriff built up his nemesis (insisting, for example, that Billy had killed 21 men), creating a myth that, by 1926, with the publication of Walter Noble Burns' *The Saga Of Billy The Kid*, had turned a character branded a vicious killer into an innocent, forced into violence by cruel fate.

Billy has been played as a martyred illiterate by Paul Newman in Arthur Penn's *The Left Handed Gun* (1958), as a conventional mixed-up good lad by Geoffrey Deuel in *Chisum* (1970), as a punk by Michael J. Pollard in the squalid *Dirty Little Billy* (1972) and as a self-indulgent revolutionary martyr by **Kris Kristofferson** in *Pat Garrett And Billy The Kid* (1973). Recent additions to the canon – Christopher Cain's *Young Guns* (1988) and Geoff Murphy's *Young Guns II: Blaze Of Glory* (1990) – stick closer to the known facts. But no movie interpretation has offered as convincing, albeit mythologized, a portrait as Michael Ondaatje's remarkable experimental novel *The Collected Works Of Billy The Kid* (1970).

The Left Handed Gun
dir Arthur Penn, 1958, US, 102m, b/w

Paul Newman makes a decent fist of Billy as a rebel without a cause, although, as the first truly childish Kid, he has some annoying moments. Further scrutiny of the photograph of William Bonney later revealed that Billy was right-handed, though left-handed may have been a euphemism for suppressed homosexuality. The intriguing aspect here is the way Billy is betrayed, finally, for failing to live up to his legend.

Dirty Little Billy
dir Stan Dragoti, 1972, US, 100m

Michael J. Pollard plays Billy as a cheeky, none-too-bright punk, who gets the shakes whenever he has a gun in his hands – a defect that might have shortened his life and diminished his fame. But this gritty, entertaining Western has satirical energy, no reverence for history and an authentically bleak, claustrophobic, manure-splattered feel.

Kit Carson

Frontier scout, Army officer, trapper and rancher Kit Carson (1809–68) was for a time, as Vardis Fisher says in his historical novel *Mountain Man*, "the most famous man of all". Stories of how many men he had killed, and women he had slept with, were retold and embellished across the frontier.

Born Christopher Houston, he became famous as the superheroic guide who helped explore the Rocky Mountains, Oregon and California in 1842. His defence of America's occupation of Los Angeles against Mexico in 1846 only fuelled the myths. As an Indian agent in New Mexico during the Civil War, he brutally persecuted the Navajo, forcing their surrender in 1864.

Carson was the first great Western icon, celebrated in biographies, fiction and dime novels from the 1840s to the 1870s, and dubbed "the greatest Indian fighter the world ever produced". Yet, when the Western matured as a movie genre, he was largely ignored. In the 1940s the actor Winifred Maurice Harrison exploited the name, appearing as Sunset "Kit" Carson in several routine oaters.

Butch Cassidy and the Sundance Kid

The afterlife of Butch Cassidy (1866–1937?) and the Sundance Kid (1867–1908) is as intriguing as their criminal career as recounted in George Roy Hill's movie. Moving as that final freeze frame is, evidence suggests that Butch – or Robert LeRoy Parker as he was born – survived that shoot-out and returned to America under an alias.

As a boy, Parker hero-worshipped a Utah ruffian called Mike Cassidy, later taking his surname – and Butch after working in a butchers – for his new identity. He robbed banks, rustled cattle and, from 1896, with a Pennsylvania gunman called Harry Longabaugh (Sundance) and the **Hole in the Wall Gang**, robbed so many trains and banks that the Pinkerton detective agency – the real-life equivalent of the super-posse in Hill's movie – started investigating. Butch, Sundance and Sundance's mistress, the Texan prostitute Etta Place, fled to South America. Bruce Chatwin recalls the legends they inspired in South America in his classic memoir *In Patagonia*.

In November 1908, Butch and Sundance fought in the famous shoot-out with Bolivian troops in the town of San Vicenze. Hill's film presents one account of that final battle, but in 1929 a sister of Robert LeRoy Parker's was paid a visit by a man called William T. Phillips who she recognized as her outlaw brother. He claimed, in his memoir *The Bandit Invincible*, that he had survived the shoot-out (though Longabaugh died), and returned to the US to run his own company. Phillips/Parker/Cassidy – if that's who he was – died in 1937.

Though their crimes inspired Edwin Porter's *The Great Train Robbery* (1903), the Western took a while to warm to this criminal duo, possibly because there is no proof Butch or Sundance ever killed anyone. It took Hill and William Goldman to see the potential of outlaws who were heroes simply because they were cooler than anyone else, didn't kill innocent bystanders and had a sense of humour.

Hole in the Wall member **Harvey Logan**, in contrast, became one of America's most wanted men after killing sheriffs in three states. In 1904, after giving up his dream of joining his old compadres in South America, he shot himself, while mortally wounded, in a gunfight with a posse in Colorado.

General Custer

General George Armstrong Custer (1839–76) would relish the historical irony that has seen him become more famous than any other US Cavalry officer. His notoriety would not dismay him – this was a man whose ego had survived finishing last in his class at West Point and being court-martialled for harshly treating his troops. He famously fought two battles that became massacres. In the first, his 7th Cavalry did the massacring – at the Battle of Washita in 1868 – and in the second they were massacred, at Little Bighorn in 1876.

That "last stand" image was enhanced in paintings – one mass-distributed by the Anheuser-Busch brewing company – ceaselessly advocated by his widow Elizabeth, and restaged in **Buffalo Bill**'s Wild West show. The image of Custer, pistols blazing until the end, is one of the most powerful in the West's iconography, even though it is pure conjecture.

Custer's bravery as an officer – fighting Confederates and Indians – was probably exceeded only by his incompetence as a military strategist. He was far more effective as a self-publicist. The power of his legend meant that he was usually a hero on film until Ford, fresh from World War II, confronted the myth by stealth in *Fort Apache* (1948), with **Henry Fonda**'s snobbish

martinet dying in a moving last stand. Other directors took note: *Two Flags West* (1950), *The Last Frontier* (1955), *Run Of The Arrow* (1957) and *The Glory Guys* (1965) all had Captain Queeg/Bligh Indian-hating officers modelled on Custer. Robert Shaw's angry, neurotic taskmaster in *Custer Of The West* (1968) looks forward to Richard Mulligan's overplayed psycho Custer in *Little Big Man* (1970).

Don't Touch The White Woman (Touche pas à la femme blanche)
dir Marco Ferreri, 1973, Fr/It, 109m

The unlikeliest movie Custer ever, Marcello Mastroianni is gloriously indulgent as the general plotting to drive the Indians off their land, while romancing Catherine Deneuve and telling his lusty Indian sidekick: "Don't touch the white woman!" This bizarre parody climaxes with a gory re-creation of Little Bighorn that feels like *Soldier Blue* done in the style of *Blazing Saddles*.

Wyatt Earp and Doc Holliday

The West's whitest hats were worn by Henry Fonda as Wyatt Earp (1848–1929) and Victor Mature as Doc Holliday (1851–87) in Ford's *My Darling Clementine* (1946) which, like many great Westerns, never let the facts ruin a great story.

Earp had, Ford insisted, told him how the OK Corral shoot-out really happened. Earp, who appeared uncredited in Douglas Fairbanks' *The Half-Breed* (1916), had soon learned that moviemakers would believe any fable he told them; it was the truth they found hard to swallow. As a man promoting his myth, Earp was hardly likely to tell Ford, for example, that he and his brothers were dubbed "the fighting pimps" by their enemies. *My*

Darling Clementine makes more sense as a World War II re-enactment – the Allies/Earps downing the Nazis/Clantons – than as a re-creation of what happened at the OK Corral.

The real story of Earp's life would have made a great, dark, *Citizen Kane*-style biopic. His first wife died of typhoid, and he later wed a laudanum addict, Mattie Blaylock, who died in the late 1880s after he abandoned her to prostitution and drugs. Wyatt started out as a horse rustler and buffalo hunter before becoming a hired gun for establishment interests but he and his brothers called themselves "sportsmen". Such sport probably included, as Frank Perry noted in *Doc* (1971), prostitution, gambling and protection. The 1881 OK Corral gunfight was not the last time Earp's life was touched by controversy. He refereed a world title boxing match in 1896 which, typically, he was accused of throwing.

Little of this infuses **John Sturges'** *Gunfight At The OK Corral* (1957), with **Burt Lancaster** as Earp and **Kirk Douglas** as Holliday, though their relationship has a homoerotic strain. Odd, too, how two prime pieces of Hollywood beefcake (Mature and Douglas) played the weedy, consumptive Holliday, their only concessions to his condition being the occasional theatrical cough into a handkerchief.

Tombstone (1993) and *Wyatt Earp* (1994) get fully stuck into the sordid details but *Tombstone* is clearer on the history (and has the finest moustaches), and **Val Kilmer**, historians say, best captures the grim cheer of Holliday who was, in real life, a mercurial, alcoholic racist.

The OK Corral

The real gunfight at the OK Corral on 26 October 1881 was a messy confrontation that lasted about 30 seconds. The truest celluloid rendering of this affair is in **George P. Cosmatos**'s *Tombstone* (1993), although historian Ben Traywick points out six major inaccuracies in the finale, including phoney confrontations between the Doc and Johnny Ringo, and Earp and Ike Clanton.

Cosmatos accurately conveys the milieu of this lawless silver town. The Earps were representing business interests who wanted Tombstone cleaned up. The biggest obstacle facing them was an anarchic confederation of outlaws, rustlers and small ranchers called "the cowboys", led by the Clantons. At stake was six million dollars' worth of silver produced by local mines every year. The Earps, as investors, didn't want that business threatened by worries about law and order.

The Earps determined, on the morning of 26 October 1881, that the town's escalating tensions must be resolved in a showdown, and they found their opponents in Fremont Street, near the OK Corral. Wyatt is reported to have told the Clantons and their allies: "You sons of bitches, you've been looking for a fight, now you can have one." Holliday almost certainly then shot – and missed – to start the gunfight. Three of the Clanton faction – the McLaury brothers and Billy Clanton – were killed. As Tom McLaury and Ike Clanton were unarmed, the killings were widely condemned. "Murder in the streets of Tombstone", said a sign in one hardware store. The Earps and Holliday were acquitted of murder but the feud continued, with Virgil Earp invalided for life, Morgan Earp assassinated and the Earps killing two more Clanton allies.

All in all, the OK Corral gunfight was a shabby, ambiguous affair that required the considerable mythmaking talents of Earp, his hagiographers and **John Ford** to become a fable about justice and heroism in the Wild West.

There's a theory that *Easy Rider* is Peter Fonda's stoned reprise of his father's most famous roles. Fonda's character, whose name is Wyatt, may, with his bordello-frequenting, drug-selling ways, be closer to the real Earp than Henry got.

🎬 Doc
dir Frank Perry, 1971, US, 96m

Sacrilegiously tampering with the story mythologized by Ford and Sturges, Frank Perry's film is a decent Western. With Stacy Keach as Doc, Faye Dunaway as his girl and Harris Yulin as Earp, the central trio don't resemble any earlier incarnation. Though there's some inappropriate soul-searching, the movie has a good feel for the West and ends with a brief, terrible, shoot-out.

Geronimo

Like the hero in a classic Western, the Apache leader Geronimo (or Goyathlay, as he's known to Native Americans) was driven to violence by revenge. His wife, children and mother were slaughtered in 1858 by Mexican troops and Geronimo (c.1829–1909) was tasked with uniting the Apaches in retaliation. He fought the Mexicans with such ferocity that, legend has it, they christened him Geronimo after the saint (Jerome) they prayed to for help against a man who fought like someone who believed the story that he was mystically immune to bullets.

Under **Cochise**, Geronimo largely kept the peace until 1876 when his community were evicted from a reservation that contained part of their homeland and moved to San Carlos Reservation in Arizona – Hell's Forty Acres as it was known. He and his followers often escaped from the reservation but, in 1886, after his band of thirty or so warriors had been pursued for months by 5000 US soldiers, he surrendered permanently.

He spent his last 23 years in curious captivity. He was taught how to be a cowboy, was invited to **Theodore Roosevelt's** inaugural and supported his family by selling autographed pictures of himself. His autobiography was published in 1907. Two years later, he died – not from a bullet, but from pneumonia.

So fearsome did Geronimo seem that he was demonized even in the 1950s. The decade started with a B Western called *I Killed Geronimo* (1950) which, to be accurate, would have had to star a disease. After that he generally played bad Injun – banging his chest, donning warpaint and generally throwing a tomahawk in the works whenever peace looked likely – to Cochise's good Injun. The portrait grew slightly subtler in Arnold Laven's flawed *Geronimo* (1962), although Chuck Connors plays the Apache legend as a macho misogynist. In structure, this anticipates Walter Hill's *Geronimo: An American Legend* (1994), the best in an unsatisfactory canon of movies about an enigmatic, charismatic hero.

🎬 Geronimo: An American Legend
dir Walter Hill, 1994, US, 115m

There's something slightly odd about the fact that Wes Studi, as the eponymous hero, gets fourth billing in a movie that purports to be a biopic of the Apache hero. In truth, Walter Hill's impressive, thoughtful film is as much about the Army's professional Indian fighters in pursuit of Geronimo as Geronimo himself. John Milius's script makes some cogent points about racism and violence on the frontier, the landscapes are beautiful and Ry Cooder's score enhances the regretful mood.

Wild Bill Hickok

It's safe to say that James Butler Hickok (1837–76) and Martha Jane Canary were not entirely accurately portrayed by Howard Keel and Doris Day in the 1953 musical *Calamity Jane*. Gary Cooper's solid, dignified interpretation in Cecil B. DeMille's 1936 epic *The Plainsman* doesn't ring true to Wild Bill's flamboyant reputation either.

Hickok was the first gunfighter to become a national icon as the "prince of pistoleers". A scout, lawman, gambler, spy, helper of fugitive slaves (as a youngster in Illinois) and gunfighter, Hickok is one of the few heroes of the West whose life almost lives up to the myth.

Fancily dressed, with brown flowing locks, piercing blue eyes and his six-guns worn with their butts thrust forward, Hickok had a striking physical presence that helped him thwart a lynch mob in Civil-War-torn Missouri. (This incident earned him his nickname when a woman in the crowd cheered: "Good for you, Wild Bill!") He won the 1865 gunfight in Springfield, Missouri, that inspired countless movie walk-downs. He once killed a man for repeatedly calling him a hermaphrodite, suffered from poor eyesight, probably the legacy of gonorrhoea, and never really liked being a lawman, especially after he accidentally killed a friend and deputy in 1871.

In his declining years – his mid-30s – he was arrested for vagrancy. Uncomfortable with his own celebrity, he never warmed to his parts in Buffalo Bill's shows. In 1876, he was mysteriously shot in the back by gambler Jack McCall who claimed he was avenging his brother – but turned out not to have one.

Bizarrely, given such fertile ground, Hickok's celluloid star has slipped. You get something like the real Hickok with Jeff Corey's cameo role as a highly strung gunslinger in *Little Big Man* (1970) and Jeff Bridges' portrayal in Walter Hill's *Wild Bill* (1995).

Wild Bill
dir Walter Hill, 1995, US, 97m

A flawed, disillusioned epic, *Wild Bill* cruelly exposes the Hickok legend and his dismal declining years. Ellen Barkin dresses down, but still looks better than contemporary accounts of Calamity Jane – once dubbed "the ugliest woman God ever abandoned to the frontier" – suggest. America didn't relish seeing a national icon as a drug-addicted, haunted, homicidal monster. Jeff Bridges is unusually expressive as Hickok but the thunderous flashbacks of gunplay that start the movie are easier to watch than the sad decline.

Jesse and Frank James

The casting of 1921's *Jesse James Under The Black Flag* gives a clue about its portrayal of the rebel guerrilla turned armed robber and multiple murderer. The main role was played by Jesse Edward James, son of the man himself.

The casting was pretty sympathetic in the first big-budget portrait, too. In Henry King's *Jesse James* (1939), **Tyrone Power** and **Henry Fonda** played Jesse (1849–92) and Frank (1843–1915) as two peaceable young Missouri farmers driven to outlawry by rapacious railroad barons. While the driving of the railway through the mid-west wasn't always conducted in accordance with best rural development policies, it's stretching the point to make this the reason for the James boys' career path. A veil is also drawn over the parts they played in the Civil War's nastiest campaign when they rode with William Quantrill's Confederate Raiders and participated in the execution of 25 unarmed Union soldiers.

With Frank and the Younger brothers, led by Cole (who had been one of Quantrill's lieutenants), they staged, in 1866, the first daylight bank robbery in peacetime America. In 1873 they diversified into robbing trains, even though Jesse had become a devout Baptist. He married his lifelong sweetheart Zee in 1874. A year later, his half-brother died – and his mother lost a hand – in a suspicious blaze at their farm, fuelling popular sympathy for the gang.

In 1881, Jesse resumed his career as a train robber, increasing the reward on his head and leading, directly, to his being shot in the back by **Bob Ford**. Yet Ford became the villain – "the dirty little coward" of the song – while James's mother sold stones from her son's grave.

This is the tale King puts such a romantic, image-defining gloss on. For a more accurate telling, see *The Great Northfield Minnesota Raid* (1971) and Walter Hill's *The Long Riders* (1980). Brad Pitt adds his name to the outlaw list in

2006 with *The Assassination Of Jesse James By The Coward Robert Ford* – proof that the James legend (which has intrigued filmmakers from Bulgaria to the Philippines) is a continual inspiration.

The Great Northfield Minnesota Raid
dir Philip Kaufman, 1971, US, 90m

The opening narration – "everywhere men from the railroads were driving poor, defenceless families from their homes" – is crude propaganda to justify the ensuing lootin' and shootin'. Robert Duvall's Jesse, a wild-eyed Bible-bashing zealot, hovering on the wrong side of sanity and desperate to continue the Civil War by any means, runs amok with Cliff Robertson's more thoughtful Cole Younger. This feels very 1970s now – the brothel seems to be populated by Playboy bunnies and the baseball sequence drags – but is an intriguing reading of a familiar story.

How the West was spun

The West wouldn't have become the Western without impresarios like Buffalo Bill and artists like Frederic Remington and Charles B. Russell.

Buffalo Bill

William F. Cody (1846–1917) did not invent the Wild West show – the first live exhibition of Western scenes was staged in 1837 – but, by making it a mass entertainment, he was the key figure in the historical West's transformation into the Western. When his show closed in 1913,

America was already gripped by nostalgia for a romanticized West that had never existed.

An army scout and hunter, Cody was only 23 when he met dime novelist **Ned Buntline** (real name: Edward Judson) and agreed to become the hero of Buntline's fiction, initially in a series called *Buffalo Bill, King Of The Border Men* and subsequently in 357 dime novels. In 1872, Buntline wrote a play called *The Scouts Of The Plains*, in which Cody starred, laying the basis for his legend and almost creating the Western. Cody's press agent John M. Burke went even further, marketing Buffalo Bill as an epic hero on a par with Kit Carson and Daniel

Sitting Bull and Buffalo Bill Cody both became legends thanks to General Custer and the Battle of Little Bighorn.

For a decade, Cody toured theatres in the winter and rode West in summer, guiding celebrities or scouting for the army. In 1876, weeks after the Little Bighorn, he took what he called "the first scalp for Custer" after a duel with an Indian. His costume for this skirmish – a Mexican suit of black velvet, slashed with scarlet and trimmed with silver buttons and lace – would influence the dress code for fancy dan Western stars to come.

In 1883 he launched his Wild West show, with which he toured for the next thirty years, involving famous Westerners like **Sitting Bull** and sharp-shooting **Annie Oakley** in his spectacles, staging Indian attacks on the Deadwood stage and incorporating such current events as the Boxer rebellion. In 1913, Cody made his first true movie, *The Indian War*, focusing on his efforts to achieve a truce in the Sioux's Ghost Dance uprising and starring General Nelson Miles. The footage, sadly, is lost.

When he died in 1917, he was globally famous as the elegant, patrician Westerner, skilled with a gun, lasso and horse. Cody's career was so varied, and epic, that it has dazzled Western filmmakers. Directors have often either used him as a flamboyant cameo or taken him largely at face value (William Wellman's *Buffalo Bill*, 1944), though *Wild Times* (1980), with Sam Elliott, conflates Cody and a gunman called Doc Carver in its intriguing tale of a sharp-shooter turned showman.

Buffalo Bill And The Indians
dir Robert Altman, 1976, US, 123m

The least entertaining, most outraged movie Robert Altman made in the 1970s, this does what William Wellman balked at in 1944: exposing Buffalo Bill as a hollow fraud. Released in America's bicentennial year, Altman's past-as-now re-creation, trampling on old national myths to question new ones, was about as welcome as a Ku Klux Klan member at a Black Power convention. A pity, because Paul Newman gives a fearless performance as Bill.

Boone and telling his client he was a legend so often that, in old age, Cody liked to say: "I stood between savagery and civilization almost all my early days."

Frederic Remington

The illustrator, sculptor, author and painter Frederic Remington (1861–1909) was as influential with images as his friend Owen Wister was with words in defining our vision of the West.

An easterner – born in New York and briefly a student at Yale School of Art – Remington headed West as a young man although, ironically, he never lived there. So obese it helped kill him – he died from complications after appendicitis – he didn't even look like a Western hero. But such paintings as *Fired On*, seen today, feel like stills from a classic Western.

Remington presented the Westerner as a stoic, independent, romantic hero, portraying cowboys, mountain men, cavalry officers and Indians in paintings that captured the American public's imagination, showing them the West as they wanted it to be.

His direct influence on the Western movie is most obvious in *She Wore A Yellow Ribbon* (1949). Ford later admitted: "I tried to copy the Remington style there, you can't copy him one hundred per cent but you can get the colour and the movement." You can also see his influence in *The Culpepper Cattle Co.* (1972), while his paintings feature in the credits of *The Last Hunt* (1955).

Frederic Remington's iconic *A Cold Morning On The Range* inspired many Western directors.

Remington's elegiac visual style imbued such regretful masterpieces as *Monte Walsh* (1970), in which some scenes look like animated Remingtons. His only rival as a painter, in the visual stylization of the West, is **Charles M. Russell** (1864–1926), who sold paintings to William S. Hart and whose rueful masterpieces, lamenting the passing of the West, inspired *Monte Walsh*'s opening titles. Both painters influenced the lighting of Arthur Penn's 1976 Western *The Missouri Breaks*, though Penn was unlikely to share their grief at the West's passing.

The literary roots

The Western novel's roots go back to the work of James Fenimore Cooper, whose frontier romances (most notably *The Last Of The Mohicans*) started rolling off the presses in 1823.

By the late 1850s, dime-novel publishers were printing millions of Western-flavoured adventure tales, with heroes increasingly loosely modelled on Cooper's Hawkeye. Deadwood Dick – a handsome young hero who was, variously, an outlaw, hunter, cowboy, Indian fighter, gambler and $5000 a year miner – later replaced Hawkeye as the prototypical hero. But, from the 1860s onwards, dime novels increasingly embellished, distorted and popularized the "exploits" of real characters like Jesse James, Buffalo Bill and Calamity Jane. From the 1880s, the heroes of these mass-market, formulaic tales were usually cowboys. Without such a shift, it would have been harder for **Owen Wister** to find an audience for his more literary tales of cowboy life.

James Fenimore Cooper

If any writer can claim to have invented the Western hero, it is James Fenimore Cooper (1789–1851) who, in his frontier romances, created Hawkeye, a white man who knows Indians so well he can virtually pass for one. This hero, loosely derived from **Daniel Boone**, is aristocratic (but not snobbish), resourceful and solitary, standing between civilization and savagery. Cooper's regret for the passing of the frontier and his proto-green appreciation of a disappearing natural way of life – as expressed in titles like *The Last Of The Mohicans* (1826) – would infuse many late-1960s Westerns. His novels, though essential Americana, have proved oddly international in their appeal, being filmed in Germany (as far back as 1912), Spain, Romania, the USSR, the UK and the USA.

The Last Of The Mohicans
dir Michael Mann, 1992, US, 112m

Forget the claims of authenticity that accompanied this movie on release – the hero is as deadly with a flintlock as Clint is with a pistol – and just enjoy the grand scale, the well-staged action sequences and Daniel Day-Lewis's performance. As Hawkeye, the big-haired frontiersman raised by the Mohicans, in love with a British officer's daughter (Madeleine Stowe) and trapped between cultures as the French, British and Indians fight, Day-Lewis exploits that sense of otherness that has usually marked him as an actor.

Zane Grey

With over a hundred Westerns derived from his works, Zane Grey is easily the most adapted writer of Western fiction. Grey (1872–1939) sold several million copies of his best-known book *Riders Of The Purple Sage* (1912) and didn't need movies to make him famous – this was just as well, as his stories rarely inspired classic movies. In the 1930s, his authorship was such a selling point that his name often appeared above the title in B Westerns. Among the best movies adapted from/inspired by his work are Fritz Lang's *Western Union* (1941), Tom Mix's *Riders Of The Purple Sage* (1925) and Henry Hathaway's *To The Last Man* (1933) and *The Thundering Herd* (1933).

Grey touched on some significant themes, condemning the slaughter of buffalo (in *The Thundering Herd*), highlighting the danger of the railroad (*The Roaring U.P. Trail*) and lamenting the plight of the Indian (*The Vanishing American*). His favourite plot device – the outlaw fighting to protect the good and finding love – would inspire **William S. Hart**.

Bret Harte

The Western fiction of Bret Harte (1836–1902), though largely forgotten now, inspired at least thirty Westerns – most filmed before 1950 – and his strong plots, sharply observed ensemble characters (covering such future Western clichés as gamblers, tarts and stagecoach drivers), and wide sentimental streak have influenced such classic Westerns as *Stagecoach* (1939).

Harte made his name with tales of the California gold camps. The oft-filmed "The Outcasts Of Poker Flat" was adapted by Ford in 1919 – the gambler looks like a rough draft of John Carradine's character in *Stagecoach* – while "The Luck Of Roaring Camp" prefigured Ford's *Three Godfathers* (1948), which prefigured *Three Men And A Baby*'s tale of forced fatherhood.

As a San Francisco man of letters, he advised one Samuel Langhorne Clemens who, as **Mark Twain**, insisted that Harte taught him how to write. As Twain virtually invented the laconic humour and tall tales that have provided comic interludes in so many Westerns, this is no small claim.

Owen Wister

A friend of Frederic Remington and Theodore Roosevelt, Owen Wister (1860–1938) shared their romanticized view of the West as a morally bracing, character-forming place where heroes like the Virginian would, as nature's aristocrats, be laconic, chivalrous, brave, yet forceful if provoked.

The Virginian (1902) made Wister a household name, pioneering serious cowboy fiction, remaking James Fenimore Cooper's prototypical hero and throwing in a shoot-out and a line he had heard out West ("When you call me that, smile") that became iconic when **Gary Cooper** said it in 1929. Sadly, Wister's novel can seem corny, flag-waving, intolerant, jingoistic, sexist and painfully slow. For all those flaws, the novel is not without power. The brave Virginian, more comfortable in the company of horses than humans, is the Western's definitive type of hero, and the author even gives us a moral code to judge these pillars of virtue by. Wister may have helped script the first movie adaptation of his most famous novel, directed by Cecil B. DeMille in 1914.

The Trail: the history of the Western

Drums Along The Mohawk (1939) was a rare venture – for the Western and for John Ford – into the prehistory of the American West.

The Trail:
the history of the
Western

The Western and the movies were made for each other. When the first cowboy rode onto the big screen, it was obvious that the horse opera – blessed with a strong narrative, an epic landscape and a heroic simplicity that harked back to ancient mythology – was here to stay. The Western has been pronounced dead many times but any genre that has given us Gary Cooper, John Ford, John Wayne, Sergio Leone and Clint Eastwood is never really going to ride off into the sunset…

The silent era

Even as it was being tamed, the West was being mythologized – in shows starring Buffalo Bill and Wild Bill Hickok, poems and songs, dime novels that sensationalized lawmen and outlaws, the paintings of Frederic Remington, and frontier stories by Mark Twain and Bret Harte.

America's infant film industry soon focused on Western stars. In 1894 **Buffalo Bill**'s troupe were filmed performing a rodeo for Thomas Edison's new Kinetoscope Parlors. The Western as a genre truly arrived with **Edwin Porter**'s *The Great Train Robbery* (1903), which in ten exciting minutes established outlaws, gunplay, fisticuffs and the galloping getaway as cinematic staples and featured, in a bit part, the first genuine celluloid cowboy star, Bronco Billy Anderson, who made over 300 Westerns. Within five years, the movie had inspired sequels, outright imitation and spoofs and made "the Western" a staple in nickelodeons throughout America.

The story of the silent Western is incomplete, obscured by myth, spin and neglect. Hundreds of pioneering horse operas – including DeMille's first adaptation of *The Squaw Man* (1913) and many films starring Tom Mix – are missing, presumed dead. Yet the silent era is, in many ways, the most fascinating part of the Western's history – a pioneering time when the classic stereotypes were being defined and when many of the outlaws and heroes that would become so central to the genre were still alive.

When Porter's movie was released, Butch Cassidy and Sundance were still robbing banks in South America, marshal Bill Tilghman was pursuing train robber Al Jennings and Wyatt Earp was prospecting for gold. By 1910, Jennings would star in his own film, *The Bank Robbery*, photographed by Tilghman. The great pioneering film directors **D. W. Griffith** and **Thomas Ince** both rose through Westerns. Griffith made *Ramona* (1910), a tragic tale of inter-racial romance with Mary Pickford as the lovelorn Indian maiden, and two wagon train dramas, *The Last Drop Of Water* and *Fighting Blood* (both 1911). Ince's *Custer's Last Fight* (1912) was a more conscientious depiction of the Little Bighorn than many later versions.

The first film studios were on the East Coast but before long film pioneers were heading West, drawn by the climate and scenery. In 1909 William Selig (producer of the Bronco Billy Anderson two-reelers) built the first motion picture studio in Los Angeles, where he launched rodeo champion **Tom Mix** as a movie star. In 1913 **Cecil B. DeMille** began filming *The Squaw Man* on location in Arizona. He found the terrain unsuitable, got back on the train and took it to the end of the line – amid orange and avocado groves, a quiet little town called Hollywood. One of the first full-length features, *The Squaw Man* was a smash. Other filmmakers followed the trail, and the rest is show-business history.

The Great Train Robbery is the first proper Western we can still watch.

Living legends like **Wyatt Earp** and erstwhile desperado Emmett Dalton found their way to California, capitalizing on their celebrity as advisors to film colony fans. Out-of-work cowboys and expert rodeo riders were in demand as stunt men and some became actors, like Mix, Buck Jones, Yakima Canutt and, decades later, Ben Johnson and Richard Farnsworth. Actor-director **William S. Hart**, a Broadway Shakespearean, made scores of successful, influential Westerns from 1914 to 1925, strictly adhering to no-frills realism out of genuine love for the real cowboys and Indians he had known and admired when wandering the West.

But Hart's down-to-earth, authentic style lost ground to action-oriented, daredevil fare like Mix's films, and to more romantic fables like Ford's first Western, the 1924 epic *The Iron Horse*, which set out themes, characters and human interest sub-plots universally recognized ever after as the Western formula.

Even at this early juncture in the genre's history, the Western was already a worldwide phenomenon. European audiences, for whom the West had a mystical glamour, were so keen that the French made their own horse operas before World War I.

Nineteen twenty-five was a vintage year for Westerns, with 227 produced. The best of them were Hart's masterly *Tumbleweeds*, the Wallace Beery vehicle *The Great Divide* (daring enough to allude to rape), Buster Keaton's spoof *Go West* – he had already sent up the genre in 1922 with *The Paleface* – and a film of Zane Grey's *Riders Of The Purple Sage*, in which Mix rode to mega-stardom. Two years later, the psychological Western – usually regarded as a 1950s invention – was born with William K. Howard's eerie bleak Western *White Gold*, a family conflict saga starring the beautiful Jetta Goudal. But the best

silent Western was Victor Sjöström's *The Wind* (1928), a harrowing, powerful movie.

The age of sound – with microphones initially confined to potted plants on indoor sound stages – was expected to kill the Western. In 1928, **Raoul Walsh** proved the doomsayers wrong with *In Old Arizona*, the first all-sound Western to feature proper locations. But the genre needed a star to replace the fading Mix and Hart. Luckily an actor called **Gary Cooper** made two Westerns in 1929: a ludicrous singing horse opera called *Wolf Song* and, far more significant, *The Virginian*, which defined his laconic image, revitalized the Western and made a mint.

The Great Train Robbery
dir Edwin Porter, 1903, US, 12m, b/w

The plot – a gang robs a train, shoots a passenger, and is pursued by sheriff and posse – provided the matrix for countless Westerns. Some incidental touches – the saloon-hall bully firing at the floor forcing someone to dance, the fight on top of the moving train – prefigured thrills to come. Well edited, with real suspense, clever panning shots and, for its time, a sophisticated narrative, Edwin Porter's smash holds up well.

Tumbleweeds
dir King Baggot, 1925, US, 78m, b/w

William S. Hart's attempt to rival *The Covered Wagon* is certainly as good and as sweeping as Cruze's epic but *Tumbleweeds* didn't salvage his stardom. A pity, because this tale of the 1889 Oklahoma land rush – in which Hart's ranch hand helps clear cattle out of the territory so farmers can move in – has real power, and a stunning land rush sequence, superior to that staged in Wesley Ruggles' Oscar-winning *Cimarron* (1931). Re-released in 1939 with Hart's impassioned, melodramatic introduction, the movie was, oddly, even more stirring.

The Wind
dir Victor Sjöström, 1928, US, 79m, b/w

The first great psychological Western, *The Wind* is dominated by an extraordinary performance by Lillian

As the Virginian, Gary Cooper defined his own image and the classic Western hero.

Gish as the fragile Virginia girl who finds Texas bleak, too windy and full of coarse men who won't take no for an answer. Driven mad by crime, guilt, the wind, and, in one unforgettable scene, an ominous white stallion, Gish holds on only because preview audiences found the original bleak conclusion too depressing.

In Old Arizona
dir Raoul Walsh, 1929, US, 63m, b/w

The first true talkie Western starred miscast Warner Baxter as the Cisco Kid, a Mexican guitar-strumming swashbuckler, in love with cheating temptress Dorothy Burgess. The phoney Mexican accents – the first of many – are hilarious but Walsh keeps the pace so frenetic you don't always notice. Baxter won an Oscar and his last line is a classic. "Her flirting days are over, she's about ready to settle down", he says of his beloved – after her death.

The 1930s

In 1930, a svelte furniture mover, under his recently acquired stage name **John Wayne**, played a buckskinned scout in Raoul Walsh's epic $2 million migration Western *The Big Trail*. The film was supposed to make him a star but recouped less than half its budget. That failure – together with lacklustre takings for De Mille's latest remake of *The Squaw Man* (1931) and the poor performance of *Cimarron*, which won the best picture Oscar in 1931 yet lost $500,000 – usually gets the blame for sinking the A Western for almost a decade. But sound – despite Walsh's example – had already proved a deterrent: in 1930, before all the bad news from the box office, Hollywood's output of major Westerns

was less than half of what it had been in the mid-1920s.

Instead, Hollywood turned to B Westerns. They were so cheap, easy to make and reliably profitable – on their limited terms – that Hollywood probably made 300 of these a year throughout the 1930s. They had their own stars – the only truly iconic figure to emerge from the mire was John Wayne – and their own staple plots. Bob Steele's films, for example, often involved him avenging his father's death by infiltrating an outlaw gang. These budget oaters reached what purists saw as a new low with

The worst Westerns

In the 1930s, the truly abysmal Western – often made by budget studios – came into its own. The most desperate attempt to inject novelty into a threadbare formula was probably Sam Newfield's notorious midget Western *Terror Of Tiny Town* (1938). But the 1930s had no monopoly on Westerns that stank, as this selection shows.

The Terror Of Tiny Town
dir Sam Newfield, 1938, US, 62m, b/w

An evil, diminutive gunslinger comes to town, a vertically challenged saloon girl is obscured by the bannister she's walking alongside, a cellist gets his bow stuck but the music keeps on flowing: these are the few highlights of a poor B Western with only one distinguishing feature – the cast are midgets.

Cowboy Commandos
dir S. Roy Luby, 1943, US, 55m, b/w

The highlight of this B Western – in which the Range Busters triumph over Nazi spies – comes when resident comic relief Slim sings "I'm Gonna Get Der Führer, Sure As Shootin'", in which he lovingly imagines spanking and lynching Hitler.

Jesse James Meets Frankenstein's Daughter
dir William Beaudine, 1966, US, 88m

Once the novelty of the juxtaposition has worn off, you feel William "One Shot" Beaudine made this in a stupor. You'll probably find yourself in a similar condition.

Shalako
dir Edward Dmytryk, 1968, US, 113m

It might seem churlish to damn any Western that finds home on the range for Sean Connery, Brigitte Bardot, Honor Blackman, Jack Hawkins, Woody Strode and Eric Sykes, but the only fun to be had in this dismal *Hombre* retread is spotting the canyon-sized holes in the plot.

Dirty Dingus Magee
dir Burt Kennedy, 1970, US, 91m

Originally, the titular villain was 19 but the casting of the then 55-year-old Frank Sinatra occasioned a hasty, hefty rewrite. One of many low points is the scene where Sinatra makes out with the chief's young daughter with the chief's blessing – an excruciating "paleface take-um Injun girl" moment.

John Ford's *Drums Along The Mohawk* is arguably the best Revolutionary War Western, though it skirts around the harsher tactics used to defeat the Indians.

Cavalry, John Ford, Henry King, Allan Dwan, George Marshall, Michael Curtiz and De Mille all made top-quality Westerns in 1939. In this annus mirablis, seven great Westerns spanned the entire genre.

Ford, with *Drums Along The Mohawk* and *Stagecoach*, stated many of the themes that would define his mythos and championed two of the Western's greatest icons – John Wayne and Monument Valley. He also perfected a gallery of stock characters that other directors would play with for years to come.

King's biopic *Jesse James* positioned the outlaw as a Robin Hood figure and proto-gangster, a shrewd move in a decade when the dirty rats had dominated the box office. (Lloyd Bacon's *The Oklahoma Kid*, starring James Cagney, tried to apply the staccato rhythms of the Warner gangster movie to the West but it wasn't as convincing or successful as King's iconic biopic.)

De Mille's *Union Pacific* revitalized the epic nation-building Western, while Curtiz's *Dodge City* (with Errol Flynn) and Dwan's *Frontier Marshal* (with Randolph Scott) were strong town-taming Westerns. In Marshall's glorious spoof *Destry Rides Again*, James Stewart rode over the horizon and Marlene Dietrich was the definitive sultry saloon girl.

the advent, in 1934, of the singing cowboy films (initially starring **Gene Autry**) and, a year later, the *Hopalong Cassidy* series.

Some decent A Westerns were made – notably Edward L. Cahn's *Law And Order* (1932), De Mille's *The Plainsman* (1937) and George Stevens' *Annie Oakley* (1935), in which Barbara Stanwyck shows real gusto as the sharpshooting gal. But by 1938, the Western was dominated by tumbleweed troubadours in lollipop costumes, creating a moronic stereotype that the genre has never quite shaken off.

Help was at hand. In a rescue mission as implausible as any mounted by the 7th

Ushering in such stars as Wayne, Stewart and Henry Fonda, and refreshing the genre, the 1930s were a prequel to the glories of the 40s and 50s.

Law And Order
dir Edward L. Cahn, 1932, US, 75m, b/w

Based on a novel by W.R. Burnett, who wrote *Little Caesar*, this successful fusion of gangster and Western mores makes no bones about the fact that enforcing law and order leads to a corral full of corpses. Walter Huston is the Earp-like lawman, "the killingest law officer who ever lived", who, true to his reputation, is the only man standing after the beautifully staged shoot-out.

The Phantom Empire
dir Otto Brower, B. Reeves Eason, 1935, US, 245m (12 episodes), b/w

In this loony sci-fi Western, Gene Autry speaks the language of the dead – a language with which, judging from the dialogue, the writers are fully conversant – runs a ranch, keeps getting kidnapped and taken underground to a civilization run by a very boring queen, and, if he doesn't return to the ranch by 2pm, his radio show will be cancelled! It's odder than it sounds.

Way Out West
dir James W. Horne, 1937, US, 65m, b/w

Best known as the film where Stan encompasses every octave known to man and budgerigar crooning "Trail Of The Lonesome Pine", this Western spoof is rich with comic genius. Laurel and Hardy ride to Brushwood Gulch to tell a girl she's inherited a goldmine but fall foul of nefarious saloon owner Mickey Finn (James Finlayson) and an irate sheriff. Some of the set pieces – like the duo's attempt to steal the goldmine's deed back – are spectacular, but the real wonder is how many laughs the two can get from a low-key soft-shoe dance routine.

Drums Along The Mohawk
dir John Ford, 1939, US, 103m

In Ford's first colour Western, the lush cinematography and scenery sometimes overshadow the story. Newlywed farmers Henry Fonda and Claudette Colbert must adjust to frontier life in a movie which shows the American people overcoming disaster and hardship through effort and common purpose much as, Ford implies, they must to defeat Fascism. Yet the optimism is qualified: the civilization the couple build will not achieve the romantic harmony between man and nature Ford prizes. The gross simplifications of Revolutionary War history don't spoil the entertainment.

Hearts Of The West (aka Hollywood Cowboy)
dir Howard Zieff, 1975, US, 102m

Howard Zieff's charming, nostalgic, eccentric comedy, inspired by the experiences of Western author Zane Grey, strikes a balance between wittily revealing the threadbare nature of B-movie production and capturing the innocent spirit of the series Western in its 1930s heyday. Jeff Bridges is engaging as the unpublished writer who becomes an extra in B Westerns, but is almost outshone by Andy Garcia as the veteran extra and Alan Arkin as the producer prone to making serious motivational speeches. This gentle comedy is more fun than the movies it pays homage to.

The 1940s

The Western made its very own epic journey in the 1940s. A decade that started out with innocent optimism ended with the Oedipal generational conflict of *Red River* (1948) and the lonely heroism of John Wayne's Nathan Brittles in *She Wore A Yellow Ribbon* (1949). Along the trail, the Western would enthusiastically discover sex (in *The Outlaw*, 1941), absorb noirish pessimism and cynicism in such dark tales as *Pursued* (1947) and, in films like *The Ox-Bow Incident* (1943), begin to question its own mythology.

Howard Hughes' critically panned *The Outlaw*, which started filming in 1940, was famously promoted by a poster with the slogan

The Ox-Bow Incident confronted vigilante justice, ushering in a new, more ambiguous, era for the Western.

"What are the two reasons for Jane Russell's rise to stardom?" positioned over her prominent cleavage. It would be too simple to say the Western lost its innocence with its virginity but in the 1940s Hollywood's West became a more cynical, psychologically complex place in which heroes were flawed, villains sympathetic and shibboleths open to question. Film noir, which dates from the start of the decade, infused the Western, shaping *The Ox-Bow Incident*, and

inspiring a respectable sub-genre of Westerns, often starring **Joel McCrea** or the young **Robert Mitchum**, which introduced gifted young directors like Jacques Tourneur and André De Toth to the Western. *The Ox-Bow Incident* is often regarded as the first "grown-up" Western because it discussed a social issue – lynching, prejudice – while telling a story, pioneering a tradition that culminated gloriously in *High Noon* (1952).

King's *Jesse James* had proved there was financial and artistic profit in blurring the black hat/white hat rigid separation of good and bad out West. A slew of outlaw-as-hero Westerns followed, immortalizing the exploits of Billy the Kid, the Dalton gang and, in a significant deviation from the macho formula, Belle Starr, glamorously played by Gene Tierney. The best of these was Fritz Lang's *The Return Of Frank James* (1940). Even the B Western wasn't immune to this trend – good old Roy Rogers was roped into the boom in *Jesse James At Bay* (1941).

When Ford returned from war duties, he made *My Darling Clementine*, mythologizing town-taming as a heroic pre-requisite of the civilizing of the frontier. Yet only two years later, in *Fort Apache*, Ford begins – initially through a soft target, an officer of Custer-like rashness – to criticize the mythology that inspired him. As Ford was, by the 1940s, the acknowledged master of the Western, that was quite a sea change.

In *Red River*, **Howard Hawks** created an epic tale that is still the definitive cattle-drive movie and proved to Ford that John Wayne could act. The revelation paved the way for Wayne's first performance of subtle greatness in *She Wore A Yellow Ribbon*. Although McCrea made more fine Westerns in the 1940s than the Duke, by decade's end it was Wayne who symbolized the genre.

Yet the box-office receipts – the evidence studios heeded but critics ignored – showed that only five Westerns made over $4 million in the 1940s and only one of them, *Red River*, was a classic Western. The two best-grossing Westerns were the scandalous *Duel In The Sun* (1946) and *The Outlaw*, followed by a comedy (*The Paleface*), a musical (*The Harvey Girls*) and then *Red River*. Hollywood was making great Westerns but they weren't always seen by a great number of moviegoers.

Robert Wise's *Blood On The Moon* was a superb noir Western that anticipated Anthony Mann's dark masterpieces of the 1950s.

The Westerner
dir William Wyler, 1940, US, 100m, b/w

Gary Cooper hated *The Westerner*, fearing he played second fiddle to Walter Brennan's venal Judge Roy Bean, but that shouldn't stop you enjoying this darkly humorous Western. Cooper saves himself from a "suspended sentence" – yep, hanging – by pretending to own a lock of hair belonging to Lillie Langtry, who Bean is obsessed by. Though the film fractures into clichés at times, Coop is at his subtle comic best, Brennan is magnificent and the shoot-out – with bullets zinging off musical instruments in a theatre – makes for an unusual finale.

Western Union
dir Fritz Lang, 1941, US, 93m

A grand entertainment – better than either of the opening-up-of-the-West epics that preceded it (*Wells Fargo*, 1937, and *Union Pacific*, 1939) – Fritz Lang's *Western Union* celebrates the westward thrust of Dean Jagger's telegraph line. The telegraph's progress has nothing to do with profit in Lang's telling, it's all about nation-building, which is why Randolph Scott, in his best pre-Boetticher role as a reformed outlaw, must sacrifice himself.

Along Came Jones
dir Stuart Heisler, 1945, US, 90m, b/w

As Melody Jones, a gunslinger who can't shoot straight but enjoys being mistaken for a killer, Gary Cooper shows that he is, as Joel McCrea says, "the greatest exponent of the manure kicker school of acting … the idea is to scuff around barnyard dirt while muttering some phrase like 'Aw shucks, Miss Nancy'". Cooper's charming self-parody – and strong support from William Demarest and Loretta Young – lift a cowboy comedy that playfully parodies the Western's conventions.

Canyon Passage
dir Jacques Tourneur, 1946, US, 92m

Jacques Tourneur's first Western feels at least a decade ahead of its time. The dialogue is hard-bitten, the pioneer town, Tourneur cleverly shows, isn't a town at all but a collection of buildings, and the action is commented on in Hoagy Carmichael's unforgettable songs. Out of an age-old premise – Susan Hayward is pledged to gambler Brian

Donlevy but really loves reliable Dana Andrews – Tourneur spins a complex story which involves murder, brutal Indian attacks and a villain (Ward Bond) who is mean to his dog.

Blood On The Moon
dir Robert Wise, 1948, US, 88m, b/w

If you can ignore the back projection shoots, this noir Western is worth the effort. Mitchum excels as the brooding drifter with a conscience, caught up in a range war. The film owes much of its considerable power to Wise's obsessive craftsmanship: his West, mostly, looks more real than that of many other directors.

Four Faces West
dir Alfred E. Green, 1948, US, 90m, b/w

In this quaint, compassionate Western, Joel McCrea is quietly effective as the bank robber whose virtue is so obvious that a nurse (McCrea's offscreen wife Francis Dee) falls for him and the suspicions of sheriff Pat Garrett (Charles Bickford) turn to sympathetic respect. Wrongly dubbed a standard B Western, this has enough twists to suggest the genre is being quietly reinvented – for example, though no bullet is fired in anger, cartridges are turned into medicine. The lack of gunplay didn't help sell tickets and may partly explain why this movie is so neglected today.

Station West
dir Sidney Lanfield, 1948, US, 80m, b/w

The seductively slinky Jane Greer is reason enough to watch this unusual tale in which Dick Powell goes undercover to find out who is behind a crime wave in a small town. Matters get a bit tangled when he falls for Greer, the outfit's notorious leader. Greer's glittering performance is truly remarkable given that Lanfield, who had wanted to cast Marlene Dietrich, subjected her to continual abuse on-set. Burl Ives plays a hotel clerk and strums the beautiful theme song.

The Beautiful Blonde From Bashful Bend
dir Preston Sturges, 1949, US, 77m

Usually dismissed as one of the great Preston Sturges' minor works, this has the freewheeling feel of the comedies of his devoted, prolific aficionados the Coen brothers. Betty

Grable is the gun-toting saloon singer who is mistaken for the new schoolteacher and generally spreads comic chaos. There is a prolonged parody of a shoot-out, an amusing turn by Cesar Romero as Grable's boyfriend, and some fine supporting characters, including Hugh Herbert's myopic dentist. Fast moving, witty, with a tad too much slapstick, this comedy Western has improved with age.

Colorado Territory
dir Raoul Walsh, 1949, US, 92m, b/w

Raoul Walsh's Westernized remake of his *High Sierra* (1941) is better than the original. Outlaw Joel McCrea and "bad" saloon gal Virginia Mayo are the doomed lovers, with Dorothy Malone the girl who represents the road McCrea hasn't taken. The movie is as bleak as the landscape; at

one point a sheriff strikes a match on the boot of a hanged man. The memorable finale – in which a bullet-ridden McCrea reaches for Mayo as they die among the rocks – makes savage mockery of Henry Hull's line earlier in the film: "The sun goes West and so does the opportunity."

The 1950s

No decade has produced as many great, near great and just very good Westerns as the 1950s, unarguably the golden age of the Western. The genre was finally taken seriously, thanks partly to the cham-

In *Broken Arrow*, James Stewart's hero discovered that Native Americans were – shock, horror – human.

pioning of French writers and filmmakers like **André Bazin** and **François Truffaut**. The masters Hawks and Ford were joined by less famous, but talented, filmmakers like Delmer Daves, Edward Dmytryk, John Sturges, Sam Fuller, Nicholas Ray and Joseph H. Lewis, and a wealth of stars

Gregory Peck brought surprising passion and desperation to his role as the doomed gunslinger in *The Gunfighter*.

– Wayne, Cooper, Stewart, Kirk Douglas, Glenn Ford and Randolph Scott – found great roles out West. Yet, like most golden ages, this glorious era contained the seeds of its own destruction.

Nineteen fifty was a year of renewal: the Native American achieved some long-overdue dignity in a Western in *Broken Arrow*; **James Stewart** and **Anthony Mann** started their famous cycle of noirish Westerns with *Winchester '73*; and Henry King made *The Gunfighter*, in which Gregory Peck's Jimmy Ringo provided the unforgettable prototype for every weary law-man and gunslinger to come.

The tradition of anguished, troubled or just darn complex heroes led from *The Gunfighter*, through *High Noon*, *Shane*, the seven Mann/Stewart Westerns, *Man Without A Star*, *The Searchers* and the Budd Boetticher/Randolph Scott films, to culminate in *Warlock*, which virtually admitted that Henry Fonda's marshal for hire was bisexual. The darkening tones are perfectly illustrated by Cooper's screen roles. After the heroics of *High Noon*, he had to defend a pack of greedy prospectors (in *Garden Of Evil*), was tempted to steal gold (*Vera Cruz*), played a reformed outlaw (*Man Of The West*), was accused of cowardice (*They Came To Cordura*) and was a washed-up drunk (*The Hanging Tree*). Almost as shocking was the injection of cynicism into the genre, which Robert Aldrich deftly managed in *Vera Cruz* (1954).

This wasn't the Western as it had been pigeonholed. But in the 1950s the genre was marked by the paranoia among filmmakers induced by **Senator Joe McCarthy**'s anti-Communist scare campaign and by the psychological insight of Sigmund Freud, whose theories supplied the dark underpinning of many a great – or over-cooked – Western in the years to come. **Nicholas Ray**'s *Johnny Guitar* (1954) stands alone as a great, over-cooked, anti-McCarthyism Freudian Western.

The traditional Western – typified by *Gunfight At The OK Corral*, *The Big Country* and *Rio Bravo* – staged a comeback in the late 1950s, often making use of the widescreen vistas of Cinemascope. The studios, which had not seen a Western really set the box office alight since **George Stevens**' great *Shane* (1953), became interested in the genre again.

The B Western finally disappeared, to be replaced by what you might call the B+ Western – A Westerns made on a smaller budget, the most glorious of which were Boetticher's Westerns with Randolph Scott – and by television. The networks made so many small-screen horse operas that the genre's stock characters and themes were soon flogged to death. Television would, however, blood **Clint Eastwood** and **Sam Peckinpah**.

As the decade closed, the Western seemed gripped by a premonition of doom. As the 1950s wore on, many titles spun off the notion of the last – *The Last Command*, *The Last Frontier*, *The Last Hunt*, *The Last Train From Gun Hill* being only the most famous – almost as if the Western was readying for its very own last stand.

Calamity Jane
dir David Butler, 1953, US, 101m

Doris Day brings such whip-crack-away zest to this cross-dressing Western musical that it seems churlish to point out that she looks about as much like the real Calamity Jane as John Wayne did. Day's buckskins and

Joe McCarthy's Westerns

High Noon (1952) is the Western that most famously squares up to Senator Joe McCarthy, the infamous Commie-basher who terrorized America – and Hollywood – in the early 1950s. The bullying demagogue's imposing bulk, weird giggle and sinister charisma would have made him a great over-the-top villain in a baroque Western like *Johnny Guitar*. But McCarthy was all too real as the dominant figure in a campaign that, from 1949 to 1954, led America on a paranoid, hysterical search for Communist traitors.

Carl Foreman wrote *High Noon* as an allegory of what happened when McCarthy – and his predecessors – came to Hollywood. Coop, alone, has the guts to confront villains who, like McCarthy, come from the east and threaten only because the federal government is so supine. *High Noon*'s success – and similar-themed Westerns like *Bad Day At Black Rock*, *Johnny Guitar* and *Silver Lode* (all 1954) – has fuelled the myth that the genre heroically confronted the forces of evil. In truth, the Western's record was as patchy as the rest of Hollywood's.

Between 1951 and 1953 Hollywood made a few juvenile pro-McCarthy Westerns – one low-budget oater was ominously entitled *Red Snow*. This cycle reached a hysterical peak with Charles Marquis Warren's *Arrowhead* (1953), in which **Charlton Heston** is the voice of "reason", surrounded by lily-livered, bleeding-heart cavalrymen, who alone sees the real threat posed by outsiders: in this case Apaches, symbolic Reds.

The controversy split the community making Westerns. **Henry Fonda**, who rowed with John Ford and John Wayne over McCarthyism, was temporarily eclipsed as a Western star. Ford and Wayne joined the Motion Picture Alliance for the Preservation of American Ideals – sadly those ideals didn't include free speech – along with Ward Bond, Clark Gable and Gary Cooper. **Nicholas Ray** extracted ironic revenge, casting Bond, the most vociferous McCarthyite, as the head of a lynch mob in *Johnny Guitar*, while **Joseph H. Lewis** went further, using Bond as the racist patriarch in *The Halliday Brand* (1957). By then, McCarthyism was a spent force, the senator had been discredited – after TV audiences decided he was creepy – and he died of booze in 1958.

prowess with a gun deter potential suitors, especially Wild Bill Hickok (Howard Keel), so she learns to dress like a lady and finds true love. Along the way, she sings some good songs – her performance of "Secret Love" is so powerful it makes this movie feel deeper than it really is – and tomboys around with enough verve to make this a classic.

Hondo
dir John Farrow, 1953, US, 84m

Louis L'Amour's favourite adaptation of his work, *Hondo* rivals *True Grit* as the best John Wayne Western not directed by Ford or Hawks. The Duke, as the nomadic half-Indian Hondo, is more natural and less invulnerable than in, say, *Rio Bravo*, and his quiet-spoken style makes his intimate scenes with Geraldine Page's settler more effective. The emotional nuances are sometimes obscured by the plot (Wayne must confront Page's no-good husband) and the stunts – this was shot in 3-D – yet, for all that, *Hondo* is a fine, surprisingly domestic, John Wayne Western.

The Man From Laramie
dir Anthony Mann, 1955, US, 101m

The final Mann/Stewart Western is a good introduction to the series, and a fitting finale for a fruitful partnership. Stewart is an officer whose mission – professional and personal – is to find the man who sold repeating rifles to the Apache, causing his brother's death. The anxiety over the Apache's rifles seems analogous to contemporary fears of the Soviet A-bomb. But Mann is more interested in his familiar themes – families imploding, his wounded nomadic ("I belong where I am") hero, the symmetry between hero and villain, the juxtaposition of men and landscape.

Run Of The Arrow
dir Sam Fuller, 1957, US, 85m

Think of this as *Dances With Wolves*, more economically told, with none of Costner's look-at-me correctness, made on a fraction of the budget. Virginia infantryman Rod Steiger, after surviving the "run of the arrow" ritual, joins the Sioux, and even finds an Indian sweetheart (Sarita Montiel). But, after complications with the US Cavalry and the Sioux's decision to skin a captured officer alive, he finally

realizes that he doesn't belong there either. After *Forty Guns*, this is the most satisfying Fuller Western.

The Big Country
dir William Wyler, 1958, US, 166m

A big theme (by Jerome Moross), big scenery (in glorious Technicolor!) and big names (Gregory Peck, Charlton Heston, Jean Simmons, Burl Ives) combine in an era when Hollywood sold its Westerns as epics, in contrast to TV's constrained oaters. William Wyler's fine, if long, movie is as much soap opera as horse opera. Peck, as probably the only Western hero to be both a retired sea captain and a pacifist, is troubled by romance (Heston has designs on Peck's fiancée Carroll Baker) and a range war.

Sheriff Of Fractured Jaw
dir Raoul Walsh, 1958, UK, 110m

Kenneth More has the conviction to carry off Raoul Walsh's conceit of sending an English toff – heir to a family firm of gunsmiths – out West where, he is told, "there's some frightful female called Jesse James and she's shooting at everyone". Understandably, More is less interested in the prospects for the family business than in beautiful Jayne Mansfield who yearns for some eastern sophistication. By the end of this odd, entertaining comedy, More has so civilized the West, he has an Indian making him tea.

Terror In A Texas Town
dir Joseph H. Lewis, 1958, US, 80m, b/w

A campy B Western – as if the title wasn't a giveaway – Joseph H. Lewis's last film is best known for its odd homage to *High Noon*, with the hero (Sterling Hayden) walking grimly towards the showdown not with a gun in his holster but a harpoon. Among other delights is an over-acting duel between Sebastian Cabot as the land-grabbing baddie and Ned Young as the gunslinger with the constantly creaking leather suit. Lewis's many intriguing compositions – note the recurring shots of trees outside the villains' houses – make up for some of the absurdities.

Ride Lonesome
dir Budd Boetticher, 1959, US, 73m

Randolph Scott is the stoic hero seeking revenge on Lee Van Cleef for killing his wife. In a risky, yet clever, twist, the arrival of the awaited villain is delayed almost to the end. Scott finally gets his vengeance – Van Cleef hangs from the same tree his wife once did – but he is ultimately alone, watching that tree burn. Budd Boetticher virtually achieves perfection here with a measured, ritualistic, assured Western that reaffirms his central conviction: that life is a game that can never be won, but must be played – alone.

The Wonderful Country
dir Robert Parrish, 1959, US, 98m

Robert Mitchum excels in this strangely neglected gem. As Martin Brady, a half-breed who crosses the border from Mexico to Texas, Mitchum must choose between the halves of his heritage. Both sides resent him, but, after witnessing the thuggery north of the border, Mitchum's hero, in an almost unprecedented decision in a Hollywood Western, drags himself and his battered sombrero to Mexico – the wonderful country. Beautifully photographed (by Floyd Crosby and Alex Phillips) and well played, Parrish's film should be better known.

The 1960s

John Sturges is not usually regarded as a pioneer but his *The Magnificent Seven* (1960) blazed the trail for the globalization of the Western. By proving that a successful Western could be made, with minimal adaptation, from a Japanese samurai movie, Sturges showed the genre could belong to anybody.

Sergio Leone would go to the same source – Akira Kurosawa's movies – and would similarly largely eschew the law-and-order Western and the traditional cowboy, taking as his heroes bounty hunters, mercenaries and gunfighters. The missing link between Sturges and Leone was provided by the German "sauerkraut" Westerns, usually based on the novels of **Karl May**, which started in 1962 and made enough money to convince Italian studio Cinecittà to produce Westerns.

With its aestheticized violence and distrust of authority, political or religious, the spaghetti Western was beautifully timed to prosper in a rebellious decade. Leone's Dollars trilogy marked the real start of the boom in 1964. In 1968, Italy made 72 Westerns – 56 more than Hollywood – and made the best Western of the year, Leone's *Once Upon A Time In The West*. Leone's revisionism was rooted in an informed, if dark, view of what the real West had been like, which may be why his movies felt more convincing, if overblown, than some revisionist exercises to come.

America reacted with scorn, incredulity and anger to what seemed, at times, like a very unexpected trade war. But by 1968, when Leone's hero Eastwood returned to star in the Leone-esque *Hang 'Em High*, American filmmakers had decided the best way to compete with the so-called spaghetti Westerns was to learn from them.

As the 1960s started, the Hollywood Western looked in rude health. Yet the old mythology was changing. Though the Duke would, by sticking to familiar ground, remain one of the top ten box-office stars throughout the 1960s, almost everyone else – even **John Ford** – was in more questioning mood. The grand celebratory Western, typified by *How The West Was Won*, looked dated even in 1962. That same year, three great Westerns – *The Man Who Shot Liberty Valance, Lonely Are The Brave* and *Ride The High Country* – were dark, sad elegies for a West that either was disappearing or had been more legend than reality. Such revisionism gave Martin Ritt's *Hud* (1963), a modern anti-Western, bitter force.

The American Western felt, as the 1960s wore on, like an increasingly nostalgic genre. **Gary Cooper** had died in 1961 and **Randolph Scott** retired the year after. The surviving age-ing heroes – Wayne, Mitchum, Stewart, Fonda – were often cast as old masters challenged to prove they could still cut it. This cycle peaked, triumphantly, with Wayne's self-parodying,

Oscar-winning turn in *True Grit* (1969). Even the younger Paul Newman and Robert Redford joined in, as the soon-to-be-obsolete heroic rogues in the mega-smash *Butch Cassidy And The Sundance Kid* (1969).

Hollywood still made fine Westerns – nota-bly Richard Brooks' *The Professionals* (1966) and Tom Griers' *Will Penny* (1968) – but often

In John Huston's melancholic Western *The Misfits*, the characters' positioning emphasized their isolation.

took out extra insurance, casting two A-list stars in the same film (*El Dorado*, *The Alamo*, *The War Wagon* and *The Way West* all tried this). The posse of comic horse operas swelled after *Cat Ballou* (1965) clicked at the box office, and encouraged other odder cross-genre experiments, notably the James O'Connolly/Ray Harryhausen dinosaur Western *Valley Of Gwangi* (1968). Yet two of the most interesting Westerns of this era – *The Shooting* and *Ride In The Whirlwind* – were produced in 1966 on little money by a maverick director called **Monte Hellman**.

Bizarrely, the old black hat/white hat simplicities did prosper east of the Iron Curtain where East Germany and Yugoslavia made Westerns which were as predictable as any routine oaters, although their heroes were often Indians or partisan fighters.

Only Peckinpah had the guts to take the Italians on, shot for shot, with *The Wild Bunch* (1969). Infused with his shocking personal vision of a violent, amoral West, the gunplay legitimized by Leone's success, it was, however, badly distributed and wasn't the box-office smash that it deserved to be. Therein lay the problem for Peckinpah and those who emulated him. Their vision of the West would not deliver audiences as reliably as lesser Westerns like John Wayne's *McLintock!* (1964).

Moving with – or slightly behind – the times, the Western became sexually, racially and criminally more explicit in the 1960s. Prostitutes no longer had to be "saloon girls", deaths were more bloodily realistic – though sometimes shot with balletic beauty – and filmmakers examined the West's racial politics in films like *Flaming Star* (1960), *Hombre* (1966) and *Tell Them Willie Boy Is Here* (1969). The genre was ahead of the curve with Vietnam.

Though Hollywood made no major anti-war picture while the conflict was running, the war was commented on, obliquely, as early as 1964 in Peckinpah's *Major Dundee*.

The Misfits
dir John Huston, 1960, US, 125m, b/w

The Misfits is a sad, troubling movie about cowboys with no place in the world, chasing "misfit" wild horses (so named because they're too small to ride) for dog food. Huston's moving film – from Arthur Miller's script – uses distance, space, the erratic movement of figures, to suggest the uneasy isolation of its central characters: Marilyn Monroe, a fragile mother superior, and the cowboys – Clark Gable, Montgomery Clift and Eli Wallach – drawn to her. Monroe is poignant, vulnerable, if not always convincing. Clift is good as the young embittered rodeo loser, while Gable's rueful masculinity may be even finer than his Rhett Butler.

One-Eyed Jacks
dir Marlon Brando, 1961, US, 141m

This is a quirky revenge Western sabotaged by being Marlon Brando's directorial debut. He and Karl Malden are bank robbers, but Brando is jailed, while Malden becomes a sheriff. Out of jail, Brando seeks revenge. The film has two climaxes. Unfortunately, only the first – when Malden whips Brando's gun hand – is memorable. But the Monterey coast, a rare backdrop for a Western, looks gorgeous, much of the dialogue is pleasingly gritty and Malden and Brando are marvellous.

Major Dundee
dir Sam Peckinpah, 1964, US, 134m

Major Dundee exists as much in aficionados' minds – as they imagine what Peckinpah envisaged – as on celluloid. It's likely that Peckinpah planned a Western *Lawrence Of Arabia*. The difference is that Charlton Heston's Major Dundee invents a war, pursuing the Apache into Mexico, partly in fear he will never get such an opportunity in the US Army. Those looking for broader meaning – there are obvious parallels with Vietnam – must face the fact that *Major Dundee* both gloats over and abhors bloodshed yet doesn't seem to give a damn about life or death.

Rio Conchos
dir Gordon Douglas, 1964, US, 107m

Westerns are often unfairly judged on the magnitude of their stars or the record of their director. Gordon Douglas's splendid, strange Western suffers on both counts – the biggest star on show is Richard Boone, while Douglas made some truly awful Westerns. Yet this baroque epic, in which Edmond O'Brien's megalomaniacal Confederate colonel continues the Civil War by arming the Apaches, and Boone, Jim Brown, Tony Franciosa and Stuart Whitman try to stop him, is energetic and inventive – and builds to an unforgettable climax.

Hombre
dir Martin Ritt, 1966, US, 111m

A classic stagecoach-as-microcosm-of-society Western in which Paul Newman's despised, alienated, tough outsider John Russell, a white man raised by Apaches, reluctantly defends the ingrates he's travelling with but is killed, trying to stop the cheating Indian agent's wife dying of thirst. For some the tragic denouement is forced, but Newman's anti-hero has no place in society and is, for all his superficial cynicism, fatally innocent.

The Professionals
dir Richard Brooks, 1966, US, 123m

The magnificent four – Burt Lancaster, Lee Marvin, Robert Ryan and Woody Strode – are hired by Ralph Bellamy to rescue his wife Claudia Cardinale who has been kidnapped by nasty Mexican revolutionary Jack Palance. So far, so John Sturges – but when the four find Cardinale, she doesn't want to return. Rousing, implausible, funny, Brooks' film decries a decline in professionalism – not just out West, but by extension in Hollywood and America – and lightly anticipates *The Wild Bunch* (1969). Oddly, given the male leads' combined star-power, Cardinale steals the movie.

100 Rifles
dir Tom Gries, 1969, US, 110m

Cherished for a shower scene which shows you more of Racquel Welch than you'll see in any other movie, *100 Rifles* was briefly controversial for an inter-racial kiss between Welch and co-star Jim Brown. As Sarita, the patron saint of oppressed Mexicans, Welch takes over the movie – even before she takes her clothes off, in a scene that really is artistically justified. Gries cheats a little, making Welch, an American icon of voluptuousness, a Mexican and having her pay for her "sin" by dying, but this is fine entertainment, made with the panache of a good Hollywood pirate movie.

The Stranger's Gundown (Django il bastardo)
dir Sergio Garrone, 1969, It, 107m

A horror Western spun off the famous *Django* franchise, this crude, yet not ineffective, tale is an obvious inspiration for Eastwood's *High Plains Drifter* (1972) and *Pale Rider* (1985), his supernatural take on *Shane*. As the mysterious stranger, Anthony Steffen walks like a man recovering from rigor mortis – appropriately, since he is a reincarnated Civil War veteran seeking revenge. In the same series, Giulio Questi's remarkable *Django, Kill* (*Se sei vivo, spara*, 1967) is even more gruesome, with murderers roasted, children shot, and human limbs scattered across the dusty street.

The 1970s

By the end of the 1970s, John Wayne, John Ford, Howard Hawks, Raoul Walsh and Henry Hathaway were all dead, Henry Fonda and James Stewart were virtually retired, Sergio Leone and Sam Peckinpah had made their last Westerns and the TV Western had ridden off into the sunset with the cancellation, in 1975, of *Gunsmoke*.

In 1973, Hollywood made only sixteen Westerns – compared with 150 in 1950. For some, the Vietnam War, so detrimental to the image of American heroism, made the genre culturally and politically obsolete. For others, the decline was a matter of decrepit stars, too much revisionism and changing tastes. Yet the action movie – especially starring an updated sheriff

Acid Westerns

The acid Western was essentially a Western you needed to be on acid to make or watch, typified by moments of profound, existential significance, a preference for mood – or message – over such reactionary concepts as plot, and a neophyte in the director's chair. For some, **Monte Hellman**'s *The Shooting* and *Ride In The Whirlwind* (both 1967) were the first acid Westerns – though they are more coherent than many that followed – but the sub-genre really took off after *Easy Rider* (1969) with Westerns like *The Hired Hand* (1971), *The Last Movie* (1971), George Englund's migraine-inducing *Zachariah* (1971), *Kid Blue* (1973) and *El Topo*. The heyday of the acid Western had passed by the mid-1970s, though the label is often applied to almost any offbeat Western.

The Hired Hand
dir Peter Fonda, 1971, US, 90m

Marred only by the usual acid Western blights of obtrusive symbolism and fuzzy camerawork, *The Hired Hand* is an atmospheric, haunting, minor classic in which nomadic hero Peter Fonda tries to buck his destiny and must, by order of the drifter's code, die. This unsettling Western, well scripted by Scottish writer Alan Sharp, is an intimate chamber piece which some consider superior to the same year's *McCabe & Mrs Miller*.

Cowboys (1971) – before his magnificent farewell with *The Shootist* (1976).

The craze for "mud-and-rags" Westerns, which aimed to show the grim reality behind old myths, replaced the genre's traditional optimism with despair in such films as *The Great Northfield Minnesota Raid* (1971), *Bad Company* (1972) and *The Culpepper Cattle Co.* (1972). But these films didn't strike much of a chord with audiences. And they weren't necessarily any more realistic than the Duke's old Westerns, but simply remade the West with different preconceptions. Writer Brian Garfield complained, rightly, that some films were so preoccupied with other movies and mythology that they lost the feel for the West that had marked so many of the greatest Westerns.

The conventional wisdom is that it was in the 1970s that the genre's death throes became painfully apparent. Yet any decade that produced Westerns of the calibre and range of *Pat Garrett And Billy The Kid*, *Little Big Man*, *Jeremiah Johnson*, *McCabe & Mrs Miller*, *Monte Walsh*, *High Plains Drifter*, *Ulzana's Raid*, *When The Legends Die*, *Soldier Blue*, *Blazing Saddles*, *El Topo* and *Heartland* must be considered one of the most fruitful in the genre's history. Nineteen seventy-six was a truly golden year, with the release of a trio of impressive American Westerns: *The Shootist*, *The Missouri Breaks* and *The Outlaw Josey Wales*. The comedy Western, after **Mel Brooks**' glorious *Blazing Saddles* (1974), fell on hard times as the genre being parodied became so unfamiliar to audiences that laughs were much harder to find.

Commercially, *Blazing Saddles* was the most successful Western of the 1970s ($45 million at the US box office), followed by Sydney Pollack's *The Electric Horseman* ($31 million). Money doesn't just talk in Hollywood: it has a way of ending conversations. By decade's end, the

like Eastwood's Dirty Harry – had usurped much of the Western's traditional domain, bringing the bad guys violently to book in a contemporary urban setting that suited an increasingly urbanized America.

As the 1970s started, the spaghetti Western was already in self-parodying decline, and the traditional Western was struggling. **John Wayne** heroically soldiered on, though his formula had begun to falter – he even died on screen in *The* money men knew that there were, in the age of *Jaws* and *Star Wars*, easier ways to make money than producing Westerns.

A Man Called Sledge
dir Vic Morrow, 1970, It, 93m

A grotesque, stylized Western which isn't quite as clever as it likes to think, Vic Morrow's tale of what gold and greed can do to a gang of outlaws (even a gang including the likes of Dennis Weaver and James Garner) is unlike any other Western. There are no heroes in this film and not much hope either. A recurring ballad about gold and greed scores the action which, at times, is hallucinatory, surreal and sexually sadistic. Garner, out of his normal range, is convincing, even when he straps a crucifix to his arm to shoot his accomplices.

Bad Company
dir Robert Benton, 1972, US, 92m

In this bitter take on the myth of Tom Sawyer and Huckleberry Finn, draft-dodger Barry Brown and roguish Jeff Bridges discover the harsh reality of a life of adventure. Robert Benton had written the script for *Bonnie And Clyde* (1967) and uses, not always successfully, some of that film's elliptical narrative style. Yet *Bad Company* grows on you, partly because it has a nice slice-of-life quality to it and partly because, unlike some revisionist Westerns, it doesn't strain too far to make its point.

J.W. Coop
dir Cliff Robertson, 1972, US, 112m

A labour of love for its director and star, *J.W. Coop* makes the rodeo so real you can almost taste the dust. Cliff

Blaxploitation

In the early 1970s, a cowed, panicky Hollywood discovered a new genre of exploitation movie: the blaxploitation action film. While **Melvin van Peebles'** *Sweet Sweetback's Baad Asssss Song* (1971) genuinely reflected the racial pride of the Black Power movement, many of the movies that followed – including the *Shaft* series – were made by whites for black audiences.

Most blaxploitation films were urban action movies, but a few were Westerns. The success of *Shaft* (1971) made it easier for **Sidney Poitier** to make *Buck And The Preacher* (1972), hailed, in its day, as the first black Western. It was nothing of the kind – that honour may belong to *A Trooper Of Troop K* (1917), an independent production recalling the exploits of the black 10th Cavalry regiment, which starred black actors and had a black director, writer and producer. Noble Johnson, who played the trooper hero, would star in 33 Westerns.

Other black independent Westerns followed. Bill Pickett, a famous black rodeo star, starred in black cowboy movies, notably *The Crimson Skull* (1921).

By the 1930s, Herb Jeffries was riding the range as a black singing cowboy in such movies as *Harlem On The Prairie* (1937). But these films adhered to the colour caste convention – villains were dark-skinned blacks, heroes and heroines were light-skinned – and had little to do with authentic black culture.

John Ford's *Sergeant Rutledge* (1960) wasn't a black Western but was a landmark in the genre's treatment of the black experience of the West, making an icon of **Woody Strode**, as the wrongly accused black sergeant. The civil rights struggle was reflected in the increasing racial and political diversity of Hollywood Westerns. By the end of the 1960s, black gridiron star **Jim Brown**, one of Hollywood's leading men, had starred in such Westerns as *100 Rifles* (1968), while Brock Peters, as a black Civil War veteran, fought vicious bigot Jack Palance in *The McMasters* (1970), a pointer to blaxploitation Westerns to come.

Moving the urban heroes of movies like *Shaft* out West smacked of desperation. Though these Westerns made money, the titles alone – *The Legend Of Nigger Charley*, *The Soul Of Nigger Charley*, *Boss Nigger* (all starring another gridiron graduate Fred Williamson)

Robertson is Coop, a rodeo rider who, out of jail, can't find his place in a cynical, commercialized world. The film does rather betray its age with its embarrassing portraits of hippie life, and there's not much plot. But Robertson has an impressive gallery of characters, economically conveys the hero's confusion after such a long absence and probably captures decaying small-town life better than Bogdanovich's *The Last Picture Show* (1971).

My Name Is Nobody (Il mio nome è nessuno)
dir Tonino Valerii, 1973, It/Fr/W. Ger, 117m

Produced by Sergio Leone, directed by Tonino Valerii, *My Name Is Nobody* metaphorically kills the Western. Henry Fonda is the gunfighter tempted into a last showdown by young Nobody (Terence Hill). Producer, director and composer Ennio Morricone send themselves – and the

Western – up beautifully. In the finale, when Fonda's gunfighter stages his death to retire, it's as if Leone, Valerii and Fonda are retiring the Western. This is Steven Spielberg's favourite Leone movie. Look out for Sam Peckinpah's name on a gravestone.

Westworld
dir Michael Crichton, 1973, US, 89m

Robotic gunfighters in a theme park malfunction in what feels, in retrospect, like Michael Crichton's first stab at the idea that would hit paydirt in *Jurassic Park* (1993). The movie's message is slightly confused – Crichton is both warning us against relying too much on technology and inviting us to marvel at it – but veteran star Yul Brynner is far more compelling and convincing as the indestructible gun-totin' android than he ever was as the King of Siam.

– betray a dull, single-minded attempt to play to the lowest common denominator. Shaft himself – **Richard Roundtree** – rode out West as a black deserter in *Charley One-Eye* (1973), only to be defeated by the script. Mario van Peebles' *Posse* (1993) does at least engage with historical reality, with its tale of black war veterans confronting racism out West.

Sergeant Rutledge
dir John Ford, 1960, US, 111m

Woody Strode almost had a nervous breakdown while being directed by John Ford on this movie. Later, though, he recognized its importance – to him and the genre – saying "You had never seen a Negro come off a mountain like John Wayne before." The movie flopped but is still powerful, if a tad static, today, a rare race-relations Hollywood Western which pulls few punches about the kind of justice a black soldier might expect on the frontier.

Buck And The Preacher
dir Sidney Poitier, 1972, US, 102m

A black reworking of *Wagon Train*, in which the Indians – not the 7th Cavalry – ride to the rescue, Sidney

Poitier's movie is virtually the only black 1970s Western that prefers experience to exploitation. The story of freed black slaves heading West after the Civil War has had scandalously little screen time in the Western and, though it is not perfect, this is a worthy, watchable, well-cast movie that redresses that omission. Harry Belafonte, as the conman preacher whose slickness turns to virtue, brings a much-needed edge to proceedings.

Posse
dir Mario van Peebles, 1993, US, 111m

You can't fault Mario van Peebles for lack of ambition. Here, he tries to reconcile black consciousness, historical reality and the Western in a flashy, hyperactive, entertaining movie that appalled many and cheered some. *Posse* is almost worth watching just to count the number of other Westerns alluded to. Van Peebles' direction doesn't always help the material, but he impresses as the leader of a magnificent six, a posse of mostly black war veterans, who take on a racist sheriff and a psychopathic colonel. The eclectic cast – which includes Woody Strode, Pam Grier, Isaac Hayes and the director's dad Melvin – adds to the fun.

Bite The Bullet
dir Richard Brooks, 1975, US, 131m

Richard Brooks' inspiring, allegorical Western about a cross-country horseback race is an obvious source for Joe Johnston's *Hidalgo* (2004). Brooks makes dazzling use of locations, especially the White Sands national monument, and handles the strong cast (Candice Bergen, Gene Hackman, James Coburn and Ben Johnson) with aplomb. Though sometimes the film pauses for too many asides, there is a lovely scene where Hackman, recounting a famous cavalry charge to Bergen, turns, admits "That wasn't the way it was at all", and tells her the real story.

The Missouri Breaks
dir Arthur Penn, 1976, US, 126m

Even if *The Missouri Breaks* stank, it would be worth watching for the acting duel between Marlon Brando and Jack Nicholson. When Brando's Mansonesque killer and master of disguise shares scenes with Jack Nicholson's amiable horse thief, the competitive thespianry is mesmerizing. At times, Arthur Penn just seems to sit back and watch. But what the film lacks in coherence, it makes up for with wit, allusion and a fresh view of frontier life. Once seen, the sight of Brando in a spinster's bonnet and pinafore by the bonfire is never forgotten.

Heartland
dir Richard Pearce, 1979, US, 96m

If Ken Loach made Westerns, they'd be like *Heartland*. Based on the memoirs of Elinore Randall Stewart, this demythologized Western is shot in docu-drama style. But its tale of pioneer rigours never becomes merely grim – though there's pain aplenty – partly because of the quality of the central performances. Rip Torn is wonderfully taciturn as the rancher who buys housekeeper Conchata Ferrell and marries her, while Ferrell brings the historical detail to life. In such a macho genre, it's a refreshing change to see a washing-line strung across the Wyoming hills.

The 1980s

As the 1980s started, the Western looked as dead as the 7th Cavalry at Little Bighorn. After watching **Michael Cimino**'s *Heaven's Gate* (1980) lose $38 million, Hollywood decided the genre was box-office poison – even though Walter Hill's *The Long Riders*, released the same year, had made $23 million on a budget of $10 million. Cimino, perfect symbol of the lunatic, pretentious, budget-busting directors who were taking over the Hollywood asylum, was due his comeuppance and, for a time, the genre sank with his folly.

In 1985, Eastwood rode to the rescue, with *Pale Rider*. A conscious attempt to restyle *Shane* (1953) for a contemporary audience, it made $60 million at the box office and, critically, marked the decisive stage in the recasting of Clint as a filmmaker of craft, intelligence and wit. The genre's modest revival was confirmed by the release, the same year, of *Silverado*, which its director Lawrence Kasdan called his "Western *Raiders Of The Lost Ark*".

In the late 1980s, the Western continued its recovery with **Christopher Cain**'s Brat Pack Western *Young Guns* (1988) and *Lonesome Dove* (1989), an award-winning TV adaptation of the **Larry McMurtry** novel which attracted 40 million viewers in the US.

A few directors had proved that not every Western was a banknote-burning exercise and, as cable TV arrived in America, the genre's massive archive was rediscovered, with nostalgic affection. Yet by now, the historical reality that underpinned the genre was too distant for almost any cinemagoer to remember. The Western had become a historical genre and that, as much as fashion, directorial excess or political correctness, meant it would never be as influential again.

Clint Eastwood rode to the Western's rescue with the box-office hit *Pale Rider*.

Heaven's Gate
dir Michael Cimino, 1980, US, 148m/219m

Some have acclaimed *Heaven's Gate*, at full length, as a lost masterpiece. Yet at nearly four hours, Cimino's confused tale of Wyoming range wars sprawls; at two and a half hours it just feels insipid. There are moments when Cimino's vision compels – notably the set-piece battle and the roller-skating scene – but these are outweighed by many moments when his failure to engage with individual characters kills the movie. Don't believe the hype – this is neither as bad nor as good as you may have heard.

The Long Riders
dir Walter Hill, 1980, US, 99m

Walter Hill's take on the James–Younger gang casts two pairs of brothers as the James and Younger siblings:

James and Stacy Keach are Jesse and Frank; David and Keith Carradine are Cole and Bob Younger. Hill seems more interested in Cole Younger as the brains behind the gang than in James Keach's Jesse, a dour, cold figure, inured to violence. Splendidly shot by Ric Waite, unobtrusively scored by Ry Cooder, *The Long Riders* is well made, more realistic than previous biopics but ultimately lacking a certain chutzpah.

Last Night At The Alamo
dir Eagle Pennell, 1984, US, 80m, b/w

One of two mid-1980s movies that made ironic reference to the heroic myth of the Alamo – the other being Louis Malle's *Alamo Bay* (1985) – Eagle Pennell's honest, low-budget movie recalls the last night of the Alamo bar in Houston. Local actor Sonny Davis is the cowboy who, despite his fantasies of becoming a Hollywood star, realizes the bar is the only thing that matters to him. Neither his desperate efforts – nor his gun – can save the place from the wrecking ball in this grimy, well-made modern Western.

Pale Rider
dir Clint Eastwood, 1985, US, 116m

Clint is the mysterious knight errant, answer to a maiden's prayer, who rides into town to save the poor and decent from robber barons who are bad for the West and – in a deliberate attempt to play to 1980s mores – bad for the environment. A mystical retread of *Shane*, *Pale Rider* isn't as compelling as the George Stevens classic. Clint's superhero preacher is so dominant – saving the town and (unlike Shane) bedding the woman (Holly Hunter) who the heroic prospector (Michael Moriarty) loves – that it unbalances the movie.

Rustlers' Rhapsody
dir Hugh Wilson, 1985, US, 88m

Funnier than John Landis's better-known *¡Three Amigos!* (1986), *Rustlers' Rhapsody* pulls off the difficult feat of spoofing a genre – the singing cowboy movie – which never took itself that seriously anyway. Tom Berenger is the cowboy crooner who uses his knowledge of genre conventions – he knows every town he rides into will have a pretty, but asexual, schoolmarm and an idealistic young newspaper editor – to his advantage. It's funny (predating the same conceit in *The Last Action Hero*) and, because Berenger has the sense to play it straight, charming.

Near Dark
dir Kathryn Bigelow, 1987, US, 94m

Indisputably the best vampire Western, *Near Dark* is genuinely scary, comic without being camp, yet lyrical in its depiction of the doomed romance between cowboy Adrian Pasdar and vampire Jenny Wright. In one great scene, Pasdar spots Wright licking an ice cream, and says, "Sure ain't met any girls like you", to which Wright replies: "No, you sure haven't." Bigelow cleverly parallels the lifestyles of the saddle tramp and the vampire, brilliantly stages the gun battles and creates moments – an undead cowboy slitting a redneck's throat with his spur – that stick in the memory.

The 1990s and beyond

After gulping at the ratings for *Lonesome Dove*, Hollywood executives decided they would finance **Kevin Costner**'s ambitious pet project. Released in 1990, *Dances With Wolves* became the first Western in almost sixty years to win the best picture Oscar, was sympathetic enough to Native Americans to be deemed politically correct and, just as crucially for an industry nervous about horse operas, made over $420 million.

The surprising return of the genre was confirmed with Eastwood's *Unforgiven* (1992), a compelling, debunking, "mud-and-rags" Western which also nabbed the best picture Oscar. Ominously, the tale of a pig farmer who reverts to his old gunslinging ways was explicitly constructed as Clint's farewell to the genre he had graced since the 1960s. But for the moment, fans who had almost starved in the great Western famine of the early 1980s didn't know where to look. In 1993 alone there was a shoot-out between two OK Corral movies – *Tombstone* and *Wyatt Earp* – a black revisionist Western (Mario Van Peebles' *Posse*), a feminist revisionist Western (*The Ballad Of Little Jo*) and Walter Hill's weighty biopic *Geronimo: An American Legend*.

John Sayles' *Lone Star* (1995) and **Jim Jarmusch's** *Dead Man* (1996) were even more satisfying, while Stephen Frears' *The Hi-Lo Country* (1998) harked back to the Freud-on-the-range sagas of old. There was a brief fad for Western heroines, with Madeleine Stowe, Andie McDowell, Mary Stuart Masterson and Drew Barrymore taking up gunslinging in *Bad Girls* (1994) and Sharon Stone starring as a Clint-ette in Sam Raimi's *The Quick And The Dead* (1995).

Though the output remains small, the 21st century has already seen three striking Westerns – *Open Range* (2003), *Brokeback*

Mountain (2005) and *The Proposition* (2005) – and more are already scheduled. The Western lives on, just.

Yet only two Westerns have made more than $200 million at the global box office: *Dances With Wolves* ($424 million) and, if you allow that it is a Western, the Antonio Banderas/Catherine Zeta Jones/Anthony Hopkins epic *The Mask Of Zorro* ($233 million). As a run-of-the-mill blockbuster can now earn $300 million

worldwide, these figures help to explain Hollywood's failure to return to the Western genre with any consistency.

Tombstone
dir George P. Cosmatos, 1993, US, 129m

A decent attempt to capture the real story of the West's most famous gunfight, *Tombstone* is unshowy, intriguing, but overlong. If there was an Oscar for authentic facial hair, *Tombstone* would have swept the nominations.

With a bullet lodged next to his heart, *Dead Man* star Johnny Depp could be forgiven the odd moment of self-pity.

The gay Western

Brokeback Mountain (2005) was christened the first gay Western so often it was tempting to believe it. In a literal sense, it is beaten to the title by **Andy Warhol**'s fetishistic Western *Lonesome Cowboys* (1968). Donna Deitch's contemporary Western romance *Desert Hearts* (1985) depicted love between two women in subtler tones than the lesbian feminist cowgirls in Gus Van Sant's *Even Cowgirls Get The Blues* (1993). Yet there is a bigger truth here – that the Western has never been quite as straight and macho as John Wayne liked to think.

In **Raoul Walsh**'s *In Old Arizona* (1932), Warner Baxter and Edmund Lowe caress each other's strategically placed guns, slyly remarking on their remarkable size. This scene was replayed, albeit toned down, in *Red River* (1948), where the homoerotic undertones peak as Montgomery Clift, then a closet gay, and John Ireland check out each other's pistols. The gun/penis metaphor is extended to its fantastically illogical conclusion in **Sam Fuller**'s *Forty Guns* (1957). The chapter of Fuller's memoirs devoted to this film is aptly entitled "Stuffed With Phalluses".

As most Westerns feature a relationship between a hero and a sidekick, a group of men doing a difficult job or a contest between hero and villain that seems motivated by more than differences over morality, you can find sub-texts under every rock and on any ranch. The young tyros in the John Wayne Westerns *Rio Bravo* (1959) and *El Dorado* (1966) are named for places – Colorado and Mississippi – a Western device often used to indicate a prostitute's territory (like Dallas in *Stagecoach*, 1939). For critic Robin Wood, James Caan's Mississippi in *El Dorado* is the virtual love interest, his character echoing Angie Dickinson's Feathers in *Rio Bravo* – they even have the same piece of trickery with cards.

Two glaring examples are *Butch Cassidy And The Sundance Kid* (1969), which Paul Newman called "a love affair between two men", and *The Far Country* (1954), in which loyal James Stewart and devoted Walter Brennan bicker like a married couple. *Warlock* (1959) is more explicit, referring to the satin sheets Anthony Quinn and Henry Fonda travel with. It's impossible to understand Quinn's character unless he had, at the bare minimum, a crush on Fonda's marshal. In the 1960s, such campery was trumped by the outrageous marauding cowboy gang with a predilection for male rape in Giulio Questi's bizarre *Django, Kill* (1967).

Cross-dressing has a fine tradition in the Western, the definitive example being *Calamity Jane* (1953) in which Jane, Wild Bill and an entertainer all wear the other sex's threads, though it's impossible to believe, given the film's antediluvian attitude to the sexes, that there's any subversive intent. This tactic was revived by Marlon Brando in *The Missouri Breaks* (1976) and Iggy Pop in *Dead Man* (1995), and was used as a strategy for survival by the heroine of *The Ballad Of Little Jo* (1993).

In such a context, the gay cowboy controversy seems forced and fallacious. The Western has always, whatever its heroes and detractors say, had some very surprising sexual undercurrents.

Kilmer's Doc Holliday is so good, it reminds you that Kurt Russell's Wyatt Earp isn't really that good at all. Cosmatos suggests that the Earps probably were, just, preferable to the Clantons and stages the OK Corral shoot-out brilliantly, replacing clichéd images of the classic gunfight with something far messier, more realistic and less heroic.

 Dead Man
dir Jim Jarmusch, 1995, US/Ger, 120m, b/w

Johnny Depp, Jim Jarmusch and Neil Young may be strangers to the celluloid range but they combine beautifully in this bizarre, quirky, mystical Western. Depp is sublime as the clerk called William Blake who gets a sentimental education out West, is pursued by bounty hunters and is mistaken for his namesake, the English poet. Jarmusch's trademark deadpan humour is as sharp as ever but the looser structure makes this feel a few degrees warmer than some of his other efforts. Young's electric guitar score is just one of the things about *Dead Man* that will haunt you.

Open Range
dir Kevin Costner, 2003, US, 139m

Open Range is a tough, muscular, satisfying Western that tries to return the genre to the heroic mode of John Ford, Anthony Mann and John Sturges. Robert Duvall gives one of his finest performances as a trail boss who, with pal Kevin Costner, is provoked into taking a stand by the brutal bluster of Michael Gambon's Irish cattle baron – we know Gambon is evil because he uses barbed wire. The script has the odd bad line, and Costner's fatal flaw – sentimentality – intrudes occasionally, but this is an outstanding Western.

Brokeback Mountain
dir Ang Lee, 2005, US, 134m

In what has been hailed as the first gay Western, Heath Ledger and Jake Gyllenhaal magnificently convey the pain of suppressed love. The coupling that intrigues Ang Lee is of souls, not limbs. Adapted by Larry McMurtry from an Annie Proulx story, the film is not without political implications – the central locations, Texas and Wyoming, are the home states of the president and vice-president – but working-class life is viewed sympathetically from afar, rather than intrinsically understood. John Wayne might not have approved but, if he'd seen it, he might have had the guts to admit it is a good Western.

Opposite: George Roy Hill's *Butch Cassidy And The Sundance Kid* (1969) is the perfect example of the radical chic Western.

The Canon: 50 classic Westerns

The Top Ten Westerns

1 Shane
1953; see p.117
Consciously mythic, *Shane* satisfies on a visceral level with thrilling juxtapositions, superb characterization and, in Alan Ladd, the ultimate ethereal, but deadly, hero.

2 Once Upon A Time In The West
1968; see p.101
This is Leone's meisterwork: with a sensational use of landscape and score, masterly storytelling, textbook pacing of thrills throughout the movie, and a triumphant use of Henry Fonda and Claudia Cardinale.

3 The Searchers
1956; see p.114
Ford and Wayne are at the top of their game in this powerful, disturbing Western that doesn't try to settle every internal contradiction.

4 Pat Garrett And Billy The Kid
1973; see p.107
Magnificent, incoherent, elegiac, Peckinpah's take on the West's greatest legend is surprisingly historically authentic and incredibly moving.

5 Johnny Guitar
1954; see p.81
A surreal Western packed with allegory, metaphor, symbolism and unforgettable imagery, *Johnny Guitar* is the ultimate feminist Western.

6 Warlock
1959; see p.142
A clever deconstruction of the Earp/OK Corral myth, full of subtexts (political and sexual), in which Fonda is at his subtle, ambiguous best.

7 The Outlaw Josey Wales
1976; see p.104
Clint's warm, entertaining, violent post-Vietnam Western eschews revenge for reconciliation as a bunch of misfits reintegrate the cold-blooded hero into society.

8 Red River
1949; see p.111
The Western *Mutiny On The Bounty*, featuring the greatest cattle drive ever, Oedipal allusions and towering performances from the Duke and Montgomery Clift.

9 Bad Day At Black Rock
1954; see p.52
This intelligent anti-McCarthy Western defies the genre's customary monosyllabism with some classic lines and a cast – especially Spencer Tracy and Robert Ryan – to match.

10 The Tall T
1957; see p.129
A miniaturist masterpiece, economically told and played, from a filmmaker, Boetticher, and a star, Randolph Scott, who are still seriously underrated.

The Canon:
50 classic Westerns

With over 8000 Westerns to choose from, selecting 50 that are essential to the genre is an arduous task, doomed to provoke incredulity and debate about inclusions and omissions. This list of Westerns tries to show as many facets of the genre as possible and include only movies of a certain quality that the author can wholeheartedly recommend.

To that end, this list does not include *Rio Bravo* – although *El Dorado* is recommended, with an explanation of why, in the author's opinion, it is a better film – or *Gunfight At The OK Corral*, a famous Western that did much to boost the genre with Hollywood studios but doesn't live up to its fame when you watch it. If it wasn't for the quality of thespianry on display from Burt Lancaster, Kirk Douglas, Rhonda Fleming and Jo Van Fleet the film would be flatter still. Director John Sturges may have been dissatisfied with it – he returned to the story with *Hour Of The Gun* (1967), a less well-known but more satisfying take on the saga.

So what about the puzzling inclusion of *Heller In Pink Tights*? George Cukor's Western is vastly underrated – though French critics were quick to appreciate it – partly because it belongs to an unfashionable microgenre (the showbiz Western), was directed by a filmmaker associated with "women's films" and features none of the genre's traditional screen icons. Yet for all that, it is an entertaining Western that repays reviewing, as Louis L'Amour, who wrote the story the movie is based on, recognized. And L'Amour, whether you read his books or not, knew a thing or two about Westerns.

Bad Day At Black Rock

dir **John Sturges, 1954, US, 81m**
cast **Spencer Tracy, Robert Ryan, Anne Francis, Walter Brennan, Lee Marvin, Ernest Borgnine, Dean Jagger**
cin **William C. Mellor** *m* **André Previn**

The first major Hollywood movie to highlight the unjust treatment of Japanese-Americans in World War II, John Sturges' *Bad Day At Black Rock* is a movie about integrity, racism and, allegorically, the McCarthy era's persecution of suspected Communists. It is also one of the finest anti-Westerns ever made.

Spencer Tracy, who had the rare ability to be virtuous, but not sanctimonious, brings all his hard-won moral authority to the role of John Macreedy. Arriving in Bad Rock to deliver a medal to Komoko, the father of a Japanese-American GI who saved his life, he inadvertently exposes the town's shameful secret.

Macreedy, assuring the conductor that he'll only stay in Black Rock 24 hours, is told, prophetically, "In a place like this, it could be a lifetime." Before he can leave, Macreedy must confront the good (the doc, **Walter Brennan**, who tells him: "I feel for you, but I'm consumed with apathy"), the bad (**Robert Ryan, Lee Marvin** and **Ernest Borgnine**) and the lovely (**Anne Francis** who betrays him and pays with her life).

Investigations by Ryan's private eye find no proof that the one-armed Macreedy, who wears a black business suit and looks like an FBI agent, exists, suggesting that he is no ordinary mortal but an agent of a higher – divine? – justice. At first, Tracy does what any reasonable person would do when he realizes that most of the townsfolk want to kill him: he tries to escape. Foiled, he discovers that Komoko was murdered in a burst of frenzied, post-Pearl Harbor patriotism and, on Ryan's part, greedy resentment. Reluctantly, Tracy faces Ryan in an ingenious twist on the classic Western showdown.

Bad Day At Black Rock paints its characters, for the most part, in the black and white of cheap melodrama. But somehow it doesn't matter. Tracy, Ryan, Marvin and Brennan make their characters more substantial and credible than the script, adapted from Howard Breslin's story *Bad Day At Hondo*, allows. The dialogue has the urgent cynicism of film noir but then this is a classic noir work, albeit superbly photographed in brilliant, menacing, sunlight by William C. Mellor. The film's one serious flaw is André Previn's score, so intrusive it seems to be trying to seize control of the narrative.

The film's anti-McCarthyism is less striking, today, than its attitude to the West. The movie is often compared to *High Noon* but in Sturges' film the train brings not outlaws, but a hero – the town has enough outlaws of its own – and the sheriff isn't scared, yet grimly heroic, just scared. The citizens of Bad Rock don't drive cattle, but call themselves cowboys. Ryan says suspicion of strangers is a hangover from the Old West, to which Tracy replies sardonically: "I thought the tradition of the Old West was hospitality."

Tracy's hero has symbolically come from the East and, upright in his black suit, contrasts with the bad, tired, xenophobic, macho West personified by Ryan in his debased Western gear. *Bad Day At Black Rock* doesn't so much revise the Western as question the whole mythos of the American West.

The Beguiled

dir Don Siegel, 1970, US, 105m
cast Clint Eastwood, Geraldine Page, Elizabeth Hartman, Jo Ann Harris, Darleen Carr
cin Bruce Surtees *m* Lalo Schifrin

Until 1970, **Clint Eastwood** shared one certainty with John Wayne: he never died in his movies. That taboo was broken in *The*

Beguiled, a haunting Gothic Western, as much Carson McCullers as John Ford, that took less than $1 million at the US box office and might have been retitled *The Reviled* after the initial response from critics.

The Beguiled was Eastwood's idea. He had fallen in love with Thomas Cullinan's novel, about a wounded Civil War deserter taking refuge in a Southern ladies' seminary, and persuaded **Don Siegel** to direct.

Eastwood shows real range in this, though he wasn't perfect casting as the deserter who uses sex to beguile the women and ensure his safety from Confederate troops. He later said, rightly, "It might have done better if I hadn't been in it." His fans, cherishing the powerful, violent, invulnerable persona the actor had perfected in Leone's Westerns, didn't want to see Clint as a loser, symbolically castrated – he has his leg amputated in one especially excruciating scene – and poisoned to death. Clint's image was so one-dimensional in 1970 that other moviegoers who might have enjoyed what one critic called "a rarefied slice of Southern gothic" didn't watch either. Perhaps the original plan to cast Jeanne Moreau in Geraldine Page's role as the headmistress whose tortured psyche drives events might have helped broaden the film's appeal.

Beautifully shot by **Bruce Surtees**, directed with impressive control and a fine sense of place by Siegel, *The Beguiled* is an unusual blend of mystery, horror and sensuality which never becomes farcical or implausible. The movie does reinforce the stereotype of sexually repressed Southern belles, which may explain why some, notably Judith Crist, found it morose and misogynist. But the film, as shaped by star and director (who both bravely refused efforts to soften the ending), does imply that the fate of Eastwood's crass, insensitive gigolo is not entirely undeserved.

For Eastwood, the "failure" would make him more cautious as a director and an actor but, alongside *The Outlaw Josey Wales*, this is, by some measure, his best post-Leone Western before *Unforgiven*. A rare, great, horror Western, *The Beguiled* can trace its ancestry back to such works as John Ford's *Seven Women* and McCullers' *Reflections In A Golden Eye* while its descendants include *Play Misty For Eye* (and so, therefore, *Fatal Attraction*) and *The Draughtsman's Contract*.

Blazing Saddles

dir **Mel Brooks, 1974, US, 93m**
cast **Cleavon Little, Gene Wilder, Madeline Kahn, Mel Brooks, Slim Pickens, Harvey Korman**
cin **Joseph Biroc** *m* **Mel Brooks, John Morris**

Has Mel Brooks ever heard a joke he didn't like? On the evidence of this comedy Western – which, in an absurd Brooksian twist, became the fourth most profitable Western of all time on its release – the answer must be no.

Corrupt attorney general Hedley Lamarr (Harvey Korman) sends **Cleavon Little** as a black sheriff to Rock Ridge, which is being terrorized by his hired thugs, as he schemes to force the citizens off their land. But Little, backed by alcoholic gunslinger **Gene Wilder** ("I've killed more men than Cecil B. DeMille"), foils the bad guys, and tames their moronic monster Mongo so that sheriff and reformed outlaw can ultimately ride off to "nowhere special" together.

To some critics, notably Kim Newman, this is a "party drunk of a movie" that outstays its welcome. If you're looking for the kind of qualities that are praised in film school – like structure, visual style or subtlety of characterization – *Blazing Saddles* isn't the comedy, Western, or comedy Western for you. But it's hard not to warm to the movie's nothing-succeeds-like-excess shtick, as the gags come quicker than arrows at the battle of Little Bighorn.

There are enough moments of sheer comic genius – the black

Cleavon Little and Gene Wilder: a rare black/Jewish partnership in a genre dominated by white, Anglo-Saxon, protestant men.

workers singing an a capella "I Get A Kick Out Of You"; **Madeline Kahn**'s songs, rhyming habits and rabbit, as she spoofs Marlene Dietrich; Slim Pickens' dopey henchman; the endless cries of "nigger!" from the townsfolk – to disguise the misfires. Brooks knows his Westerns – **John Wayne** loved the script – never lets the pace drop and, with the Frankie Laine title song, created a parody so finely judged that it surpasses many theme songs that were meant to be taken seriously.

Brooks had one very large slice of luck. Gig Young, hired to play the alcoholic gunfighter partly because he really was an alcoholic, was too drunk to continue in the role so Wilder stepped in. As Philip French notes, Wilder's persona, as the complete antithesis of the traditional Western hero, encouraged Brooks to make his film partly a Jewish Western, even appearing as a Jewish governor out West and a Yiddish-speaking Native American chief. The Jewish jokes don't always work – they don't all miss either – but they reduce the dependence on the initial comic premise of a black American who accidentally becomes a sheriff out West, and Wilder's presence gives the film an unusual flavour. The other lucky aspect of Wilder's arrival was that he made Brooks promise to film *Young Frankenstein* (1974).

The recent DVD release features a rambling interview in which Brooks discusses the panic the use of the word "nigger" and the notorious beans-around-the-campfire scene spread among studio executives. Cowboys had never farted on screen before. Truly, as Brooks says, *Blazing Saddles* "broke ground – and broke wind".

Butch Cassidy And The Sundance Kid

dir **George Roy Hill, 1969, US, 110m**
cast **Paul Newman, Robert Redford, Katharine Ross, Strother Martin, Henry Jones**
cin **Conrad Hall** *m* **Burt Bacharach**

Too charming and commercially successful for its own good, *Butch Cassidy And The Sundance Kid* infuriates many with its anachronistic

A timeless freeze: Paul Newman and Robert Redford go out all guns blazing in George Roy Hill's deceptively sad Western.

humour, the sugary soft-focus pop-video interlude and its tacit refusal to admit that it is, erm, actually a Western. For all that, George Roy Hill's movie still works, as a whimsical revision of the genre, as a classic buddy movie prefiguring such blockbusters as *Thelma And Louise* (1991), as an exercise in what Tom Wolfe called radical chic, and as pure entertainment. Don't be deceived by the gloss, the easy chemistry between **Paul Newman** and **Robert Redford**, or the gags in William Goldman's too-witty-for-some script: this is, at heart, a very sad movie.

In real life Butch Cassidy was almost the genial criminal mastermind of Newman's portrayal. He ran the Hole in the Wall Gang, robbing banks with little unnecessary violence, and mediating between the human race and his pal Sundance, a volatile killer known to shoot up saloons when drunk or stressed. Redford's Sundance is no maniac, but he is menacing, with the most ambiguous smile since the Mona Lisa's, quicker with his gun than with his wits.

Roy Hill's movie doesn't dwell on their glorious criminal heyday, speeding through some entertaining gunplay, a knee in the groin for a gang member who challenges Butch and the arrival of Sundance's girl Etta (**Katharine Ross**). Newman insisted the girl was largely irrelevant – that the film is "a love affair between two men" – but her arrival is the cue for the cute singalong of "Raindrops Keep Falling On My Head", a last dollop of sweet sentiment before the mood sours.

The strange return of the Hole in the Wall Gang

In the 1970s, a group of liberation socialists and anarchists in Britain, involved in planting bombs at the homes of leading establishment figures, signed a communiqué to the media, justifying their deeds, as "Butch Cassidy and the Sundance Kid". They signed a later statement "The Wild Bunch".

These pseudonyms were soon superseded, as a group called **The Angry Brigade** – which may or may not have been the same people – upped the ante, mounting attacks in retaliation for the Conservative government's industrial relations laws. The Angry Brigade famously stood trial in 1972, although the case was one of the more inglorious episodes in British legal history. And the communiqués – and attacks – disappeared thereafter.

In his fine memoir *Granny Made Me An Anarchist*, Stuart Christie, who was acquitted at the Angry Brigades trial, recalls being interviewed by two senior detectives. While side-stepping their line of questioning, Christie's response suggests why the group might have chosen those pseudonyms. Asked, "What do the names Butch Cassidy and the Sundance Kid and The Wild Bunch mean to you?", he replied: "Great films, all about honour and redemption and friendship – and sticking it to the bad guys."

Robbing a train on its way west and on the return journey seems an inspired idea, providing some hilarious moments, but, after their second robbery, as the gang catch the banknotes fluttering through the air, a super posse emerges to begin a grim pursuit of Butch and Sundance. The chase, punctuated by the query "Who are those guys?", is too protracted for some but from hereon in, the stars' charisma and Goldman's jokes merely serve to make the inevitable tragedy bearable.

Escape to Bolivia doesn't work – Etta leaves, preferring not to watch them die – and Butch and Sundance are soon surrounded by an army almost as large as that which besieged John Wayne's Alamo. The film's serious gunplay is reserved for its romantic, thrilling and brutal penultimate scene before the heroes perish to become myths in the famous freeze frame. Before Butch and Sundance go ad-libbing to their doom they highlight some of the tale's bitter ironies, Butch declaring: "If he just paid me what he's paying them to stop me robbing him, I'd stop robbing him."

Borrowing from many movies – notably *The Wild Bunch*, *Jules Et Jim* and *Bonnie And Clyde* – *Butch Cassidy And The Sundance Kid* doesn't, as a film, have quite as much personality as its stars or script. But Newman and Redford, playing off each other beautifully, are at their most watchable as the charmingly flawed heroes rendered obsolete by big business and technology – as symbolized by the train from which their nemeses emerge.

Dances With Wolves

dir **Kevin Costner, 1990, US, 180m**
cast **Kevin Costner, Mary McDonnell, Graham Greene, Rodney A. Grant, Floyd "Red Crow" Westerman, Tantoo Cardinal, Robert Pastorelli, Charles Rockett**
cin **Dean Semler** *m* **John Barry**

Epic, moving, long, romantic, historically suspect, simplistic, yet engrossing, **Kevin Costner's** *Dances With Wolves* could be the most remarkable directorial debut since *Citizen Kane* (1941). Spiralling costs led to this being dubbed "Kevin's Gate" before release but, unlike Michael Cimino, Costner swept the Oscars and the box office.

As the movie opens, Lieutenant John Dunbar (Costner) tries to kill himself, leading a suicidal charge against Confederate troops. Decorated, rather than decapitated, he asks to be posted to the frontier, to see it before it is gone, and is sent to isolated Dakota where he plays Robinson Crusoe before making contact with the Native Americans. He prefers the saintly Sioux to the perfidious Pawnee, acquires his own name, Dances With Wolves, and is encouraged in his wooing of Stands With a Fist (**Mary McDonnell**), a white woman raised by the Sioux.

The movie's reputation peaked as it swept the Oscars. As Costner's stock has plummeted since, *Dances With Wolves* has come under sustained attack for being boring and historically ignorant and for making its white characters – Costner excepted – as one-dimensionally bad as Indians in a B Western.

Despite some humanizing touches, the Sioux are almost too noble, dignified, eloquent, environmentally sensitive, spiritually rich

Kevin Costner's lieutenant has a Robinson Crusoe meets Man Friday moment in *Dances With Wolves*.

and virtuous. To be fair, the director's cut on the DVD gives a more complex picture, showing Costner alienated after a Sioux massacre in a scene cut from the commercial release. The Pawnee, however, are shown as obsessed with slaughtering the Sioux which, as they were in reality outnumbered 25 to 1, would have been suicidal.

Yet *Dances With Wolves* is better than that. Historical accuracy has never determined the quality of a Western and the film is at heart a sentimental fantasy about the kind of interaction which seldom occurred on the frontier. The scene where Costner meets the Sioux on a prairie and tries to pantomime a buffalo is one of many where the right detail makes his epic story involving. The love story with McDonnell is conducted almost entirely through glances. And the ambushes, hunts and pitched battles are all dynamically handled.

Dances With Wolves is an elusive film. For Clint Eastwood, it was "an admirable project, with stunning visuals, but kind of a contemporary guy out West who was interested in ecology and women's rights and Indian rights". Even Philip French changed his mind about its quality three times in three viewings. If you ignore some of the simplicities – and catch the director's cut – it is an impressive Western.

Destry Rides Again

dir **George Marshall, 1939, US, 94m, b/w**

cast **James Stewart, Marlene Dietrich, Brian Donlevy, Charles Winninger, Una Merkel**

cin **Hal Mohr** *m* **Frank Skinner, Frederick Hollander, Frank Loesser**

Did *Destry Rides Again* really inject sex into the Western? Quite possibly. The Hays Office refused permission for saloon singer **Marlene Dietrich** to say, after stuffing some dollar bills into her cleavage, "There's gold in them there hills." The killjoys.

The chemistry between Dietrich and **James Stewart**, as pacifist sheriff Tom Destry, is not that surprising, given that their offscreen affair was so intense that Dietrich had to have an abortion. Producer Joe Pasternak was disappointed – he had cast Dietrich, in an atypical role, partly in the hope that she would show her gratitude

The name game

If you're in any doubt as to the moral status of a female character in a Western, just check out her name. Pure WASP princesses, schoolmarms and mums are often demurely dubbed Lucy or Virginia. Loose women – even if they redeem themselves – will be called something much more exotic like Frenchie, Dallas (*Stagecoach*, 1939), Vienna (*Johnny Guitar*, 1954), Lacey (in the John Wayne B Western *In Old California*, 1942) or Feathers (*Rio Bravo*, 1959). In *My Darling Clementine* (1946), the contrast is at its most pointed: the schoolteacher is Clementine, while the poor saloon girl is named Chihuahua, after a small, irritating breed of dog.

Sex in the Western

The history of sex in the Western has been traced back variously to Jane Russell lying on a pile of straw in *The Outlaw* (1941) and Marlene Dietrich's sultry vamp in *Destry Rides Again*. Devoted, as it is, to a period and place where women were rare, the Western hasn't generally put the sin into scintillating. Here are three landmarks – of different kinds – in the sexual evolution of the Western.

 The Outlaw
dir Howard Hughes, 1941, US, 116m, b/w

Apart from two obvious points of interest – Jane Russell's cleavage – this strange Western is a historical curio, notable for, in Kim Newman's fine phrase, "makeshift direction, variable acting, and the kind of bad decisions that come from three years in an editing suite with a mad genius and seventy tons of film". This odd

retelling of the Billy the Kid legend made Jane Russell a star, possibly because Jack Beutel, as Billy, is less macho than she is.

 Wild Gals Of The Naked West
dir Russ Meyer, 1962, US, 65m

This hyper-stylized, cartoonish, Russ Meyer saga only goes to prove you need more than breasts to carry a sexploitation Western. You'll probably be praying for the saloon doors to swing shut before the 65 minutes is up.

 Lonesome Cowboys
dir Andy Warhol, 1968, US, 110m

Warhol treats us to a marginalized transvestite sheriff, much female sexual humiliation, male bodies lovingly photographed, a bit of gay banter and some fun with Western myths. The only true note here is the hustling of Warhol's self-styled superstars, trying to impress their director/guru.

physically – while Dietrich's ex-lover, German novelist Erich Maria Remarque, watched on set from the sidelines.

Out of such tensions emerged a movie that, despite some longueurs, proved triumphantly that women in the Western weren't doomed to play respectable wives and mothers. Dietrich used the sexuality she had shown in *The Blue Angel* (1930), lightened it and created a stereotype so powerful that it became her trademark.

In her memoirs, Dietrich characterized Stewart as perfecting "the 'whatever happened to the other shoe' style of acting", an unfair, if insightful, remark that describes some of his apparently effortless – but in reality carefully crafted – displays of American folksiness to come and even occasionally applies to his Destry. His sheriff is mostly one of his subtler characterizations. It can't be easy playing a lawman who rides into town carrying a canary and a parasol, and orders a glass of milk at the Last Chance Saloon. His villainous opponent, **Brian Donlevy**, wants to take over the town – and retain his grip on Dietrich – and is constantly trying to provoke Destry into a gunfight. Eventually, Destry has to set aside pacifism for a final reckoning in which Dietrich, as the bad girl, makes the supreme sacrifice and fatally stops a bullet intended for the hero.

Stewart does enough to prevent *Destry Rides Again* becoming a Dietrich star vehicle, though it's a close run thing, especially when she sings "The Boys In The Back Room" and fights with **Una Merkel**, a combat fought for real on set until Dietrich was drenched with water. So compelling was this spectacle that it was re-enacted by Shelley Winters and Marie Windsor in *Frenchie* (1951), a routine Western knock-off based on Dietrich's character, and Mari Blanchard and Mary Wickes in *Destry* (1955).

The critics hated the film – even Graham Greene found it "rather tired" – possibly perplexed by the mix of action, satire and music, but it was a surprise box office smash. *Destry Rides Again* helped define the onscreen persona of one of the Western's most enduring stars and perfected a stereotype – the sultry saloon singer – which the genre's directors would never tire of.

Duel In The Sun

dir **King Vidor (and six uncredited directors, including Josef von Sternberg), 1946, US, 138m (129m in TV version)**
cast Jennifer Jones, Gregory Peck, Joseph Cotten, Lionel Barrymore, Lillian Gish
cin Lee Garmes, Ray Rennahan, Hal Rosson *m* Dimitri Tiomkin

David O. Selznick's fascinating, uneven, overblown, ambitious epic is the work of a mad genius haunted by the fear that he'd never make another smash as big as *Gone With The Wind*. The producer's grandiose vision created – and stymied – an epic romance, cooked in the Arizona sun, shot in vivid Technicolor, with a cast of 2500 and only 2443 fewer directors.

Selznick's future wife Jennifer Jones is a beautiful half-breed who, after her father's execution, moves in with distant, wealthy relatives. Disapproved of by crusty old patriarch Lionel Barrymore, she falls for both his sons: virtuous Joseph Cotten and abusive, bad, Gregory Peck. The plot thickens but never quite coheres. The story's psychological complexity is undermined by some cheap lines ("I'm trash I tell ya – trash" cries the doomed heroine) and Selznick's commitment to squeezing in as much sex and violence as the censors would stand. Yet somehow the movie survives all this to, for the most part, entertain.

Some sneered that the film should be entitled "Lust In The Dust" (and indeed a poor spoof made many years later took that name). The movie ended, controversially, with Jones and Peck shooting each other but snatching one last lip-lock. Peck has a fine old time as the villain. Jones is gorgeous but looks more nervous, an understandable reaction given Selznick's obsession with the contribution her breasts would make to the movie. Best of all, Lillian Gish quietly steals every scene from her on-screen husband Barrymore.

A movie censor in Memphis wrote to Selznick to say that the picture "contains all the iniquities of the foulest human dross". He wasn't entirely wrong. Four-year-old **Martin Scorsese**, who saw it with his mother, couldn't watch by the end – "it was all so frightening, Dimitri Tiomkin's music made it seem almost like a horror film". He has since declared the movie ahead of its time.

Duel In The Sun is as much of a personal vision as, say, Peckinpah's *Pat Garrett And Billy The Kid*. It's just that, in this case, the movie is the vision of a memo-spewing producer. Selznick, coaxing King Vidor into the director's chair, had described the film as "an intimate story of people". Inevitably, though, it swelled to become something grander. Vidor, assisted mainly by Josef von Sternberg, does his best to make it work. Most of the time he succeeds. There's still no other Western quite like this.

El Dorado

dir Howard Hawks, 1966, US, 126m
cast John Wayne, Robert Mitchum, James Caan, Edward Asner, Charlene Holt
cin Harold Rosson *m* Nelson Riddle

Howard Hawks gave us three versions of his take on the trio Western – the heroic Wayne united with a broken down lawman and a green, brave kid. Despite the formidable reputation of *Rio Bravo* (see box), *El Dorado* is the best of the bunch.

Wayne is a gunman hired by land baron Bart Jason (Asner) to get rid of a small rancher. But when he arrives in town to find that the local sheriff is his old buddy **Robert Mitchum**, he turns down the job and helps his drunk, dishevelled old mate take on Jason and his hired baddies with the help of **James Caan**, a youngster who is keen but so bad a shot that he has to carry a shotgun not a pistol.

Made at a smarter pace than *Rio Bravo* – shaving fifteen minutes off the running time – *El Dorado* is less self-important and much better cast. *Rio Bravo*'s Dean Martin is entertaining, but not especially credible, as the regenerated alcoholic lawman, more at ease

The most overrated Western: *Rio Bravo*

In 1959, **Howard Hawks** made a Western called *Rio Bravo* which he, the critics and cinema audiences liked so much that he made it twice more: as *El Dorado* (1966) and *Rio Lobo* (1970).

The formula was deceptively simple. In a favourite Hawksian conceit, three men are obliged to do a difficult, dangerous job. The most upright of the three is played by **John Wayne**, the second man is a derelict hero who uses the dangerous mission to rebuild his life, while the third is an attractive bit of eye candy, a young greenhorn, essentially brave and decent, but a little raw and in need of some fatherly tuition from the Duke. In *Rio Bravo*, the trio take on an army of gunmen intent on springing their murderous pal from jail.

The film's reputation has grown to such an extent that many critics – notably Herb Fagen and Robin Wood – have acclaimed it as the classic Hawksian Western and one of the best Westerns ever made. But it leaves a vocal minority – Wayne's biographer Garry Wills, Western writer Brian Garfield, and this author – distinctly underwhelmed. Neither the backdrop – epic vistas eschewed for claustrophobic town shots – nor the story – Wayne and his allies are maintaining the West, not conquering it, a more limited mission – are on a par with his *Red River*. The film seems too slack, too hackneyed, too monotonous – enlivened mainly by the repartee between Wayne and **Angie Dickinson**'s Feathers – and the story too slight to justify 141 minutes of anyone's time. Many critics have made persuasive arguments about the film's inner subtleties, but you should be able to enjoy a Western without having to bone up on film theory.

with a glass than a gun. Mitchum, as the "tin star with a drunk pinned on it", is much more convincing and a more effective counter to Wayne. Ricky Nelson's acting as the neophyte in *Rio Bravo* is so bad that it interrupts the story, while Caan is watchable and likeable.

Though *El Dorado* is often labelled as *Rio Bravo* played for laughs, that doesn't do it justice. There is plenty of comedy here, including a scene where Hawks has a pot shot at **François Truffaut**, when Mitchum shoots the piano, rather than the player, but the movie never degenerates into a simple put-on.

The movie touches on many of Hawks's pet themes – male solidarity, professionalism, acceptance of others' faults – but it is built on a smaller scale than either *Red River* or *Rio Bravo* and is all the better for it. For a Western, an unusual amount of the action in *El Dorado* takes place at night and, underpinning the comedy, there is a sense that the valley of death is not too far away for these characters – or, for that matter, for Wayne, Hawks and the Western.

El Dorado has some appealingly vulnerable heroes – even Wayne's gunman has a bullet lodged near his spine that causes occasional paralysis – and the movie is imbued with an emotional complexity, a quiet thoughtfulness, a contemplation of autumnal years to come, that makes it genuinely moving.

The Good, The Bad And The Ugly (Il buono, il brutto, il cattivo)

dir Sergio Leone, 1966, It, 180m
cast Clint Eastwood, Lee Van Cleef, Eli Wallach, Aldo Giuffrè, Mario Brega
cin Tonino Delli Colli *m* Ennio Morricone

The Good, The Bad And The Ugly could have been completely different. Luckily, **James Coburn** and **Charles Bronson** rejected

The good – Clint – and the ugly – Eli Wallach – put a noose to good use in Leone's masterpiece.

the $15,000 Italian director Sergio Leone could pay a lead for his first Western, so he chose *Rawhide* hunk **Clint Eastwood**, who, dubious but ambitious, accepted. The two embarked on a stylish, innovative adventure, Eastwood contributing and paring down his own spare dialogue, **Ennio Morricone** composing the florid, anthemic music and Leone patenting a genre known as the spaghetti Western. Drawing on his encyclopaedic knowledge of the Western, Leone created a cynical, mocking European vision of the West's seamy underbelly in three films known as the "Dollars" trilogy after the first two in the series: *A Fistful Of Dollars* (1964, see p.170) and *For A Few Dollars More* (1965, see p.251). The films are also known as the "Man With No Name" trilogy, even though Clint's hero is variously known as Blondie, Manco and Joe throughout the movies.

The people's choice

This list, as compiled by the Internet Movie Database, is based on average member ratings (out of ten) for films that have received more than 1000 ratings. The formula, inevitably, slightly favours more recent movies and, judging by the results, the voters are more impressed by Sergio Leone than John Ford. Bearing those caveats in mind, this is a reasonable snapshot of public opinion among online movie aficionados.

1 *The Good, The Bad And The Ugly* (1966)

2 *Once Upon A Time In The West* (1968)

3 *The Treasure Of The Sierra Madre* (1948)

4 *High Noon* (1952)

5 *The Ox-Bow Incident* (1943)

6 *Butch Cassidy And The Sundance Kid* (1969)

7 *Unforgiven* (1992)

8 *For A Few Dollars More* (1965)

9 *The Wild Bunch* (1969)

10 *The Man Who Shot Liberty Valance* (1962)

Source: www.imdb.com, 2006.

The Good, The Bad And The Ugly is the most famous of the trilogy, thanks in part to Morricone's superb theme – a chart smash for Hugo Montenegro – and the long, dialogue-free, opening scene. It is also the most flamboyant and the funniest of the three. In it, Leone looks askance at the American Civil War – to the consternation of Orson Welles who told the director that the historical subject matter would certainly sink his picture – while Eastwood regularly captures and frees Eli Wallach's outlaw to collect the bounty on him. Both get caught up in a search for stolen Confederate gold, also coveted by another opportunist in Lee Van Cleef, culminating in a hypnotic, hysterically protracted face-off in a cemetery. In the increasingly operatic context of Leone's films, Wallach's villainy is glorious, not overblown, his volubility the perfect contrast to Eastwood's laconic "hero".

Leone swings between brutality and absurdity, between extreme close-ups of the actors' sweat-beaded eyes and painterly wide-screen landscapes – he studied the work of Civil War photographer Matthew Brady before shooting this – while relishing the ignoble and glorifying the double-cross.

At the same time, with his usual pedantry, he ensured that the historical details, especially the Confederate uniforms, were as accurate as he could make them. The Civil War scenes, almost a movie within the movie, are ambitious and knowing – the captain's remark that the drunkest officer wins the battle is an obvious allusion to **Ulysses S. Grant**'s boozing sessions before hostilities commenced.

At various times, Leone surprises the viewer by his rule that the ability to see is limited by the sides of the frame. What the camera cannot see, the characters cannot see, a simple conceit which helps him spring many of his surprises. Leone's fund of ideas is so great that you scarcely notice the shortage of plot. But then, this is not a film about plot, it is a celebration of bold gestures, that flirts with parody, achieves a dream-like tone at times, yet never fails to entertain or intrigue. As influenced by Chaplin's *Monsieur Verdoux* (1947) as by any single Western, Leone's third spaghetti Western was originally intended to be his last.

The Gunfighter

dir **Henry King, 1950, US, 84m, b/w**
cast **Gregory Peck, Helen Westcott, Millard Mitchell, Jean Parker, Karl Malden, Skip Homeier**
cin **Arthur Miller** *m* **Alfred Newman, Dimitri Tiomkin**

Spyros P. Skouras, head of production at 20th Century Fox, was so incensed by **Gregory Peck**'s facial hair in *The Gunfighter* that when the movie stalled at the box office he told Peck: "That moustache cost us millions."

It may have also cost *The Gunfighter* the critical acclaim it deserved – the initial reviews were mixed. **Henry King**'s masterpiece was long neglected, yet William Everson, in his *Pictorial History Of The Western*, preferred this to *High Noon* (1952), saying "*The Gunfighter* creates such a mood of inexorable Greek tragedy that no matter how many times one sees it, one is always hoping subconsciously for that accidental change that will lead to a happy ending."

The film's original director **André De Toth** was inspired by the tale of an obscure member of the Clanton gang called Johnny Ringo. This intriguing minor villain was a violent, Shakespeare-quoting gunfighter, possibly a ruined Southern aristocrat, who was killed by a man who gave him no chance to draw and then bragged he had killed Jimmy Ringo. When De Toth and Fox differed over how to film this life, King stepped in.

Peck, imaginatively cast as Ringo, portrays him as a celebrity, sick of recognition, knowing he can't escape, ultimately doomed by his peculiar fame. The saloon, where most of the action is set, is his stage and he paces across it, waiting to meet his estranged wife and son, with a sense of barely suppressed violent energy that is, from an actor who can be as wooden as Peck, something of a revelation.

One saloon customer Ringo has a drink with is a young rancher who, with his innocence and life of domestic bliss on the ranch, represents the life Ringo can no longer have. When Peck is shot in the back by a sneering adolescent, he lays a curses on his killer, saying he was simply outdrawn: instead of being hanged for murder, the man who shot Jimmy Ringo will have to live as he has done, constantly forced to prove how fast he is until he too dies.

The Gunfighter was massively influential. Zinnemann would use the film's constant references to clocks – time running out for its hero – to punctuate *High Noon*. And King's elegiac tone infused many subsequent Westerns – from *Shane* (1953) to *Ride The High Country* (1962) and beyond. As Robert Slotkin notes in his book *Gunfighter Nation*, Jimmy Ringo is a kind of everyman. The malaise of the middle-aged man grown weary of the rat race – *Man In The Grey Flannel Suit* syndrome – is presented here as a tragedy with mythic dimensions.

Heller In Pink Tights

dir **George Cukor, 1960, US, 100m**
cast **Sophia Loren, Anthony Quinn, Margaret O'Brien, Steve Forrest, Ramon Novarro**
cin **Harold Lipstein** *m* **Daniele Amfitheatrof**

Heller In Pink Tights is a forgotten gem, arguably the most accomplished, entertaining movie to belong to that microgenre known as the showbiz Western.

This colourful, romantic, amusing fable, based on **Louis L'Amour**'s acclaimed novel *Heller With A Gun*, is one of the few Westerns to explore the tattered splendour of the small theatrical companies that toured the West in the 19th century, often with posses or creditors in hot pursuit. This is George Cukor's only Western and he makes few concessions to the genre. *Heller In Pink Tights* is less how the West was won than how the West was fun, a distinction lost on critics who, on release, panned him for giving **Sophia Loren** too much screen time (L'Amour, though, always insisted it was one of his favourite adaptations of his work).

Contemporary reviews focused on the blonde wig Loren wore as Heller. Yet there is more to her performance than wigs: she is warm, natural, funny and sexy as the actress who keeps getting into difficult situations and whose affections are briefly disputed by Steve Forrest's gunfighter and Anthony Quinn's head of the troupe. Her characterization nods to the real-life frontier favourite **Adah Isaacs Menken**, famous for performing operas like *Mazeppa* on horseback. But this is an affectionate, tongue-in-cheek homage to an era rather than a fictionalized biopic. Loren's physique inspires one great – and, given the time, very brave – visual gag in which she is shown behind a set of sliding doors

Sophia Loren lights up the West in a blonde wig and pink tights in George Cukor's Western.

adorned by a painting of a naked woman. When the doors open, Loren's head briefly looks as if it's emerging from the painted woman's vagina.

Cukor draws a gem of a performance from former child star Margaret O'Brien as the ingenue protected by a clucking stage mom and, better still, reins in Quinn who is, for once, understated and effective. In his final film, silent movie great Ramon Novarro's sinister turn as a banker is, like Loren's heroine, good enough to carry the movie.

As a portrait of a rarely screened world of sleaziness, red plush playhouses and hypochondriacal ham actors, which subtly underlines the courage needed to be a travelling player in the Old West, *Heller In Pink Tights* is hard to beat. Cukor's biographer Patrick McGilligan caught the ambience nicely when he called the film "a handshake between Toulouse-Lautrec and Frederic Remington". Loren may have won her Oscar for *Two Women*, but she's better in this.

High Noon

dir Fred Zinnemann, 1952, US, 85m, b/w
cast Gary Cooper, Thomas Mitchell, Lloyd Bridges, Grace Kelly, Katy Jurado
cin Floyd Crosby *m* Dimitri Tiomkin

The swirl of claim and counter claim over *High Noon*'s meaning is in danger of obscuring its merits as a classic Western. As Garry Wills perceptively points out, *High Noon* was not the first Western to contrast the sheriff's lone courage with a cowering populace, nor the first to ponder if its hero should renounce violence as **Gary Cooper**'s fiancée **Grace Kelly** suggests. John Wayne had faced that very issue in his 1947 movie *Angel And The Badman*.

Even the movie's political slant is controversial. Soon to be blacklisted screenwriter **Carl Foreman** saw it as an allegory of McCarthyism in Hollywood. But Coop's refusal to walk away seemed, to some foreign critics, an implicit endorsement of America's stand against "evil" in the Korean War. The right-wing

National Review magazine named *High Noon* the 57th best conservative movie ever, heartened by its critique of wishy-washy judges who let hardened criminals like the Millers loose on parole.

What makes *High Noon* different isn't all the subtexts but its stylish restatement of classic Western themes. The story – a lone hero facing his nemesis on his wedding day, troubled by the heroine insisting she won't marry him if he stays to fight – strongly echoes *The Virginian*, the Western that made Cooper. But he is much greater in this, director Fred Zinnemann extracting full value from his grim, weathered face. **Katy Jurado**, as the businesswoman

The spin-off movies

The most famous film to be made in reaction to *High Noon* is *Rio Bravo* (see box on p.65). Officially, Howard Hawks was so offended by Coop's "chicken" sheriff that he felt driven to make a movie that would refute the film's debunking of the Western myth. Here are two of the best *High Noon* spin-offs:

Silver Lode
dir Allan Dwan, 1954, US, 81m

Far more explicit in its anti-McCarthyism than *High Noon*, Allan Dwan's movie has a villain called McCarty (Dan Duryea) who rides into town claiming to be a US marshal with a warrant for the arrest of rancher Dan Ballard (John Payne). The impressively thuggish Duryea soon has the townsfolk hunting Payne down in this concise, inventive, noirish Western. In the most powerful scene, Dwan's camera tracks Payne as he runs four blocks across town. In case anyone misses the allegory, an actor calls the villain "McCarthy" in one scene.

High Plains Drifter
dir Clint Eastwood, 1972, US, 105m

A supernatural, gothic, spin on *High Noon*. In Eastwood's first Western as a director, the townsfolk must pay for standing by while their lawman was whipped to death. The guilty, acquiescent citizens of Lago are the reincarnated superhero's real adversaries – not the approaching outlaws. A grim, sardonic tale, with Felliniesque moments of cruel absurdity, *High Plains Drifter* could be the missing link between *High Noon* and *Rambo*.

who flees rather than see Coop, her old love, killed, is sympathetic yet ambiguous, transcending the genre's female archetypes and the usual stereotyping of Mexican women as peppery Latin passion pots.

Zinnemann gave his Western town Hadleyville a desperate dustiness; made the townsfolk's cowardice understandable (although it's worth noting how the church, a traditional guarantor of moral values out West, is where Hadleyville starts to betray its marshal); used the "Do Not Forsake Me Oh My Darling" theme to heighten the claustrophobic gloom; and, when in doubt, cut to the clock.

Despite what you may have read, *High Noon* does not happen in real time. It does last 85 minutes but, writer Richard Combs notes, the first clock in the film shows 10.35am which, as the movie continues for 15 minutes after the noon train's arrival, gives 105 minutes of action. (For Combs' deeper analysis of the film's ambiguities of time, see his essay "Retrospective: *High Noon*" in *The Western Reader*, Limelight, 1998.)

High Noon is a massively influential psychological Western; while harking back, it nods to the future. Children enact the shoot-out, as they would in *Shane* (1953) and Peckinpah's films. Kane is no superman but a vulnerable hero with as few illusions about his job as Peckinpah's Pat Garrett. Lon Chaney's embittered former lawman, telling Kane "Deep down inside, people just don't care", anticipates countless disillusioned or weak lawmen to come.

Dismissed as a craftsman by auteur theorists, Zinnemann does have a concern – the individual's duty to his own self – that unites this Western with his Thomas More epic *A Man For All Seasons* (1966). That concern is the most likely explanation for the iconic, much-referenced moment when Coop throws his badge in the dust.

Before someone – Howard Hawks? – convinced John Wayne *High Noon* was anti-American (see box opposite), he said, accepting the film's best actor Oscar for Coop, that he wished he'd had a script like that. The Duke knew a good Western when he saw one.

Hud

dir Martin Ritt, 1962, US, 111 min, b/w
cast Paul Newman, Melvyn Douglas, Patricia Neal,
Brandon De Wilde, John Ashley
cin James Wong Howe *m* Elmer Bernstein

In his best movie, Martin Ritt condemns the materialist destruction of the West and America. Such lofty aims are undermined slightly by casting witty, charismatic, blue-eyed **Paul Newman** as the sneering, mercenary heel Hud Bannon. Ritt casts **Brandon De Wilde** – playing off our memories of him as Joey in *Shane* (1953) – as the soon to be disillusioned nephew to magnify Hud's flaws. But Newman is still the centre of the movie, more interesting to watch than Melvyn Douglas as Hud's morally upright, too-good-to-be-human rancher father.

That misjudgement does not negate a fine contemporary Western. The upside of Newman's charm is that it keeps us watching as his character plumbs new cynical depths, trying to sell a herd infected with foot and mouth against his father's wishes and almost raping **Patricia Neal**, the housekeeper, when drunk. (His approach to the opposite sex is summed up by his remark: "The only question I ever ask a woman is 'What time is your husband coming home?'") Neal deservedly won an Oscar for her performance – her scenes with Newman provide many of the film's finest moments.

Hud does, as his father insists, respect nothing and value nothing but when he suggests that being decent isn't enough in an America of crooked TV shows, fraudulent tax returns and price fixing, he's not entirely wrong. The code of the West, personified by his father, seems inadequate, though Hud's opportunism, ultimately, proves just as self-destructive. The generational divide is a sour inversion of *Rebel Without A Cause* (1955) – this time, it's the son, not the parent, who is morally, emotionally and spiritually bankrupt. Hud's determination to dig up the ranch for oil is a greedy neglect of the old Westerner's duty to the land.

The best that can be said for Newman's anti-hero is that, as a self-confessed "cold-blooded bastard", he is just as cynical about himself. When his father dies of a heart attack, Hud is shunned by

Paul Newman's Hud is sexy but immoral;
his dad Melvyn Douglas is upright but dull.

his nephew, losing any residual sympathy we might have left for him at the same time.

Starkly shot in black and white by **James Wong Howe**, *Hud* is a harrowing, bleak drama. Neither Ritt nor the scriptwriters – drawing on Larry McMurtry's novel *Horseman Pass By* – offer any extenuating circumstances for Hud. This keeps the message intact but doesn't help us understand the central anti-hero, last seen alone on the ranch, shouting that the world is full of crap.

Trivia buffs have a special fondness for *Hud* because Newman's anti-hero, complaining about his father's refusal to exploit their land for oil, claims: "My daddy thinks oil is something you stick in your salad dressing." By the 1990s, Newman would lament that his charity-funding Newman's Own salad dressing was outgrossing his movies.

The movie obviously influenced the Coen brothers, especially the scene where Hud sucker punches a cowboy. In 1994, they would cast Newman in *The Hudsucker Proxy*, a screwball comedy sending up, among other things, American capitalism. At one point, the board of directors chants: "Long live the Hud!"

"No animals were harmed in..."

After a horse fell to its death from a cliff in *Jesse James*, public indignation led to the American Humane Association overseeing movie-making through a film and TV unit. After some debate, the AHA came up with the famous guarantee "No animals were harmed in the making of this motion picture" which has graced a million movie credits since.

Jesse James

dir **Henry King, 1939, US, 105m**
cast **Tyrone Power, Henry Fonda, Randolph Scott, Nancy Kelly, Henry Hull, Brian Donlevy, John Carradine**
cin **George Barnes, W.H. Greene** *m* **Louis Silvers**

The reputation of Henry King's biopic of "one of the doggonedest, gawl-dingedest, dad-blamedest buckaroos that ever rode across these here United States of America!", as the orator says at Jesse James's funeral, has slipped somewhat. It's tempting to think how great this could have been in the hands of a master like Ford. Slowed by too much moralizing, marred by Henry Hull's over-acting, King's film can seem formulaic at times. King wasn't a great filmmaker, though he made some great movies, but with *Jesse James* he largely invented a now familiar formula – the revisionist Western with a sympathetic outlaw at its heart.

In *Jesse James*, Henry King films the outlaws' outrages with a gleeful zest that anticipates Leone.

Tyrone Power is surprisingly effective as Jesse James, a Western Robin Hood. The real outlaw's youthful bank robbing and his bloody stint with the notorious Quantrill guerrillas is ignored. King has stacked the deck so that, for much of the movie, his crimes are a perfectly understandable response to the provocations of American capitalism. The Pinkerton Detective Agency's homicidal attack on his mother provokes him to kill the murderer in a classic Western showdown. The bullying arrogance of the railroad men who are forcing settlers off their farms makes it easy to see why **Randolph Scott**'s lawman is sympathetic to the James brothers. An early shot of Jesse swinging a scythe on the farm underlines the message that it is the railroad that is destroying every American's dream – of having a middle-class home of their own.

L'Ouestern: French critics' top ten

In 1971, 27 French critics selected their best Westerns for Raymond Bellour's book *Le Western*. The French have always had their own take on American movies in general – their veneration for Jerry Lewis is notorious – and the Western in particular. The list shows no great regard for radical revisionism. Neither *Little Big Man* (1970) nor *The Wild Bunch* (1969) even made the longer list of 87 top Westerns. Yet the masters aren't always given their due either: is Sam Fuller's *Run Of The Arrow* (1957) really, as the voting suggests, greater than *Stagecoach* (1939)? Leone's films were not deemed "true" Westerns at the point this list was made. Those omissions apart, if you wanted an entrée to the genre, watching all 87 wouldn't be a bad start.

1 *Johnny Guitar* (1954)

2 *Rio Bravo* (1959)

3 *The Big Sky* (1952)

4 *The Naked Spur* (1953), *Rancho Notorious* (1952), *Man Without A Star* (1955)

7 *My Darling Clementine* (1946), *The Left Handed Gun* (1958), *The Searchers* (1956), *Ride The High Country* (1962)

Yet, as Power becomes increasingly megalomaniacal, King uses his brother Frank, the quietly charismatic **Henry Fonda**, to offer a populist, democratic critique of an outlaw who used to lead by example but eventually leads by force. The critique isn't pushed too far. Jesse is still martyred, shot in the back by a dirty little coward while taking down a Home Sweet Home sampler. The fact that his son happens to be playing with toy trains bitterly and economically indicates capitalism's final triumph.

King is not normally renowned for the zing of his action sequences but, possibly inspired by his historical research with writer Nunnally Johnson, he creates two scenes – of Jesse riding his horse through a plate-glass window and along the roof of a train – that are among the genre's most memorable.

A descendant of Jesse's famously claimed that the film's connections with historical reality stretched about as far as the fact that the hero was called James and rode a horse. King's movie may belong to the "print the legend, not the facts" school of Western but it began a cycle of doomed outlaw movies that culminated gloriously and violently in *The Wild Bunch* (1969).

Johnny Guitar

dir **Nicholas Ray, 1954, US, 110m**
cast **Joan Crawford, Sterling Hayden, Mercedes
McCambridge, Scott Brady, Ward Bond**
cin **Harry Stradling** *m* **Victor Young**

The *New York Times* reviewer said of *Johnny Guitar*: "Nicholas Ray
and [screenwriter] Philip Yordan stuff the film with so much sexual
symbolism one wonders why they left out a train going into a

Nicholas Ray's *Johnny Guitar* is the ultimate feminist Western. The men – Sterling Hayden, left, and Scott
Brady – are incidental, while Joan Crawford's saloon owner Vienna is the focus.

tunnel." Why indeed. *Johnny Guitar* is, as **François Truffaut** put it, a baroque "hallucinatory Western" which owes more to Sigmund Freud than Zane Grey, takes a few pot shots at McCarthyism yet, in the relationship between its titular hero and his saloon-owning love, is infused with a deep, glorious romanticism.

Sterling Hayden's stiffness serves him – and the movie – well as the guitar-strumming gunslinger called to defend **Joan Crawford** from an angry mob, led by jealous Mercedes McCambridge, bitter because the object of her affections is obsessed with Crawford. Ray cast Crawford partly because he was attracted to her. She repays him with a fine performance that goes beyond camp or melodrama.

Truffaut is right to compare Ray's Western to a dream. The violent colours in which it is shot emphasize the strangeness. There are some haunting images – notably Crawford, in a white dress, playing the piano in her saloon, with a candlestick and a pistol beside her – and some beautiful arrangements. Note the way the members of the patrol at Crawford's saloon arrange themselves into the V of migratory birds.

Johnny Guitar is simply raging with undercurrents. Crawford's saloon owner is tougher, more macho, than the passive, lovestruck gunslinger she is supposed to be relying on, his tag line "I am a stranger here myself" reflecting his marginal importance to events. The villainess, as played by McCambridge, was described by a *Time* reviewer as "a sexological square knot who fondles suggestively and gets unladylike satisfaction from watching a house burn down". Her resentment of Crawford's heroine is often seen in lesbian terms though, given the *New York Times*'s valid point about the quantity of symbolism on offer, it would be foolish to be too categorical about this.

Ray and Yordan's obsession with nuance and neurosis makes *Johnny Guitar* a compelling, weird and rich Western. Crawford later said that she should have had her head examined for taking part in this but no diva could resist lines like: "Down there, I sell whiskey and cards but all you buy up these stairs is a bullet in the head. Which do you want?"

Little Big Man

dir **Arthur Penn, 1970, US, 147m**
cast **Dustin Hoffman, Faye Dunaway, Chief Dan George, Martin Balsam, Richard Mulligan**
cin **Harry Stradling Jr** *m* **John Hammond**

Dustin Hoffman's Jack Crabb may be the West's most unreliable historian.

Arthur Penn's picaresque revisionist Western – drawing stunningly obvious parallels between the US Army's massacre of Native Americans and the slaughter of Vietnamese civilians at My Lai – is one of the biggest-grossing Westerns of all time.

The movie is based on Thomas Berger's novel of the same name. **Dustin Hoffman** is Jack Crabb, aka Little Big Man, an allegedly 121-year-old white man who was raised by Cheyenne. In flashback, he selectively recalls his life, drawing on memories of Western "heroes" (such as Custer and Wild Bill Hickok), massacres and last stands.

Penn's film is epic, funny, intelligent, neatly constructed (note how many of the key opening characters – Hickok, Custer, the preacher's wife, the limb-losing quack – reappear "fulfilled" later on) and ambitious. Crabb's recollections touch on every stock character in the Western's gallery, and credit him with many lifetimes' worth of adventures: he's a gunfighter called Soda Pop Kid (the name surely an allusion to the soda pop Alan Ladd buys in *Shane*, 1953) and exacts terrible revenge on Custer by goading him to his death. Crabb is a teller of tall tales in the **Mark Twain** tradition, though his stories are not necessarily any more unreliable than the "official" history of the West, enshrined in classic Fordian Westerns.

But the comic tone gives way, oddly, to massacres and speeches after an hour. Some of the caricatures and the over-acting grate, particularly **Richard Mulligan**'s Custer. At times, notably in one Indian raid scene, the revisionism is so crude and facile, you can see why *Pravda* praised this for exposing "the enormous crimes that have marked the path of capitalism". Cheyenne life is portrayed by Penn as a countercultural idyll, in which the effeminate homosexual Little Horse is cherished, Old Lodge Skins (**Chief Dan George**) is mystically at one with nature and Hoffman is allowed to indulge in a semi-incestuous sexual marathon with his Cheyenne wife's three sisters. Kim Newman argues that Penn has diluted Berger's novel and created Cheyenne characters that – Chief Dan George apart – feel no different, in a revisionist sense, from the Cheyenne in Ford's *Cheyenne Autumn* (1964).

The problem may be that Penn, unlike Berger, has little genuine feeling for the West, a disregard that is more striking in his *The Missouri Breaks* (1976). The same detachment that allows him to cheerfully stand the genre's conventions on their head means that, sometimes, he gets the nuances wrong.

Yet, for all that, *Little Big Man* has enough momentum, humour and power to keep you watching. Hoffman's hero, Jeff Corey's Hickock, Balsam's quack and Chief Dan George's Old Lodge Skins are fine performances. *Little Big Man* is an audacious Western, worth watching for a tone and scenes unlike almost any other film in the genre and for what it says about the time it was made. *Little Big Man* is Penn's attempt not so much to revise the Western as to dismember it.

Lone Star

dir **John Sayles, 1995, US, 135m**
cast **Chris Cooper, Elizabeth Peña, Kris Kristofferson, Matthew McConaughey, Frances McDormand**
cin **Stuart Dryburgh** *m* **Mason Daring**

John Sayles' *Lone Star* is the most neglected fruit of the 1990s Western revival, neither sweeping the Oscars like *Dances With Wolves* (1990) nor storming the box office like *Unforgiven* (1992).

Sayles' story is superficially an entertaining police procedural. Sam Deeds (**Chris Cooper**) is the small-town sheriff confronted with a skeleton and a badge belonging to one of his distant predecessors, a vicious sheriff (**Kris Kristofferson**) who made the law up as he went along. All the signs are that he was killed by Deeds' own father (**Matthew McConaughey**), who was the monstrous lawman's deputy in the 1950s. In the course of his investigations, he comes across an old flame (Elizabeth Peña) – a romance that dried up, we assume, because it crossed the racial divide.

Sayles has a gift for intricately interwoven stories and, in *Lone Star*, he has created a subtle masterpiece where the story seems to unfold from the characters, not from the mechanical dictates of a Hollywood crime story plot.

Chris Cooper's small-town sheriff confronts the sins of the past in *Lone Star*.

That said, the final twist is, in context, more shocking than the final surprise in *The Crying Game* (1992). Telling his story in flashbacks and through unhurried conversations, Sayles uses a tight, clever script to more than compensate for a tight budget.

Like much of Sayles' work, *Lone Star* lacks pace at times, but he uses the extra screen time to analyze character and community in a way seldom seen in the modern cinema, creating a movie that is far richer than any plot summary can convey.

Murder and romance are only part of what Sayles has to offer. To emphasize the way the sins of the past are haunting the present, his camera tracks from a conversation in one part of the room to a conversation in another part, 25 years earlier. Deeds' investigation is accompanied by scenes – such as the school board arguing over textbooks, really debating which version of history will be taught in the schools – which subtly highlight the blight of racism. Sergeant Cliff admits that his girlfriend's family don't mind he is white – they are Spanish — because they had worried their unmarried daughter might be a lesbian. His fellow sergeant nods, saying "Yeah, it's always heartening to see a prejudice overcome by a deeper prejudice."

For a director who got his big break directing Bruce Springsteen videos, this is a remarkable achievement — although you don't need too much imagination to see a common theme between *Lone Star* and some of the Boss's tales of small-town desperation.

Lonely Are The Brave

dir David Miller, 1962, US, 107m, b/w
cast Kirk Douglas, Gena Rowlands, Walter Matthau, George Kennedy, Michael Kane
cin Philip Lathrop *m* Jerry Goldsmith

If **Kirk Douglas** had prevailed, this would have been called *The Last Cowboy*, a smaller step away from its source, *The Brave Cowboy*, Edward Abbey's acclaimed Western novel. But *Lonely Are The Brave* fits Douglas's view of the film's theme — "If you try to be an individual, society will crush you" — and suits the occasional stridency that mars what is otherwise a fine, entertaining Western.

Douglas and Matthau are subtly excellent in two roles that could have led, easily, to scenery chewing. They are ably supported by Gena Rowlands, William Shatner and Carroll O'Connor, though George Kennedy is a tad predictable as the thuggish cop.

Douglas is Jack Burns, the itinerant cowboy and escaped convict — he got himself into jail to persuade a buddy to escape only to find that his friend, in flagrant violation of the old Western code, prefers to sit out his time behind bars — trying, on his horse Whiskey, to evade Matthau's sheriff, who has jeeps, walkie-talkies and helicopters at his disposal.

As an individualist and a cowboy ("a Westerner hates fences, and the more fences there are the more he hates them"), Douglas's obsolescence is underlined in one unforgettable scene where he tries to ride across a highway full of trucks. His character is never quite explained — he seems as much a man whose head has been turned by too many B Westerns as he is an authentic cowboy caught fatally out of time, lamenting the days when the range was open and not fenced and signed off. Though we are invited to identify with him, Matthau's reluctant lawman is almost as sympathetic and Douglas's hero is aware of his flaws, declaring: "I'm a loner clear down deep to my guts. And you know what a loner is? He's a cripple."

Screenwriter **Dalton Trumbo** was blacklisted for much of the 1950s and his identification with his persecuted hero is sometimes too intense, leading to some too obvious speeches and seriously heavy-handed imagery – could all that cross-cutting to a truck full of toilets signify symbolism speeding into view? You betcha. The film comes alive most in small moments – a hug between Douglas and Rowlands hinting at past love and Douglas's soliloquy on signs while washing his hands.

David Miller's direction is variable, as Douglas later admitted, but, once seen, *Lonely Are The Brave* is not easily forgotten, with Douglas at his considerable best in an ambiguous role. The opening – in which the peace Douglas is enjoying is shattered by the roar of an aeroplane – is a tour de force.

To see the same story remade, to lesser but enjoyable effect, in feel-good Frank Capra fashion, try Sydney Pollack's *The Electric Horseman* (1979), starring Robert Redford, Jane Fonda and Willie Nelson.

McCabe & Mrs Miller

dir **Robert Altman, 1971, US, 121m**
cast **Warren Beatty, Julie Christie, Rene Auberjonois, Hugh Millais, Shelley Duvall, Keith Carradine**
cin **Vilmos Zsigmond** *m* **Leonard Cohen**

Robert Altman has many gifts as a director but possibly his most consistent quality is his ability to divide reviewers. His *McCabe & Mrs Miller* was described by Roger Ebert as a perfect movie, had Pauline Kael rhapsodizing "it was a beautiful pipe dream", but left one critic complaining that it was "like reading a novel without half its pages, the ones in which the interesting things happen".

Altman set out with the stated intent of destroying "the myths of heroism in the Old West" but this masterpiece is much richer and more satisfying than a simple deconstruction. **Warren Beatty** gives probably his finest performance as McCabe, the cocky gambler who's no smarter than he ought to be, and sets up a brothel in a small mining town. **Julie Christie** is also at her best – despite her dodgy Cockney accent – as Mrs Miller, the whorehouse madam who coaches him but can't, ultimately, prevent him killing himself through stupidity.

The "&" in the title reflects the corporate, not romantic, association between the title characters – she still charges him $5 to enjoy her favours. Big business, ultimately, dissolves the partnership when a corporation decide to take over and, after McCabe refuses their initial offer, send hired guns into town to get rid of him.

McCabe & Mrs Miller is a truly sad film that, possibly, doesn't need the accompaniment of Leonard Cohen's mournful music. Altman's frontier is not heroic, the townsfolk have little constructive to do, life isn't just cheap, it's valueless. Keith Carradine's kid dies in a gunfight mainly because he is crossing the wrong bridge at the wrong time. The bleak, wild landscape is beautiful, yet ominous – at times, as wintry as a Pieter Bruegel painting – its threat ultimately fulfilled in a spectacular finale in which Beatty succumbs as much to the snowy wastes as to his wounds.

Altman's film has some similarities with Anthony Mann's *The Far Country* (1954), although, ironically, given Mann's strengths, *McCabe & Mrs Miller* has a far better sense of place. Though Altman has taken many of the genre's stock themes and situations – the loner who shakes up a town, the whore with a heart – he subverts them brilliantly to produce a fine, unusual Western.

The Magnificent Seven

dir **John Sturges, 1960, US, 138m**
cast **Yul Brynner, Steve McQueen, Eli Wallach, Horst Buchholz, Charles Bronson, Robert Vaughn, Brad Dexter, James Coburn**
cin **Charles Lang** *m* **Elmer Bernstein**

In the face of stiff competition from a TV schedule bursting with rootin'-tootin' Westerns, *The Magnificent Seven* represents Hollywood playing its trump card, offering – count 'em – seven gunfighters in one film!

Remaking **Akira Kurosawa**'s *The Seven Samurai* (1954) meant Sturges could merge the conventions of the traditional gun-fighter film and the platoon war movie, giving us a smorgasbord of Western stereotypes: the crazed neurotic, the aloof loner, the ethnic outsider, the populist, the wild "Kid", the conflicted gunfighter, the professional interested in testing his skills. These mysteriously motivated misfits had a simple mission: to stop a Mexican village being terrorized by vile, sardonic **Eli Wallach**, playing a role which now seems like a dry run for his turns as one of Leone's bad guys.

Sturges had a flair for choreographing action sequences, composing scenes and handling actors. The armed truce on set between **Steve McQueen** and **Yul Brynner** never quite erupted into open conflict – Brynner's threat to remove McQueen's hat if he kept trying to steal scenes settled the issue – but the tension between them works well on screen. The other five are almost as magnificent – even the casting of German Horst Buchholz as a half-Mexican works.

The movie benefits from the genius of **Elmer Bernstein**, whose iconic hummable theme tune, later used to advertise Marlboro cigarettes, was the highlight of a memorable Oscar-nominated score.

Though the film's optimistic mood recalls simpler days, *The*

Yul Brynner scans the horizon, daring Steve McQueen to upstage him.

Shooting lessons

When the Mexican peasants are taught to shoot in *The Magnificent Seven*, director John Sturges is celebrating one of the genre's most persistent motifs.

The shooting lesson is part of the essential structure of a Western, marking the point at which the hero, often a gunfighter, starts to become integrated into a community, while underlining their prowess.

The pupil is usually a boy or a youth – see *The Shootist* (1976) and *Man Without A Star* (1955), in which **Kirk Douglas** advises, "Get it out fast and put it away slow." But sometimes the pupil is a woman (Robert Taylor teaches a wagon train full of gals in *Westward The Women*, 1951) or just socially disadvantaged, like the Mexican peasants in Sturges' film. In revisionist Westerns or comedies, the ritual is stood on its head – **Dustin Hoffman**'s sister teaches him to shoot in *Little Big Man* (1970), while Jayne Mansfield shows Kenneth More in *Sheriff Of Fractured Jaw* (1958). In *El Dorado* (1966), Howard Hawks takes the deconstruction a stage further: his greenhorn James Caan never learns to shoot straight.

The most inspiring shooting lesson – though interrupted by a concerned mother – is **Alan Ladd**'s tuition of Joey in *Shane*. The prowess is impressive but it is Ladd's analysis of other gunfighters' tricks, like an old sports coach dissecting opposing teams' tactics, which lingers in the memory.

A master class: Shane teaches Joey the art of gunplay.

Magnificent Seven was oddly prophetic, cinematically and politically. The picture can be read, as Robert Slotkin amusingly shows in his book *Gunfighter Nation*, as a prophecy of American policy in Vietnam that Nostradamus would be proud of. Interestingly, it was the second Western in 1960 – the other being *The Alamo* – in which lionized brave Americans defended freedom and justice against Mexican tyrants and hopeless odds to triumph through martyrdom. Only three of the seven are left alive at the end of the movie.

The adaptation of Kurosawa, the Mexican backdrop, the use of mercenary heroes (even if they ultimately are not motivated purely by money) and vigilante justice – these recur throughout many 1960s Westerns. But Sturges' film is sunnier and more optimistic than any of those by Leone and Peckinpah which used elements of it. In *The Magnificent Seven*, the villagers fight in their own defence; they're not helpless or corrupt, but, in their way, as magnificent as the seven.

Three sequels, many parodies (¡*Three Amigos!*, 1986, with Chevy Chase and Steve Martin, is amusing, if not hilarious) and countless imitations later, *The Magnificent Seven* is a reminder, as *The Onion* noted, "that entertainment on a grand scale doesn't have to jettison good storytelling".

Man Of The West

dir **Anthony Mann, 1958, US, 100m**
cast Gary Cooper, Julie London, Lee J. Cobb, Arthur O'Connell, Jack Lord
cin **Ernest Haller** *m* **Leigh Harline**

Man Of The West is, simply put, the darkest Western **Anthony Mann** and **Gary Cooper** ever made. Jean-Luc Godard hailed it as "an admirable lesson in modern cinema". A tale of Oedipal sub-texts, rape, murder, revenge and insanity, Mann's masterpiece is, despite some flaws, the finest expression of his creed: "I always tried to build my films on opposition of characters. By putting the accent on the common points of the two characters – the good guy and the bad – then making them collide, the story acquires much more intensity."

Mann had fallen out with frequent collaborator **James Stewart** so Cooper became Mann's tortured hero, a reformed criminal on a train robbed by his old evil mastermind (and father figure) Lee J. Cobb. Cooper's only chance to escape – and save saloon girl Julie London – is to make Cobb believe that he has reverted to his bad old ways.

The casting is slightly problematic. Cobb is too young to be a father figure to the 57-year-old Cooper, and his stagey style doesn't quite sit with Coop's understated mastery though Mann makes good use of the contrast. The ambiguous hero is secretive about his past – when it is shockingly revealed by Cobb, we are left wondering what kind of hero Cooper is playing – while Cobb's villain becomes increasingly unhinged, finally raping London to humiliate Cooper. *Man Of The West* is a rare Hollywood Western in which the raped woman doesn't die. Her ordeal would usually have disqualified her as the hero's partner but there are scenes of tender, erotic power between Cooper and London and Mann does not, finally, spell it out that the hero will definitely shun the saloon girl to return to his family.

Mann's mastery of location and landscape is at its most sure here. The farmhouse, though set in a truly bucolic farm, is nastily claustrophobic. The rock formations suggest the silent witness of an ancient amphitheatre, while the gunfight is set, not in a main street at high noon, but in a ghost town, with both participants supine as if they were already corpses. In death, Cobb's bad guy rolls, unceremoniously, down a mountain incline after an unfair fight.

High Noon writer Carl Foreman called *Man Of The West* an "exercise in pure sadism". Cooper felt that films "where the good guy overcomes tremendous odds to lick the bad guy" were justified in a more violent portrayal of life out West. For Mann, all this talk of good guys and bad guys was slightly irrelevant: his hero is forced to admit that, in wanting to kill all villains like Cobb, he is just like them.

The Man Who Shot Liberty Valance

dir John Ford, 1962, US, 121m, b/w
cast John Wayne, James Stewart, Vera Miles, Lee Marvin, Edmond O'Brien, Andy Devine, Woody Strode
cin William H. Clothier *m* Cyril Mockridge

The Man Who Shot Liberty Valance is now probably better known as the source of the immortal line "When the legend becomes fact, print the legend" than it is as a movie. But this is one of Ford's most unusual and misunderstood works, a dark, disenchanted, even bitter, artistic summation sceptically examining American mythology, predicting a loss of faith in government and acknowledging the increased brutality of America and the Western.

Ransom Stoddard (**James Stewart**) is the politician whose rise is based on his reputation as the man who, as an idealistic young lawyer, shot villainous Valance (**Lee Marvin**), even though the fatal bullet (which, in a departure from Ford's usual mythos, strikes Valance in the back) probably came from the gun of Tom Doniphon (**John Wayne**). That said, as Kim Newman notes, Stewart had the guts to face a man he seemed to have no chance of out-gunning while Wayne,

Liberty Valance meets the men who would shoot him: James Stewart and John Wayne.

even if he did kill Valance, did so unheroically from the shadows. Ultimately, the town's newspaper reporter, given the chance to debunk a Western hero, decides that the legend must endure, regardless of the factual truth.

Ford chose, for artistic not budgetary reasons, to shoot this in black and white, deliberately stylizing the movie as if it were a silent Western. He confined the action to sound stages, dispensing with the scenic grandeur that typified much of his work. The two leads are used in interesting ways, their iconic status taking precedence over notions of realism, especially in the flashbacks to their "young-er" days. Wayne's larger than life "hero" is doomed to become as obsolete as Marvin's deliberately showy villain Valance, losing his girl Vera Miles and the West to Stewart's everyman, a shift Ford seems deeply ambivalent about.

The dark tone was reflected on set, with Ford being especially monstrous to Wayne. The Duke, though he resented his character, fearing that Stewart and Marvin both had better parts, makes the most of the movie's toughest role. Stewart, who requires a greater suspension of disbelief as the young idealist in the flashback scenes, is almost as good. Ford's gallery of players is expanded marvellously to include Edmond O' Brien's gloriously over-the-top newspaper editor and two actors who would become synonymous with younger Western directors: Strother Martin, a Peckinpah favourite, and Lee Van Cleef, a Leone regular, as Marvin's psychopathic accomplices.

Liberty Valance feels, at times, like Ford's farewell to the Western – and the West. The absence of Monument Valley reflects not, as some suggested at the time, directorial fatigue but Ford's loss of faith in the American frontier ideal. The shocking whipping of O'Brien's editor is Ford's comment on brutalities to come in the genre. Some restaurant scenes were said to be staged in mocking tribute to **Howard Hawks**. Some of the music – strangely Gene Pitney's Burt Bacharach/Hal David theme "The Man Who Shot Liberty Valance" wasn't used – came from Ford's movie *Young Mr Lincoln* (1939). And when the camera shows a stagecoach in mothballs – an obvious allusion to one of Ford's greatest Westerns – it's hard not to wonder if this is the director's bitter comment on his own canon.

Monte Walsh

dir **William A. Fraker, 1970, US, 108m**
cast **Lee Marvin, Jack Palance, Mitch Ryan, Jeanne Moreau, Jim Davis, Bo Hopkins**
cin **David M. Walsh** *m* **John Barry**

It always seems to be dusk in this romantically elegaic Western, probably because middle-aged cowboys Monte Walsh (**Lee Marvin**) and Chet Rollins (**Jack Palance**) happen to be living in their own personal twilight.

The two have been made redundant by a remote corporation which is remorselessly fencing off land and firing cowboys. Palance, bowing to the inevitable, gives up cow-punching and marries the

Gunfights with a twist

The abattoir in which Lee Marvin has his climactic showdown with hot-head Mitchell Ryan provides a suitably unusual backdrop for *Monte Walsh*'s elegiac finale. Yet many directors have – through wit or lack of budget – devised intriguing variations on the time-honoured gunfight.

• **Bad Day At Black Rock** (1954). Spencer Tracy defeats trigger-happy Robert Ryan with a necktie, some petrol and an empty whiskey bottle.

• **Day Of The Evil Gun** (1968). An unusual denouement: Arthur Kennedy challenges ex-gunslinger Glenn Ford to a duel. Ford won't draw. A bystander, trying to prevent cold-blooded murder, shoots Kennedy dead.

• **The Mercenary** (*Il mercenario*, 1968). A rodeo clown, a camp adventurer and a Polish gunfighter settle matters in a bull-ring in a grand finale to Corbucci's quirky Western.

• **One-Eyed Jacks** (1961). Not an actual gunfight, but the scene in which dad Karl Malden whips his son Marlon Brando, crushing mumbling Marlon's gun hand, is a striking Freudian sado-masochistic interlude.

• **Pat Garrett And Billy The Kid** (1973). Billy The Kid and Jack Elam promise to take ten paces, turn and draw. Both cheat, only Billy cheats faster.

• **Terror In A Texas Town** (1958). Poor old Sterling Hayden enters his "gunfight" clutching a harpoon.

town's "hardware widow". The wedding provokes Marvin into some none too thorough soul-searching and the thought that he might marry **Jeanne Moreau**, the town whore. All three principals play their parts beautifully, but the movie's truly transcendent moment comes when Moreau is asked what she thinks about getting married. "I like it", she says after a luminous hesitation, adding, "Of course marriage is a common ambition in my profession."

Marvin, however, decides that cowboys aren't suited to marriage. He toys with the idea of stunt-riding in a Wild West show but can't face all those concrete cities and, after taking a look at the show itself, says "I ain't gonna spit on my whole life." Before things turn truly desperate, there is a fine sequence in which Marvin, trying to disprove his own irrelevance, tames a bronco and destroys half the town. Hearing of Moreau's death by pneumonia – and Palance's slaying by a short-tempered fellow cowboy Mitchell Ryan – Marvin faces his friend's killer in a shoot-out set in an abattoir.

William A. Fraker's directorial debut, adapted from Jack Schaefer's episodic novel of the same name, is a funny, profane, true, Western that captures the difficult charm of Schaefer's original – while telescoping the action – and deserves to be much better known. It is rare to see Marvin and Palance laugh without malice, and Fraker, a gifted cinematographer who had just shot Marvin for *Paint Your Wagon* (1969), makes the most of his leads, coaxing a nicely restrained performance from Palance. Marvin is an even greater joy to watch; as fan and novelist George Pellecanos says, "he is at his best in scenes with no dialogue".

Monte Walsh is a light tragedy, with quiet humour, beautifully shot by David M. Walsh to recall the landscapes of Frederic Remington. There is a striking, if occasionally intrusive, score from John Barry (the highlight being **Mama Cass** singing "The Good Times Are Coming" over the opening credits). The story is set at the same historical and era-changing moment as *The Wild Bunch* (1969) and *The Professionals* (1966), a time when gunslingers are facing redundancy. But *Monte Walsh* deals with this moment with a tad more thought and realism. Even in the movies, not every gunslinger can take half of Mexico with them to their doom. A well-observed, meandering story of one anachronistic cowboy's life, *Monte Walsh* is still criminally underrated – as a cult book and a great melancholy Hollywood Western.

My Darling Clementine

dir **John Ford, 1946, US, 97m, b/w**
cast **Henry Fonda, Linda Darnell, Victor Mature, Cathy
Downs, Walter Brennan, Tim Holt, Ward Bond**
cin **Joseph P. MacDonald** *m* **Cyril Mockridge**

Of all the Wyatt Earp movies, Ford's graceful, lyrical, deeply romantic
interpretation of the legend is the quintessential, most low-key, and
most affecting version of the story. Of course, it is also entertainingly
climaxed by the gunfight with Walter Brennan's dastardly Clanton
gang at Tombstone's OK Corral, as described – if inaccurately – to
Ford by Earp himself.

The story of Earp's taming of the town of Tombstone, and his
own transformation from drifter cowboy to civilized lawman, had
been filmed many times before. Superficially a superior remake
of 1939's *Frontier Marshal* (Randolph Scott's stab at Earp), *My
Darling Clementine* is quite distinctive in tone. It is full of rich
detail, memorable vignettes, signature scenes like the town dance
on the floorboards of what is to be the church, and classic Western
dialogue ("There's a stage leaving in thirty minutes. Be on it.").

A seasoned **Henry Fonda**'s still, restrained Earp prompts warm
mirth with his hop-skip style on the dance floor and cuts a perfectly iconic figure lounging on the porch with his boots up and his
Stetson brim down. A surprising **Victor Mature** is unforgettable as
the tortured, tubercular Doc Holliday, entranced by a drunken thes-
pian's Hamlet soliloquy on a tavern table. **Linda Darnell**'s vibrant
saloon floozy Chihuahua sacrificially takes a bullet, eliminating the
complication in Earp's courtlier romance with **Cathy Downs**' virtuous schoolmarm Clementine. The fact that the movie is named after
her, not Earp or the gunfight, is the most glaring statement of Ford's
intentions. The gunfight is less significant and life-changing for Earp
than Clementine's arrival in Tombstone.

The shift in emphasis rather obscures what was historically at
stake in this conflict, which was as much about prosperity as it was

So many Western icons in one frame: Henry Fonda, a front porch and, in the distance, the iconic cactus.

about peace. It also marginalizes the Clanton gang, an alliance of relatives and their allies who, in essence, were economic rivals to the Earp party and their big-business sponsors. Good as Brennan is at being bad, Ike Clanton was probably not any more villainous than Holliday.

The inevitable shoot-'em-up – to make Tombstone a town in which a man can have a shave without having his head blown off – is thrillingly staged, but this is no rootin'-tootin' adventure. Rather it is a profoundly wistful and bittersweet reflection on civilization versus savagery, order versus anarchy and natural wonder (beautifully shot Monument Valley) contrasted with man-made horror.

The weary Earp defers his dream of a peaceful life as a cattleman and reluctantly assumes responsibility for a cowering community in

Taming the town

There is a modest historical truth behind the town-taming Western. Lawmen did try to keep the peace in unruly towns like Dodge City, Wichita and Abilene. But this sub-genre mainly springs from the inaccurate, self-serving, glamorized recollections of **Wyatt Earp**.

The hero, either motivated by an anachronistic sense of noblesse oblige or alerted to injustice by personal tragedy, does what a real man's gotta do, using his skill and guts to confront the villains and make a once wild and lawless town fit for decent folk. These heroes, usually but not always lawmen, often find that, in establishing peace, they have made themselves obsolete – but they obviously keep this realization to themselves because the genre teems with lawmen who face this dilemma afresh, as if for the first time.

Taming the town was, until the 1950s, a simple, heroic business, definitively rendered in *Dodge City* (1939). The villains, bizarrely, were often presented as mob bosses, rather than trigger-happy outlaws. Ford's *My Darling Clementine* (1946) gives taming Tombstone a mythic dimension. But even here, a price must be paid. If the town is to become truly, irrevocably, civilized, it's not enough that baddies like the Clantons should perish. The likes of **Doc**

Holliday, that walking, coughing symbol of vice, must bite the bullet too, so the Tombstones of the West can be fit for school teachers and such. And once characters like Doc die or hightail it out of town, the bad girls will vamoose as well, so families can be raised, barns be put up in record time and square dancing become popular.

Even in the 1950s, the straightforward heroic narrative was skewed in films such as *Man With The Gun* (1955), in which the town has to hire a mercenary to save them. These movies begat what Kim Newman calls the "who-will-save-us-from-the-man-we-hired-to-save-the-town?" sub-genre of films such as *Invitation To A Gunfighter* (1964). The fiendish *Warlock* (1959) manages to straddle both micro-genres: you get the hiring-a-mercenary and the who-will-save-us shtick in one!

Westerns increasingly begged the question of whether the town was worth taming – a point famously made in *High Noon* (1952), in which the price of freedom is a continued vigilance that asks too much of the easily frightened townsfolk, but reiterated in Burt Kennedy's *Welcome To Hard Times* (1966), *Firecreek* (1968) and *High Plains Drifter* (1972). Even Ford, having created the great *My Darling Clementine*, deconstructed the very idea of town-taming in *The Man Who Shot Liberty Valance* (1962).

an archetypal Ford scene, monologuing at his murdered younger brother's grave. The message of duty above vengeance or personal desire is fundamental in Ford's finest work.

The Naked Spur

dir **Anthony Mann, 1952, US, 91m**
cast **James Stewart, Janet Leigh, Robert Ryan, Ralph Meeker, Millard Mitchell**
cin **William C. Mellor** *m* **Bronislau Kaper**

James Stewart, Clint Eastwood noted, "had a great way with violence – when he had been wronged, was mad about something, it was much more intense than with other actors".

It took **Anthony Mann** to unlock the inner rage in an actor hitherto chiefly famous for his folksy charm, but in five Westerns – *Winchester '73* (1950), *Bend Of The River* (1952), *The Naked Spur*, *The Far Country* (1954) and *The Man From Laramie* (1955) – he remade Jimmy Stewart as an actor and icon.

Like most of Mann's Western "heroes", Stewart is burdened by past bitterness – his fiancée's departure – and barely in control of himself or events, waking screaming from a nightmare and spending much of the time faint from blood loss. Becoming a bounty hunter, he tracks murderous **Robert Ryan** hoping to use the $5000 reward to buy back the ranch his absconding fiancée sold. Collecting a grizzled prospector and a dangerous gunman along the way, Stewart finally captures Ryan – and his beautiful companion, Janet Leigh, who he nearly kills – but Ryan cleverly turns his captors against each other. The tension is enhanced by the constant threat of half-seen Indians. After a three-way shoot-out, Stewart emerges victorious but, having come close to losing his reason, decides he'd be richer with Janet Leigh than with the reward.

The progress of Stewart's tormented hero is marked by two climbing attempts. He fails to overcome a bluff in his early pursuit of Ryan but, at the end, surmounts a similar obstacle even though he's severely wounded. Like many of Mann's overachieving heroes, he can only grow when he's been taught a lesson.

The Naked Spur was shot entirely on location in the Rocky Mountains. Once again, Mann brilliantly matches landscape and mood. For French critic André Bazin, *The Naked Spur* showed Mann's "natural gift for direct, discreet use of the lyrical and his infallible sureness of touch in bringing together man and nature, that feeling of the open air, which in his films seems the very soul of the Western". Put more prosaically, the arduous journey – Stewart always seems to be dodging boulders, being flung off ledges, and scaling cliff faces – emphasizes how close to the psychological, emotional and physical edge they all are.

Leigh felt that the contrasting acting styles of the major players made the tensions between the characters more authentic. Stewart's performance is a gem – especially when, in 90 seconds, he has to convincingly repudiate the obsessed character he has played for the last 90 minutes of the film – but Ryan's is every bit as powerful.

Mann's grubby, noirish, reinvention of the Western in movies like this and *Man Of The West*, the moral ambiguity of his West, and even the motif of the bounty hunter – hitherto largely scorned in Hollywood's Western mythos – all anticipate Leone's bloody revisions of the traditional horse opera.

Once Upon A Time In The West (C'era una volta il West)

dir **Sergio Leone, 1968, It, 165m**
cast **Henry Fonda, Claudia Cardinale, Charles Bronson, Jason Robards, Frank Wolff, Jack Elam**
cin **Tonino Delli Colli** *m* **Ennio Morricone**

When *Once Upon A Time In The West* was released, *Time* magazine sniffed that it "proves that he [Leone] is simply a serious bore". That was sadly typical of the initial American reaction to a movie now recognized as one of the greatest Westerns ever made.

Once upon a time in the West, Sergio Leone's films suggested, such grim, sudden violence was the order of the day.

After Leone finished his slightly tongue-in-cheek "Man With No Name" trilogy, he thought he was done with the Western. Luckily, the difficult gestation of his gangster epic *Once Upon A Time In America* (1983) sent him back to the genre to make a movie more ambitious and epic than any other Italian Western, a truly operatic tale that matched the richness of **Ennio Morricone**'s score. His initial thought of saying goodbye to his "Dollars" films by casting Clint Eastwood, Eli Wallach and Lee Van Cleef vanished when Clint turned the film down – a very fortunate refusal.

Put simply, this is the story of the "civilizing" of the West through the mechanical impersonal force of the railroad and the feminization of the region, beautifully symbolized by Jill (**Claudia Cardinale**), who has inherited land which lies in the line of the railroad. Although the two civilizing forces conflict, they are finally reconciled, with Cardinale looking after the railroad workers. Three men complicate matters: **Jason Robards'** mysterious bandit, **Henry Fonda's** assassin (called Frank – a homage to his Frank James role?) hired to kill Cardinale and **Charles Bronson's** mysterious stranger pursuing Fonda who, we learn, is out for revenge.

The scale of the movie enables Leone and his scriptwriters (Bernardo Bertolucci and Dario Argento, initially, with Sergio Donati taking the shears to their wordy draft) to pack in homages to their favourite American Westerns. Leone's biographer Christopher Frayling has cited over thirty significant allusions to such diverse Hollywood Westerns as *The Iron Horse* (1924), *Dodge City* (1939), *Shane* (1953), *Johnny Guitar* (1954) and *The Magnificent Seven* (1960).

The game of allusion, reference and quotation never becomes tedious, cumbersome or intrusive. Novelist Graham Greene praised the balletic quality of the eight-minute sequence in which three men wait for a train – a parodic tribute to the outlaws killing time in *High Noon* (1952) before the showdown.

The shocking killing of a child – and the pan to the clear blue eyes of Fonda – is justly famous but the film is full of astonishing imagery: a dying tubercular man crawling to a puddle in the desert; painterly long shots that give proceedings a Biblical grandeur; the sudden revelation of a family's corpses on picnic tables. The synthesis of story and Morricone's score is at its most haunting in the scenes of Jill riding on a buggy through the desert.

This isn't really a spaghetti Western at all. For a start, Leone deliberately moved his story to Flagstone, Arizona, so he could – in an act of "sacrilege" which angered many traditionalists – briefly occupy Monument Valley, the cinematic space almost monopolized by his idol **John Ford**. The pace isn't as relentlessly rapid-fire as the "Dollars" films, and the movie's perspective on the civilizing of the West is more firmly rooted in grubby historical reality than some of Ford's epics.

Leone said his aim was to take the genre's most stereotypical characters and, by making them take part in a dance of death, tell a story about the birth of a nation. The deaths can be actual or implied. Bronson may kill Fonda but, in a land where money increasingly talks louder than guns, his own demise – along with that of Robards' doomed, romantic bandit – is only a matter of time.

The Outlaw Josey Wales

dir Clint Eastwood, 1976, US, 134m
cast Clint Eastwood, Chief Dan George, Sondra Locke, Bill McKinney, John Vernon, Paula Trueman
cin Bruce Surtees *m* Jerry Fielding

When this movie was released, one reviewer complained: "If only the actors hadn't got in the way of all this beautiful scenery, it would have been a great film", while *Variety*'s critic saw only a formula Eastwood slaughterfest, "*Death Wish* on the prairie". Today, *The Outlaw Josey Wales* is fondly regarded as the ultimate post-Vietnam reconciliation Western.

The healing message is especially ironic as the film was based on the novel *Gone To Texas* written, under the pseudonym Forrest Carter, by **Asa Earl Carter**, a former Ku Klux Klan chapter leader who famously wrote the "segregation now, segregation tomorrow, segregation forever" line in a speech for Alabama Governor George Wallace.

Eastwood didn't know all that when he bought the screen rights. He was just intrigued by the tale of Josey Wales, a Southerner who refuses to surrender his arms after the Civil War, and leaves a bloody trail as he flees a posse across the south-west. On screen, *The Outlaw Josey Wales* becomes a much richer story, taking two traditionally exclusive Western themes – the loner who turns his back on civilization and the group heading West whose destinies become interlaced in the face of danger – and combining them in the same film. "As if", as Roger Ebert noted, "*Jeremiah Johnson* were crossed with *Stagecoach*."

Eastwood, on the run from Union soldiers who cold-bloodedly killed both his family and his surrendering comrades, becomes embroiled with other drifters and refugees, including a wise old Native American and a family nearly slaughtered on their way West. The depiction of the family's suffering – in which Sondra Locke is nearly gang-raped – was one of the issues which led Eastwood to fire director Philip Kaufman. The star felt, rightly, even judging by the final footage, that Kaufman was letting the camera linger in pure sexual exploitation. This community of oddballs finally helps Wales defeat the bounty hunters, reintegrating him into "society" as represented by the weird little ghost town of Santa Rio.

Fletcher (John Vernon), Wales's former commander, has pursued him because he fears the outlaw will kill him in revenge for letting their old comrades die. Fletcher eventually agrees to report that Josey has probably fled to Mexico, even though he knows it's not true. To which Josey replies "I guess we all died a little in that damn war", a line that applies to the American Civil War and to the Vietnam War, which ended only the year before this movie was released.

For a film so full of killing which doesn't downplay the horror of violent death, *The Outlaw Josey Wales* is a surprisingly warm, optimistic Western. The arrival of **Chief Dan George** as Lone Watie, Wales's Cherokee sidekick (a brilliant casting decision by Kaufman), thaws hero and movie after the initial horrors. Their exchanges provide many of the film's finest, funniest moments, with Chief Dan George's cynical, open humanity a perfect match for Eastwood's closed, taciturn, sharp-shooting superhero.

The wisdom of Lone Watie

"I myself never surrendered, but they got my horse and it surrendered."

"I'm an Indian all right but they call us the civilized tribe. They call us civilized because we're easy to sneak up on. White men have been sneaking up on us for years."

"Get ready, little lady, hell is coming for breakfast."

Wales: Whenever I get to likin' someone they ain't around long.

Watie: I notice when you get to dislikin' someone they ain't around long either.

The Ox-Bow Incident
(aka Strange Incident)

dir **William Wellman, 1943, US, 75m, b/w**
cast **Henry Fonda, Dana Andrews, Anthony Quinn, Henry Morgan, Jane Darwell, Frank Conroy**
cin **Arthur Miller** *m* **Cyril Mockridge**

Movie moguls get so much of the blame for what happens in Hollywood that it seems fair to give them credit when they rarely deserve it. Walter Van Tilburg Clark's anti-lynching novel would never have become a movie if 20th Century Fox boss **Darryl Zanuck** hadn't read the book and told director **William Wellman**: "I don't think it'll ever make a dime but it's something I want my studio to have."

Zanuck's generosity had limits. He made Wellman agree to make two other pictures sight unseen and restricted the budget so Wellman was forced to make a "serious" studio-bound picture, prompting the critic James Agee to dismiss the film as "respectable, and sympathetic – but suffers from rigor artis".

There's something in Agee's criticism. But the story of three men in a small town lynched for a crime that turns out never to have taken place is saved from mere liberal goodness by Wellman's vivid noirish characterization. Frank Conroy's sadistic fake Southern major ("he never even saw the South until after the war", fumes Fonda), Jane Darwell, superbly cast against type as the cackling lewd old woman who relishes the melodrama, and **Henry Fonda**, as the moral, but impotent, hero, lead a strong ensemble cast.

Fonda and Henry Morgan ride into a desolate street in a small Nevada town to hear a rumour that a farmer has been murdered and a posse is being formed. Fonda joins in reluctantly, partly out of self-preservation, but becomes increasingly disturbed by the posse's actions and tries to prevent the mob's bloodlust from being fulfilled. Watched today, Fonda's eloquent anguished hero is reminiscent of a similar more famous role as the juror impassioned for justice in *12 Angry Men* (1957).

A minority have found the movie simplistic – and some of the novel's subtleties are lost in Lamar Trotti's screenplay – but Wellman seems to be aiming for the simplicity of a modern parable. The script is full of speechifying, especially at the finale, but Wellman boldly shoots the scene so Fonda's eyes are shielded by Morgan's hat, and lets the simple eloquent decency of Fonda's voice dominate the scene. The rhetoric is over-the-top but, almost against your will, it brings a lump to your throat.

The Ox-Bow Incident might have had an easier time at the box office if the original plan – to have Mae West serving the cowboys food and singing – had gone ahead. It would, however, have ruined what Orson Welles once said was his favourite picture and the Western that, Clint Eastwood later recalled, he admired most as a boy.

Pat Garrett And Billy The Kid

dir **Sam Peckinpah, 1973, US, 121m**
cast **James Coburn, Kris Kristofferson, Bob Dylan, Katy Jurado, Jason Robards, Slim Pickens**
cin **John Coquillon** *m* **Bob Dylan**

Having the chance to film the story of Billy the Kid was a dream fulfilled for Peckinpah – he'd first tackled it over a decade earlier

Old friends, new enemies: Billy the Kid and Pat Garrett reflect on changing times in Peckinpah's Western.

when he wrote a script for *One-Eyed Jacks* which was accepted, then spurned, by the studio. But, what with his starting most days' filming with a whiskey breakfast, and MGM then mutilating his cut, *Pat Garrett And Billy The Kid* was never going to have an easy ride.

Critics still debate the movie's merits but the opposing views are not necessarily irreconcilable. "The film has no motor impulse, it's a woozy, druggy piece of work", said Pauline Kael, while Lyn Silke, the wife of the movie's art director, believed: "*Pat Garrett* is the masterpiece, more complete than *The Wild Bunch*." Kael and Silke are both right. The movie does not have the drive of *The Wild Bunch* – nor does it put you in touch with your inner psycho in the same way – but it has a much more rounded feeling of life and, especially, of death.

In Peckinpah's hands, the story of Pat Garrett's pursuit and killing of his old friend Billy the Kid becomes many things. The killing marks the end of Peckinpah's beloved, slightly mythical, Old West, and the triumph of an unfeeling capitalism that kills Garrett just as he killed the Kid. The movie acts as a virtual deconstruction of the Western, subverting rituals (the gunfight in which both contestants cheat, the poker game that ends in humiliation and death) and stereotypes. Garrett's anti-heroic sheriff shoots the Kid at close range, his victim offering no real resistance. And what kind of gunfighter is Billy? A bad boy Christ, who waits, whoring and drinking in a private Gethsemane, for death to call.

Pat Garrett's meaning for Peckinpah can't be ignored. The film is invested with the kind of bitter, rueful bleakness you'd expect from a paranoid middle-aged alcoholic who equated the syndicate that ordered Billy's execution with the Hollywood syndicate that threatened his creative existence.

Like Garrett, Peckinpah was faced with the choice of changing and compromising – he had just been the hired hand directing *The Getaway* (1972) – or becoming obsolete. Yet the director also laments the demise of The Kid, his hard-drinking, fast-living anti-hero alter ego, a character closer to Peckinpah's public image. When Peckinpah, as Will the coffin maker, warns the sheriff – "When are you going to learn you can't trust anybody, not even yourself, Garrett?" – it's as if we are eavesdropping on Peckinpah's inner conflicts.

The film's flaws are real. **Bob Dylan**'s character seems pointless, while **Kris Kristofferson**'s Billy is more symbol, a Jim Morrison lookalike, than character. It's a pity that Peckinpah and screenwriter Rudy Wurlitzer never really agreed on the Kid's significance. Some dialogue is banal and there are too many self-conscious touches of "genius". But the flaws are outweighed by the quality. John Coquillon's gorgeous cinematography and Dylan's jarring, yet fitting, score accentuate the claustrophobic regret. Coburn's Garrett is a revelation from an actor typecast as a grinning, jiving conman. The emotional heart of the tale is the death of **Slim Pickens**' sheriff, mourned by Katy Jurado, an aching sadness that signifies Peckinpah's own farewell to the Western.

What the film lacks in plot, it makes up for in pessimistic coherence. In the re-released director's cut *Pat Garrett And Billy The Kid* is a flawed masterpiece, a dark, mature, compelling vision from a director too often patronized as an idiot savant.

Pursued

dir **Raoul Walsh, 1947, US, 101m, b/w**
cast **Robert Mitchum, Teresa Wright, Judith Anderson, Dean Jagger, Alan Hale, Harry Carey Jr, John Rodney**
cin **James Wong Howe** *m* **Max Steiner**

In this Hollywood Western **Robert Mitchum**'s laconic hero spends his entire life (and the duration of the film) being victimized by everyone around him. In the opinion of **Martin Scorsese**, who paid for the print of *Pursued* to be restored, it is the "first noir Western … resembling a Shakespearean drama with Freudian overtones", and one of the lost treasures of American cinema.

Pursued is a tale of intrigue, incest, slaughter and flashbacks, ably directed by Walsh, memorably scored by the great Max Steiner and beautifully photographed by **James Wong Howe**, whose shadow-haunted images, stark desert locations, noirish underlighting and low-angled interiors were innovative and experimental for a Western (and not just for a Western – this marked the first use of infrared film on a Hollywood movie).

Mitchum, as Jeb Rand, tortured by memories of the apparently purposeless slaughter of his family and by the regularity with which other people keep trying to kill him, gives one of his most impressive, low-key studies in fatalism, extracting full value from such lines

The most underrated Western: *Pursued*

So neglected that the philanthropic **Martin Scorsese** had to help pay for the print to be restored, Raoul Walsh's *Pursued* is a Western that owes more to Sigmund Freud, Emily Brontë and Sophocles than to the genre's more customary icons: Zane Grey, John Ford and John Wayne.

Pursued's critical neglect is easy to explain. As a director, especially of Westerns, Walsh has never really had his due – he's not enough of an auteur to satisfy a certain kind of critic. It's partly his own fault: he did like to hide behind a man-of-action schtick. The film's star, **Robert Mitchum**, was seriously underrated until late on in his career and, though he has since become a cult hero, the re-evaluation of his work has focused on a few predictable masterpieces – usually *The Night Of The Hunter* (1955) – and ignored much of his other quality work.

In *Pursued* Mitchum gives a performance of such world-weary reserve and sad-eyed nonchalance that he suggests, as Scorsese says, that "for him, hope was never even a possibility".

Pursued was a noirish, psychological Western before either term had seriously been applied to the horse opera. By the 1950s, Westerns as diverse as *Bad Day At Black Rock, Johnny Guitar* and *Rancho Notorious* were held up as noir masterpieces. But it was Walsh who proved that the mood of paranoid pessimism that distinguished so many 1940s crime thrillers could be applied to the Western.

as "You know I flipped this coin twice and I lost both times. Last time I left for war, this time I left the ranch." His brooding, darkly sexual, heavy-lidded performance anticipates the supposedly revolutionary style brought to the screen a few years later by Method icon Marlon Brando.

Mitchum is ably opposed by **Dean Jagger** as Grant Callum, the oily villain with incestuous designs on his sister-in-law Ma Callum (the terrific Judith Anderson). To make matters more noirishly complicated, Mitchum falls for his step-sister Thorley (Teresa Wright, who stands out even in such a strong cast). Their wedding night is marred, rather, by the bride's attempt to accelerate the "till death do us part" bit of the wedding vows as she seeks revenge for Mitchum's murder of her brother.

Confused? You won't be – Walsh handles this fusion of Freud, noir and Western with aplomb. Mitchum is the innocent victim of that old Western stand-by, a blood feud, his family killed – on Dean Jagger's orders – because his father had an affair with Ma Callum.

Pursued is not just the first noir Western, it's probably the best – and one of the finest, yet most underrated, Westerns to come out of Hollywood in the 1940s. Twenty years later, Leone paid obvious homage in *Once Upon A Time In The West*, having a character sing "Danny Boy", just as Mitchum does in *Pursued*. The psychological Western – usually said to have been invented in *The Gunfighter* (1950) – may well have started here.

Red River

dir Howard Hawks, 1948, US, 133m, b/w
cast **John Wayne, Montgomery Clift, Joanne Dru, Walter Brennan, Coleen Gray, John Ireland, Noah Beery Jr**
cin **Russell Harlan** *m* **Dimitri Tiomkin**

With *Red River*, Howard Hawks provided sensitive, cutting-edge Method actor and beauteous youth **Montgomery Clift** with his first screen role and the Duke with a turning point in his career, eliciting a revelatory performance from Wayne as the Captain Bligh of the cattle trail which prompted a startled **John Ford** to tell Hawks: "I never knew the big son of a bitch could act!"

Frequently referred to as a Western *Mutiny On The Bounty*, *Red River* has the dimensions of classical Greek tragedy (a son having to "kill" his father to prove himself), with Wayne's tyrannical rancher Thomas Dunson – conflicted, proud, obsessive, vengeful – provoking foster son Matthew Garth (Clift) to rebellion on the pioneering drive of 9000 head of cattle from Texas to Abilene, Kansas, on the Chisholm Trail. The long-awaited showdown between the two ill-matched men is as butchly emotional a scene as can be found in any Western.

The movie is notable, besides, as a mood piece of epic majesty, with a famous stampede, the much loved "Yee Haw" scene (affectionately re-enacted in Billy Crystal's 1991 mid-life-crisis cattle drive comedy *City Slickers*), a perfect supporting ensemble and two female characters

– **Coleen Gray** appearing briefly as Tom's sweetheart and **Joanne Dru** as Matt's – who are remarkably fierce as well as feminine, the macho Hawks admiring more passionate, gutsy gals than Ford or most other Western directors.

If *Stagecoach* had made Wayne's name, *Red River* defined him as a Western icon. The critic Gerald Mast famously wrote that no other Western star could "ever walk the way Wayne does, devouring space with his stride". In *Red River*, Hawks perfected a John Wayne who seemed almost as big as the frontier. Wayne's indomitable presence and his character's grand, urgent, mission gave *Red River* what is, for Hawks, a rare depth – most of the director's masterpieces were comedies like *His Girl Friday* (1939) and he probably felt more at home with *Rio Bravo* (1959), his next big Western to star the Duke.

Oedipus West: John Wayne and Montgomery Clift clash on the cattle trail in *Red River*.

The many films to pay homage to *Red River* include *The Last Picture Show* (1971), while a documentary on gay cinema, *Celluloid Closet*, impishly focused on the homoeroticism of John Ireland's Cherry Valance admiring Matt's gun. Well aware of the movie's significance in his career, Wayne continued to wear Dunson's belt with its Red River D brand on the buckle throughout many of his later pictures.

Ride The High Country
(aka Guns In The Afternoon)

dir Sam Peckinpah, 1962, US, 93m
cast Joel McCrea, Randolph Scott, Mariette Hartley,
Ronald Starr, R.G. Armstrong, James Drury, Warren Oates
cin Lucien Ballard *m* George Bassman

With a budget of $800,000, **Sam Peckinpah**'s second feature film was, for MGM, something to fill out a double bill, initially supporting *The Tartars* (a stolid epic promoted with such lines as "Orgy celebrates conquest!"). Luckily, the critics – and the judges at international film festivals – saved this masterful elegy for the Old West from oblivion.

Peckinpah sets the autumnal tone instantly with **Joel McCrea**'s former marshal almost being run over by a car and scolded "Watch out old timer". Escorting gold from the mountains, he runs into old friend **Randolph Scott**. The two – with a youthful sidekick and an eloping farm girl (Mariette Hartley) in tow – reach a mining camp that seems like a Wild Western cousin of Sodom and Gomorrah. There, in a grotesque wedding ceremony in the camp brothel, Hartley realizes she is now the sexual property of all five Hammond brothers, not just her husband. McCrea and Scott save her from their brutish attentions, differ over the gold's fate and are pursued to a final, tragic shoot-out.

McCrea and Scott have seldom been better. Hartley, herself a victim of an abusive marriage, made the most of the best female role in a Peckinpah Western. His rapid cross-cutting and percussive rhythms of violence made the final shoot-out feel more threatening than anything Ford or Hawks had filmed but, for the most part, he showed a restraint which makes this the one Peckinpah Western traditionalists and revisionists both enjoy.

Peckinpah is not to be confused with other makers of revisionist Westerns like **Arthur Penn**. Peckinpah's brand of revisionism is such that he is more likely to lament the conquering of the Old West by corrupt "civilization" than to suggest, as Penn does in *Little Big Man* (1970), that the West was conquered through genocide.

As ever with Peckinpah, you don't have to look far for personal sub-texts. The last, indelible, image of McCrea paid homage to a photograph of the director's father on his final hunting trip.

Ride The High Country is, according to Peckinpah, a movie about salvation and loneliness, but it's richer than that. His most gentle Western alongside *The Ballad Of Cable Hogue* (1970), this is full of unusual imagery – the whore gnawing on a turkey leg absently noting the vicious beating being dished out nearby – and makes fine use of the grittiness and grandeur offered by the landscape. As a filmmaker, he had found the theme/obsession – characters struggling with the fact of their own obsolescence – that would recur through *The Wild Bunch* (1969) and *Pat Garrett And Billy The Kid* (1973). When Warren Oates' villain shoots chickens, you know he's doomed – just as Billy the Kid's chicken shooters are in *Pat Garrett*.

The Searchers

dir John Ford, 1956, US, 119m

cast John Wayne, Jeffrey Hunter, Vera Miles, Ward Bond, Natalie Wood, Hank Worden

cin Winton C. Hoch *m* Max Steiner, Stan Jones

John Ford's superbly moving masterpiece, a favourite of filmmakers including Martin Scorsese, *The Searchers* has been referenced in films as diverse as *Taxi Driver* (1976), *Star Wars* (1977) and *Close Encounters Of The Third Kind* (1977) (see p.116). It was also one of the first films promoted with a making-of "plugumentary" for TV.

John Wayne dominates the film with a towering performance as terse, tormented Ethan Edwards, the wanderer driven on a relentless quest to find his niece Debbie (Natalie Wood), abducted by the Comanches who massacred his brother's family. The character's complexity shows an awareness of paradox foreign to Ford's pre-World War II Western heroes. In Ford's early mythos, cowboy and cavalry heroes built a nation over the dead bodies of savage Indians. But Ethan's obsession and racism is so bitter he intends to kill the girl he considers defiled. He remains implacable through five years of searching despite the voice of reason of his young half-Indian sidekick, Jeffrey Hunter's Martin. At the last minute he recognizes his own savagery, relents and understands that there is no place for him in the settlers' civilizing domesticity.

John Wayne's tormented hero in *The Searchers* inspired Travis Bickle in *Taxi Driver*.

The legacy of *The Searchers*

The most famous borrowing from *The Searchers* came in 1957 when **Buddy Holly** turned Ethan's catchphrase "That'll be the day" into the hook and title for his most famous hit. The British 1960s pop band The Searchers were named in the film's honour. But moviemakers have been even more enamoured of this classic than rock and roll stars.

You would expect the movie to influence Sam Peckinpah and Sergio Leone, who probably knew the movie frame by frame. But Ford's masterpiece has had as great an influence outside the genre.

George Lucas has publicly admired the film, and some *Star Wars* aficionados draw parallels between the Skywalker family saga and the troubles of the Edwards family, right down to the scene where Luke returns to the burning homestead.

Ethan's obsessive quest for his niece has inspired two **Paul Schrader** screenplays: *Taxi Driver* (1976) and *Hardcore* (1978). In both movies, the hero is a loner driven to violence and insanity by his quest to rescue a young white woman who has become the sexual prey of those he regards as sub-human. In *Taxi Driver*, Harvey Keitel's pimp Sport – who wears a cowboy hat, is known to loner Travis Bickle as "chief" and admits to once owning a horse – nods to Scar, the Comanche chief in Ford's film.

Wayne's deceptive art is to make Ethan so close to his own gestures that he doesn't seem to be acting at all – a gift which, for many years, led critics to undervalue him as an actor, as opposed to an icon.

What makes this dark parable so winning and effective is the heart in the flawed Ethan, the film's remarkable beauty, the comic, dramatic and romantic contributions of Ford's company players and the evocative, unobtrusive score. Among this emotive epic's stunning compositions is the immortal last shot of Wayne framed in the frontier home's dark doorway, purified and poised to walk away yet again from hearth and family "to wander forever between the winds".

The Searchers is a truly complex movie, with contradictions, subtexts and unanswered questions seldom found in Ford's earlier films. The glorification of Ethan, even though Ford and we recognize his obsessive and racist quest is wrong, is just one of many tensions which remain, unsmoothed over, in this great Western which anticipates the revisionism of Ford's *Cheyenne Autumn* (1964) with its painful realization that a hero who hates Indians can no longer be simply heroic.

Trivia hounds note: while their climactic crisis sees Ethan and Debbie run up a ridge in Monument Valley, the hill they scramble back down was 1200 miles away in Los Angeles' Bronson Park.

Shane

dir **George Stevens, 1953, US, 118m**
cast **Alan Ladd, Jean Arthur, Van Heflin, Brandon De Wilde, Jack Palance, Ben Johnson**
cin **Loyal Griggs** *m* **Victor Young**

When *Shane* was finished, the word on the Paramount lot was that it was just another **Alan Ladd** movie. Yet today, despite a few snipes from the likes of François Truffaut (who thought it phoney), George

This PR still from *Shane* makes the romantic triangle more blatant than it is in George Stevens' film.

Stevens' movie stands alone as a magnificent, self-consciously mythic, classic Western, and a hugely influential masterpiece.

Stevens turned **Jack Schaefer**'s novel, depicting arguably Western fiction's definitive heroic drifter, into a fine, complex movie. The conflict between the small farmers and big ranchers – alluding to the Johnson County range war in Wyoming in 1892 – is articulated in a moonlight debate on Independence Day in which **Van Heflin**'s quietly heroic farmer Joe Starrett and Stryker, the villainous rancher with hair like an Old Testament prophet, state their reasonable, if mutually exclusive, cases.

The Western hero in *Shane*

The Western movie hero is a simplified, airbrushed, mythologized representation of the real Westerner. When George Stevens set out to make the definitive Western, *Shane*, he defined the archetypal Western hero. Shane is, as Michael Coyne notes in his book *The Crowded Prairie*, "like [America's] idealized self-image, friendly, benevolent, peaceable and slow to anger, yet once roused to violence, he establishes his moral authority with thorough and often terrible finality".

A lot of retouching was needed to create this icon. Shane is, for a start, white and Anglo-Saxon, whereas the historical West was a place of some racial complexity. The first North American cowboys were Mexican vaqueros, while some estimates suggest that one in seven cowboys were of African-American ancestry. In Stevens' movie, the ethnic mix is just about diverse enough to include homesteaders with recognizably Scandinavian accents.

Shane's own accent is hard to place, possibly because, as with Wister's Virginian, we are supposed to regard him as a natural aristocrat, if not a literal one, a point underlined by his talk of haberdashery with Joe Starrett's wife Marilyn. His golden buckskin – the costume he wears as his "true" self – recalls **James Fenimore Cooper**'s frontier scout Hawkeye, the prototypical loner template for many Western heroes.

Shane's mysterious arrival in the valley indicates that he has come west to seek regeneration – one of the most persistent American frontier myths. He has a wistfulness that hints at emotional wounds unhealed, a motif amplified in Boetticher's and Mann's acclaimed Westerns of the 1950s.

A true Western hero, Shane is, as a sidekick says of Errol Flynn in *Dodge City* (1939), "the most movin' on man you ever saw". At the time *Shane* is set, with the frontier closing, moving on was no longer so easy but his need to do

Ladd's casting has been criticized, but it is hard to think of any other leading man who could so effortlessly have played Shane. His restraint, when taunted and humiliated, is believable, as it would not have been for John Wayne or Robert Mitchum. When he finally magnificently beats **Jack Palance**'s lean, mean, sneering hired gunfighter Wilson to the draw, he is convincing in a way that Montgomery Clift, originally cast as Shane, could never have been. Ladd looks, in Raymond Chandler's famous phrase, "like a small boy's idea of a tough guy" and in *Shane* he is given a small boy, Joey Starrett (played by **Brandon De Wilde**), to idolize him.

so is more about mythic resonance than historical reality, echoing the restless nomadic ways of knights in medieval romances.

Indeed, James C. Work, an expert in Western fiction at Colorado State University, has found parallels between Shane's story and the tales of **Gawain** and **Owain** the adventurer, one of King Arthur's principal battle knights, that go beyond their nomadic ways. Owain, for example, seeks revenge from a black-clad knight who has humiliated a friend of his in an uneven battle – not that dissimilar to Wilson's humiliation and murder of Torrey which Shane must avenge. And Shane's wound can be seen as a punishment for being tempted by Marilyn as Lancelot was by Guinevere.

The Western hero myth, perfected in the world's most successful capitalist economy, alludes, strangely often, to **Robin Hood**. Shane defeats the cattle barons much as Sherwood Forest's mythical hero frustrated the medieval barons on behalf of those too poor, weak or confused to defend themselves. The Robin Hood motif is not as explicit in *Shane* as in Henry King's *Jesse James* (1939), but it is present.

The audience doesn't need to appreciate this mythic underpinning for *Shane* to work, though it may explain why, for some, the film has such resonance. Shane is a compelling hero because he slays the ogre reluctantly, using his peerless, ruthless, instincts not to threaten civilization but to defend it. As Richard Schickel observed, when "everyone wore a six-shooter, complex moral conflicts could be plausibly resolved in clean, clear, violent action".

Since *Shane*, the image of the Western hero has been transformed, muddied and confused. Cowboys and gunfighters in 1960s and 70s Westerns, especially those that didn't star The Duke, were often portrayed as, at best, heroically obsolete or, at worst, psychopathic, violent, bigoted bullies. But the idealized Western hero – as exemplified by Alan Ladd riding off into the night, having made that part of Wyoming safe for, if not democracy, democratic society – remains one of the most powerful archetypes in popular culture.

But Stevens isn't just making myths. **Loyal Griggs**'s superb photography of the Grand Tetons landscape gives us a very different West to Ford's Monument Valley. The majestic mountains suggest the futility of conflict and, during Wilson's first shoot-out and the ensuing funeral, emphasize civilization's frailty in a place and time where the nearest marshal is a hundred miles away. Those who dislike *Shane* complain about its pretensions, but there is realism too. The casualties of conflict in *Shane* are blasted back into mud, or a pile of beer barrels. Stevens' juxtaposition of Joey chomping on his sweet and the punches flying in a mass brawl is amusing, thrilling and inspired.

Apart from Ladd's reluctant gunfighter, *Shane* gives us a fine gallery of Western archetypes: the homesteader, the homesteader's wife, the tyrannical land baron, the mercenary gunfighter (watch the pure joy with which Palance pulls on his gloves for the first gunfight), the hothead doomed because he's all valour and no discretion, and the storekeeper, quietly measuring tectonic shifts in local politics to stay alive.

Shane is not perfect. At times, as in the famous stump-chopping scene, Stevens' intent is too obvious, while **Victor Young**'s score can cloy. But Stevens' craftsmanship means the film repays re-viewing. Note, for example, how the town dog repeatedly shuns Wilson. *Shane* is full of delights like that. Admired by such different filmmakers as Akira Kurosawa, Peckinpah, Leone, Eastwood and Mann, *Shane* is a great Western. Joey's despairing cries of "Come back Shane!" as his wounded hero rides off into the distance – possibly to his death – resound as much today as when the film was made.

She Wore A Yellow Ribbon

dir John Ford, 1949, US, 103m
cast John Wayne, Joanne Dru, John Agar, Ben Johnson, Harry Carey Jr, Victor McLaglen
cin Winton C. Hoch *m* Richard Hageman

At the end of the 1940s, John Ford made a trio of films centred on his beloved 7th Cavalry, his microcosm of Western society at a key point in its history. Although they do not share the same characters or a through plot, the films have in common a consistency in style, Ford's core of regular actors and his romantic vision of soldierly fellowship. Thus they are universally recognized as the Cavalry trilogy: *Fort Apache* (1948, see p.227), *She Wore A Yellow Ribbon* – probably the greatest of the three, though it's not perfect – and *Rio Grande* (1950, see p.164).

In *Fort Apache*, **John Wayne** had been the sympathetic young officer, a quietly heroic contrast to **Henry Fonda**'s Custer-by-any-other-name. In *She Wore A Yellow Ribbon*, Wayne is Nathan Brittles, the very name suggesting the fragility of his position, older, more melancholy, the commander anxiously facing retirement – tantamount to exile from the only life he knows – and talking freely to his wife in her grave when hostilities with the Indians compel him to stand fast. For Wayne – and Ford – the price of leadership is isolation and celibacy, a price the Duke pays in many subsequent Westerns, though not in Andrew V. McLaglen's rambunctious *McLintock!* (1963).

Though the film opens with the 7th Cavalry flag and the words "Custer is dead", Wayne's ageing hero must act to stop war, circumventing the Custer-like zeal of lieutenant **John Agar** who wants to launch the kind of rash charge that undid Fonda in *Fort Apache*. If anything, Wayne's Brittles has more in common with his counterpart on the Indian side, Chief Pony That Walks, another old man who sees averting war as his duty. Their friendship has real poignancy and, by merely crossing the racial divide, is unusual for a Hollywood Western of this era. Perhaps the road to *Broken Arrow* (1950) starts here.

As Ford's best biographer Joseph McBride notes, this meditative Western marks the point at which the director's intolerance for the younger generation begins to mar his work. Brittles' two lieutenants – Agar and **Harry Carey Jr** – do not improve much on acquaintance, making it hard to be engrossed by their romantic triangle with Joanne Dru.

Ford's stock company are, mostly, on top form in telling and reverential vignettes (like Mildred Natwick watching the company riding off to probable death). Ford blends farce and tragedy with ease. The film won an Oscar for the grandeur of Winton C. Hoch's cinematography, which, in its use of colour, pays homage to the style of Western artist **Frederic Remington** (see p.16). In some ways, if you're watching the whole trilogy, it pays to watch this one last.

The Shooting

dir **Monte Hellman, 1966, US, 81m**
cast Jack Nicholson, Will Hutchins, Warren Oates, Millie
Perkins, Charles Eastman
cin Gregory Sandor *m* Richard Markowitz

The Shooting may just be the most famous Western hardly anybody
has ever seen. Funded anonymously by **Roger Corman**, Hellman
filmed this – and its companion existentialist Western *Ride In The
Whirlwind* – in 35 days in the Utah desert in 1965. Both were influenced by the assassination of JFK and the shooting of Lee Harvey
Oswald, though they were also shaped by the maker's reverence for
Jean-Paul Sartre, Albert Camus and more familiar Western icons
like John Ford. Hellman once famously described *The Shooting* as
"a film about other films, rather than a film about life".

    The Shooting is bookended by two enigmatic shootings. At
the start, **Warren Oates** rides in to a camp to find his brother
missing, their partner mysteriously assassinated (the grim physical detail of the death recalling the gorier aspects of JFK's death)
and the hapless Will Hutchins shooting at nothing, with vague
memories of an argument between the victim and someone who
may have been Oates's brother. Things don't get any clearer with
the arrival of **Millie Perkins**: she gets the cowboys to shoot her
horse because it's lame, but Oates realises, after killing it, that it
was healthy after all. Perkins is out to avenge the murder of her
husband and child and persuades Oates and Hutchins to join
her quest. Later still, she recruits a sociopathic gunman (**Jack
Nicholson**), though he seems as interested in goading Hutchins.
The final shooting in which Oates is the victim of crossfire is to
some enigmatic, to others inexplicable.

    Hellman's films are easily reduced to absurdity in the retelling but
they have an eerie power and a knack for productively perplexing us.
Bleak, ambiguous, with doomed characters and an intriguingly uncon-
ventional landscape for a Western, *The Shooting* is full of unusual imagery and themes. Hellman knew the Western well enough to play with
it in this way. For once in a Western, Perkins' nameless heroine is the
pivotal figure, making all the other characters react to her. Nicholson's

gunfighter is a grinning homage to Palance's hired gunman in *Shane* (1953). Characters are introduced in extreme close-ups and at one point the frame is split in two by a tree, the arrangement of the characters (Perkins on one side, Hutchins and Oates on the other) strikingly symbolic. Gregory Sandor's cinematography and Richard Markowitz's spare score brilliantly accentuate the air of existential doom.

If you're still puzzled by the finale, Hellman insists that if you watch it closely enough you can decipher it. The director has said

In *The Shooting*, Jack Nicholson pays smirking homage to Jack Palance's hired gun in *Shane*.

it is a replay of the shooting of JFK's alleged assassin **Lee Harvey Oswald**, though it recalls the violent chaos surrounding JFK's demise in Dallas. Perhaps inevitably, given the way they were shot, *Ride In The Whirlwind* is, though powerful, best seen as a companion piece to *The Shooting*, even down to the JFK theme – though the second movie dwells more on the assassination's ugly political aftermath.

Hellman and Oates would reunite, famously, for *Cockfighter* (1974) and, less famously, for a strange spaghetti Western called *China 9, Liberty 37* (1978) in which the conflict between Oates and a young gunslinger is driven mainly by their shared desire for Jenny Agutter. Sam Peckinpah has a rare cameo but, though the film has its admirers, it's not as haunting as *The Shooting*.

The JFK Western

For such an eastern president, **John F. Kennedy** exerted a strong magnetic pull on Westerns in the 1960s, even those not made by Monte Hellman. Here are two of the better movies from the era which dwell on his murder.

The Chase
dir Arthur Penn, 1965, US, 133m

In Arthur Penn's overheated, unsubtly symbolic, yet compelling, contemporary Western, the link with the JFK assassination is even clearer than in *The Shooting*, the film almost seeming, at times, like an accusation against the state of Texas, big business and the corrupt establishment. In a sleazy Texan town, Marlon Brando's decent liberal sheriff is powerless to act as the locals murder escaped jailbird Robert Redford for, as Richard Shickel put it, "no good reason other than that he stirs inchoate anxiety and happens to be in Texas". Having escaped from a lynch mob, Redford's character is shot being led into jail, just like Lee Harvey Oswald.

The Price Of Power (Il prezzo del potere)
dir Tonino Valerii, 1969, Sp/It, 108m

An unusually politicized, paranoid Italian Western, *The Price Of Power* restages the assassination of President James Garfield in 1881 to explore the killing of JFK. Valerii uses enough themes from the Kennedy tragedy – the finding and shooting of a patsy, the First Lady in a pink dress, Southern resentment over racial issues – to make his intent clear, but never reduces his movie to mere polemic. The JFK conspiracy sometimes sits oddly with the spaghetti Western conceits but Valerii's epic Western mostly works.

The Shootist

dir Don Siegel, 1976, US, 100m

cast John Wayne, Lauren Bacall, Ron Howard, James Stewart, John Carradine, Richard Boone

cin Bruce Surtees *m* Elmer Bernstein

John Wayne's last Western – and final movie – is a deliberate, self-conscious, beautifully made epitaph for the genre's greatest hero in its golden age.

Director **Don Siegel**'s intentions are clear from the opening montage of Wayne's most iconic moments from other Westerns but he rises above mere nostalgia and sentimentality to create one of the finest, most underrated, movies in the Duke's canon.

As shootist J.B. Books, Wayne is scared. Not scared of being killed, but scared he might be dying, a suspicion confirmed by James Stewart as Doc Hostetler who diagnoses cancer and advises him that waiting till the bitter end might prove bitter indeed. Today, the film is even more moving as, three years later, Wayne did die of cancer. In the film, he consoles himself through his relationship with his landlady Widow Rogers (**Lauren Bacall**) and her spiky but basically decent son (**Ron Howard**), and by challenging three old enemies to a last gunfight.

Apart from the widow and her son, no one appears unduly upset by the prospect of the shootist's imminent demise. The undertaker offers him a free funeral but, Wayne suspects, purely because he plans to "parade every damn fool in the state past me at a dollar per head and half price for children". The sheriff, a local newspaperman and an ex-girlfriend all, in their own ways, see Books' death as an opportunity, not a sadness. Unlike Joel McCrea's ageing gunfighter in *Ride The High Country* (1962), Books does not expect to die justified, just dignified. That's why he refuses to be remembered for a "pack o' lies" in the gutter press and organizes a quick death in a gunfight in a saloon, not the kind of slow painful end Wayne suffered in real life.

Siegel and his star didn't always see eye to eye. Wayne simply refused to shoot an opponent in the back, as Siegel suggested – maybe it stirred unpleasant memories of *The Man Who Shot Liberty Valance* (1962) – and insisted that the shootist die at the hands of a bartender, not in a mercy killing by the widow's son.

Less contentious – and a sign perhaps that he knew this would be his last Western – he asked for a rewrite so he could ride his trusty horse ole Dollor, seen to greatest advantage jumping fences at the end of *True Grit*, one last time on the screen.

Out of such tension emerged a greater movie – sensitively directed by Siegel and beautifully shot by **Bruce Surtees** – with, at its heart, such a powerful, dignified performance from Wayne that you don't mind the occasional clunker in the script or the odd moment when the elegiac tone becomes a tad intrusive. His scenes with Bacall (who had lost Humphrey Bogart to cancer) and Stewart are so accomplished you forget you are watching a movie. *The Shootist* is a great, moving, farewell from the Western's greatest star.

Son Of Paleface

dir **Frank Tashlin, 1952, US, 95m**
cast **Bob Hope, Jane Russell, Roy Rogers, Trigger, Lloyd Corrigan, Iron Eyes Cody, Douglass Dumbrille**
cin **Harry J. Wild** *m* **Lyn Murray, Jack Brooks**

Blazing Saddles (1974) may be the most famous Western spoof but the genre's aficionados prefer, by a landslide, Frank Tashlin's *Son Of Paleface* in which the director's cartoonist craft matches **Bob Hope's** incessant one-liners with an anarchic visual comedy.

Son Of Paleface is a sequel to – and funnier than – *The Paleface* (1948) in which Hope was a cowardly Indian fighter. Tashlin, who had written the script for the first film, stepped into the director's chair and keeps up a frenetic pace. Hope, playing the cowardly son of the cowardly Indian fighter, becomes embroiled with **Jane Russell**, a sexy singer pretending to be a bandit so she can wear tight black pants, and government agent **Roy Rogers** who is too fond of his horse Trigger to be stirred by Russell's attentions.

In just over an hour and a half of screen time, Tashlin spares no Western cliché, sending up Indian uprisings, lynch mobs, posses, ghost towns, saloon brawls (in a saloon called The Dirty Shame) and quick draws, and squeezes in as much rootin', tootin' and shootin' comedy as he can.

The pace ensures that Hope's fast-talking cowardly "hero" never becomes too obnoxious, even when, in one celebrated sequence, during a monologue about his father's Indian-killing exploits, he strikes a light on a real Native American, pauses, and starts referring to his dad as "the great Eskimo killer ... hated Eskimos".

Only Russell's physique is relatively immune to Tashlin's humour, a surprising omission which, given the director's later use of Jayne Mansfield and Marilyn Monroe, suggests he was warned off. She still looks devastating, especially when Tashlin introduces her with a pan shot up her legs while the soundtrack goes va-va-voom. Russell, relieved to be asked to do more than display her two most obvious attributes, gives one of her funniest performances, easily holding her own with Hope. Rogers sends himself up nicely while Trigger has two of the funniest scenes, chasing Hope through a house and fighting him for a blanket. As Western writer Brian Garfield says: "It's nonsense, but it's just about right."

Stagecoach

dir **John Ford, 1939, US, 96m, b/w**
cast **John Wayne, Claire Trevor, John Carradine, Thomas Mitchell, Andy Devine, George Bancroft**
cin **Bert Glennon** *m* **Boris Morros**

Stagecoach was the first Western **John Ford** had made in over a decade and it is a defining work in film history: the first great, enduring genre epic of the sound era, the vehicle that made **John Wayne** a star, and Ford's first shoot in **Monument Valley**. It also represented the introduction or perfecting of elements that would become the Western's favourite clichés, including the wronged man out to settle a score, the goodtime girl with a heart of gold, and the cavalry riding to the rescue.

A colourful group of passengers – a lawman, his prisoner (Wayne's Ringo Kid), Thomas Mitchell's drunken doctor, John Carradine's rakish gambler, an embezzling banker, a meek travelling

John Ford's *Stagecoach* offers a microcosm of society in which the usual social order is stood on its head.

salesman, Claire Trevor's Dallas (the tramp run out of town) and the pregnant wife of an officer – ride anxiously through Indian country. It's a deceptively simple story, mixing intimate character study and stupendous action into a meditation on frontier spirit, enhanced by the folkloric musical score.

As the coach makes its final run across the spectacular landscape the passengers anticipate a safe conclusion to their difficult journey when Apaches attack. The breathtaking chase is on, people at their worst and finest in the cramped confines of the coach as their ammunition runs out.

Ringo vaults from the coach onto the panicked horses, in a landmark sequence of thrilling stuntwork by the legendary **Yakima Canutt**. It's been imitated a thousand times but it's always glorious, pulse-racing viewing, especially when the bugle sounds the charge "Ta ta, ta ta, ta ta, Ta ta ta ta ta ta ta taaaa…". It would be a sufficiently exciting finish, but *Stagecoach* has yet another stunning set piece – Ringo's rendezvous with those who done him wrong, a shoot-out once seen never forgotten – before the two most deserving people are allowed to ride off together to a new life.

Ford always said that Dudley Nichols' screenplay drew heavily on the **Guy de Maupassant** short story "Boule de suif", the title of which refers to a common nickname for a prostitute. That may sound a tad high-falutin' but *Stagecoach* is, for a Hollywood Western, unusually class-conscious and the film, like Maupassant's story, neatly inverts the social order. The characters we admire by the end of *Stagecoach* are the exact opposite of those we might, through their social standing, admire at the start of the movie.

This inversion suits Ford's mythos – we are usually invited to admire soldiers not officers (and certainly not plutocrats) in his cavalry Westerns – but it is more pointed in *Stagecoach*. The most despicable character, the embezzling banker, spouts isolationist slogans ("America for Americans!") at fellow passengers and is pilloried as a fairweather patriot. As the film was released in 1939, only a year before the America First committee was formed to keep America out of World War II, it is hard, as writer Michael Coyne suggests in his *The Crowded Prairie*, not to read *Stagecoach* as an anti-isolationist, anti-Fascist Western.

The Tall T

dir **Budd Boetticher, 1957, US, 77m**
cast **Randolph Scott, Richard Boone, Maureen O'Sullivan, Skip Homeier, John Hubbard, Arthur Hunnicutt**
cin **Charles Lawton Jr** *m* **Heinz Roemheld**

The seven Westerns **Budd Boetticher** made with **Randolph Scott** between 1956 and 1960 are so consistent that many regard them as essentially one Western. Even Boetticher admitted "All my films with Randy Scott have pretty much the same story, with variants. A man whose wife has been killed and is searching out her murderer. They [the villains] have made mistakes but they are human beings, sometimes more human than Scott."

Boetticher was doing himself a slight disservice. He wasn't that micro-consistent and *The Tall T*, usually acclaimed as the best of the seven (though the director preferred *Seven Men From Now*), is one of the variants. Scott is presented with a different dilemma, how to keep himself and an heiress (**Maureen O'Sullivan**) alive after their stagecoach has been taken hostage by **Richard Boone** and his cronies.

But some things remain the same. The relationship between Scott and O' Sullivan – the centre of the Elmore Leonard story *The Captive* on which the movie is based – is pushed almost offstage, until the finale where they set out to build a better West together. *The Tall T* dwells instead on the complex conflict between Scott's laconic hero Pat Brennan and Boone's flashy villain Frank Usher. Boetticher said once: "Frank really loved Pat in the picture to the point of being terribly attracted to him physically. He would have liked to have been Pat."

In *The Tall T* – as in other Boetticher Westerns – hero and villain are mirror images. Though his films are often praised for their moral certitude, his villains are subtly drawn, with enough redeeming qualities to, so Boetticher suggests, have been the hero if fate had treated them differently. In *The Tall T*, Boone is capable of killing a 10 year old but refuses to shoot his adversary in the back and declines to take advantage of the sleeping O'Sullivan when they are alone in a cave. Before the final showdown, inevitable ("Some things a man can't ride around", says Scott quietly) but not desired by hero or villain, ideas of social justice are quietly questioned.

Like most of Boetticher's collaborations with Scott, *The Tall T* is economical with dialogue, and the viewer's time. The best Boetticher/Scott Westerns were mostly written by Burt Kennedy and his adaptation of Leonard's story is as tightly controlled as any Boetticher movie. *The Tall T* is no crowd-pleasing epic; the movie has a subtle intricacy, a refreshing refusal to do the obvious, that probably explains why, even today, it is still underrated. Then again, maybe critics just got fed up with trying to work out why it is called *The Tall T* – still the subject of a stuttering debate on the Internet.

Tell Them Willie Boy Is Here

dir **Abraham Polonsky, 1969, US, 98m**
cast **Robert Redford, Katharine Ross, Robert Blake, Susan Clark, Barry Sullivan, Charles McGraw**
cin **Conrad Hall** *m* **Dave Grusin**

Blacklisted director **Abraham Polonsky** had high hopes – and ideals – for his first movie in 21 years, the intriguing *Tell Them Willie Boy Is Here*. So it must have been a blow when the movie flopped, only to be re-released in the 1970s with the slogan "Baretta is Willie Boy!" to exploit the fact that **Robert Blake**, who plays the titular rebel, had become a famous TV detective. The movie was rediscovered again, in still more macabre fashion, in 2002 when Blake, who shoots his girlfriend in the film, was charged with shooting his wife (he was later acquitted).

Tell Them Willie Boy Is Here is not one of the best loved or most widely admired Westerns. Even Pauline Kael called it "ideology on horseback". Yet, despite its solemnity, the sense of a liberal conscience worn too visibly, the too obvious parallels between the fate of the hunted Willie Boy and the fate of characters like Polonsky in 1950s Hollywood, this is a powerful Western.

The movie draws on Harry Lawton's book *Willie Boy*, which recounts the real story of a similar manhunt at the turn of the 20th century. Blake excels as the young Paiute rebel accused of murder and forced to go on the run, after much misunderstanding, blundering and jumping to conclusions. **Robert Redford** gives one of his best studies in ambiguity as sheriff Cooper, who reluctantly sets out to find Willie Boy and his girl (**Katharine Ross**, good, but too glamorous). Hindered by a posse whose posturing he finds hard to take, he tells one member: "You ain't mayor yet judge, you're just running like Willie."

As Polonsky makes clear, Willie Boy has to die, condemned for his crimes (killing his girlfriend's father and, later, his girlfriend) and because he has no place in society, caught between two cultures and refusing to live, docile, on the reservation. But, in a touch worthy of

Anthony Mann, he suggests Cooper and Willie Boy are sides of the same character, when the sheriff places his hand into a handprint his target has left behind. After Willie Boy cons the sheriff into killing him, Cooper brings the body down and, Pontius Pilate-like, washes the blood off his hands with dirt before ensuring Willie Boy gets a ceremonial burial. Rebuked by his boss for having no corpse to show the media, Cooper sneers: "Tell 'em we're all out of souvenirs."

Polonsky is more interested in the machinations behind the hunt for Willie Boy than in explosive action – a preference which may explain the film's low standing with traditionalists. The fact that many characters refer to Redford as Coop, in Polonsky's rather obvious attempt to invoke a great Western icon, may deter others. But this is a cogent, original, Western, beautifully shot – especially in the desert scenes – by **Conrad Hall**, with Redford and Blake at their considerable best as hunter and hunted.

3.10 To Yuma

dir **Delmer Daves, 1957, US, 92m, b/w**
cast **Glenn Ford, Van Heflin, Felicia Farr, Henry Jones, Richard Jaeckel, Leora Dana, Robert Emhardt**
cin **Charles Lawton Jr** *m* **George Duning**

Those who think of the Western as the home for simple moral certainties will be puzzled by *3.10 To Yuma*. In this taut, classy movie, derived from the **Elmore Leonard** story of the same name, the relationship between hero and villain is as ambiguous as in any Budd Boetticher or Anthony Mann Western.

The plot is simple enough. **Van Heflin**'s poor farmer has volunteered to take **Glenn Ford**'s charming, Machiavellian outlaw to court in Yuma for $200 and is holed up in a hotel room while the captive's pals try to stage a rescue. But the film's psychological conflict stems from each man's envy of the other's lot in life. Some fans, noting that Daves had a messianic hero in *The Hanging Tree* (1959), have found religious symbolism in this – with Van Heflin as the Christ figure tempted by Ford's devilish rogue.

Daves is a much underrated Western director, and *3.10 To Yuma*, his finest Western, has not been granted the recognition it deserves. Though the themes of waiting and a lone lawman doing his difficult duty unaided point back to *High Noon* (1952), this Western nods to the amoral revisionism of Sergio Leone and Clint Eastwood.

Daves – and writer Halsted Welles – expand on Leonard's story, making the envy at the heart of the central relationship clearer and incorporating a scene in which barmaid Felicia Farr's ole-time sexuality persuades Ford to drop his guard. Sadly, they tamper with the

Charming devil Glenn Ford tempts Van Heflin's Christ-like farmer in the criminally underrated *3.10 To Yuma*.

ending, giving the tale a daft twist in which Ford effectively helps Van Heflin make it onto the 3.10 alive (saying "I've busted out of Yuma before"). In reward, it is implied that, after Ford has served his time, he may be reunited with Farr.

The acting varies from very good (Farr and Van Heflin, suitably stubborn, steady and sympathetic) to superb (Ford, who steals the film as the amiable, fast-talking, yet perceptive outlaw). The actors needed to click because this is surprisingly talky for a Western. Charles Lawton Jr's striking black and white photography is at its most evocative in the opening scene in which, as **Frankie Laine** wails the theme song, a distant stagecoach proceeds across a barren desert. Shame about the ending, though. The story's logic is undone by the dictates of the studio star system.

El Topo

dir **Alejandro Jodorowsky, 1971, Mex, 124m**
cast **Alejandro Jodorowsky, Brontis Jodorowsky, Mara Lorenzio, David Silva, Paula Romo**
cin **Rafael Corkidi** *m* **Alejandro Jodorowsky**

El Topo may be the definitive acid Western – but like a lot of acid movies, it isn't always coherent and is full of lines that sound deep mainly if you're high. Even Danny Peary, in a generally admiring review in his book *Cult Movies*, concluded: "That this film is beyond our comprehension doesn't make it profound."

A Chilean writer, graphic novelist, composer, tarot expert and psychotherapist, Jodorowsky made himself famous with this allegorical, surreal, mystic Western of redemption. *El Topo* became a cult favourite on the American student circuit in the early 1970s after Allan Klein, on **John Lennon**'s recommendation, bought the distribution rights. (Rows over distribution rights have since stymied the movie's release on DVD.)

The quest of Jodorowsky's hero echoes such diverse sources as *Lord Of The Rings* and Eastwood's laconic hero in Leone's "Man With No Name" trilogy, but it is odder than either. The opening scene – in which the hero rides through the desert with

Slogans on the range

"There were three men in her life. One to take her ... one to love her ... and one to kill her." An intriguing hook for *Once Upon A Time In The West* (1968).

"See the naked young Franciscans whipped with cactus. See the bandit leader disembowelled. See the priest ride into the sunset with a midget and her newborn baby. What it all means isn't exactly clear, but you won't forget it." The American studio tries to convey just how unique *El Topo* (1971) really is.

"The land had changed, they hadn't. The earth had cooled, they couldn't." A surprisingly appropriate slogan for *The Wild Bunch* (1969).

"An army of one." When you see Clint Eastwood in *The Outlaw Josey Wales* (1976), you realize the studio weren't lying.

"The hell-hot story of a hell-bent dancehall dame who climbed to the top bullet by bullet, man by man." She was some girl, the *Buckskin Lady*, as played by Patricia Medina in 1956.

an umbrella and his son – is an unforgettable twist on Western iconography. Initially, El Topo is an avenging Leone-esque angel – shooting the men behind a massacre – but events turn strange when the hero abandons his son to ride off with a woman, Mara, who urges him to prove his love for her by challenging four Masters of the Desert. After he's conquered these masters, El Topo is shot, sees the fickle Mara ride off with a woman she loves, and falls asleep for twenty years. He awakes, bald and humbled, in a cave full of deformed dwarfs. In trying to save these dwarfs, El Topo triggers their massacre and a confrontation with his grown son.

Throwing in the allusions faster than T.S. Eliot in *The Waste Land*, and maintaining a grim, remorselessly violent, pace, Jodorowsky has created a complex fantasy that has an uncanny resonance. If there is a meaning – for some there are many, for others, none – it may be about humility. El Topo starts the film thinking of himself as God, later to explicitly admit, "I am not a god, I am a man". Not that being humble was one of Jodorowsky's qualities. In his annotated script, he notes that the rock Mara hugs – and from which water squirts her – "is an exact replica of my own phallus".

True Grit

dir Henry Hathaway, 1969, US, 128m
cast John Wayne, Kim Darby, Glen Campbell, Robert Duvall, Dennis Hopper, Jeremy Slate
cin Lucien Ballard *m* Elmer Bernstein

Ned Pepper: I call that bold talk for a one-eyed fat man.
Rooster Cogburn: Fill your hands, you son of a bitch.

Is there any more exhilarating sight in any Western than **John Wayne**, as Rooster Cogburn, growling, putting his horse's reins in his teeth, taking a six-shooter in one hand and a rifle in the other, and, barrels blazing, charging Ned Pepper's gang?

Veteran director **Henry Hathaway** had made plenty of Westerns, but this confrontation is a truly transcendent moment which had audiences cheering and laughing on its release. Cheering because this one ridiculous, against-the-odds challenge defined – and celebrated – the celluloid archetype that was John Wayne, and laughing because at the same time the Duke – and Hathaway – were sending up that archetype.

True Grit is not a perfect Western. The pace is uneven. Glen Campbell, as the Texas Ranger, struggles with the loquacious script, based on Charles Portis's fine novel. Many argue that Peckinpah's *Ride The High Country* (1962) tells the same story better. Yet *True Grit* packs a hefty emotional punch, conveys a real sense of a perilous society in the making and, for a Western, offers a surprising number of laughs.

Kim Darby is simply extraordinary as Matty, the orphaned girl looking for a man with true grit to hunt down Tom Chaney, the cowardly killer of her father. She strikes a bargain with Wayne's one-eyed drunken fat old rascal of a marshal – playing Jim Hawkins to Wayne's Long John Silver – after being advised that he is the most ruthless law enforcer around. They unite with Campbell's Texas Ranger who's chasing a reward for Chaney who has also shot a Texas state senator. "It is a small reward," says Campbell, "but he was not a large senator."

This is no conventional trio Western. Their mission is made harder by the fact that they can't stop bickering with each other and by the fact that Chaney has thrown his lot in with Ned Pepper's gang of outlaws. Robert Duvall's Pepper is a subtle portrayal of a man who seems to regret that his path has crossed Cogburn's, knowing that the lawman's quest can only end in death for one of them.

Hathaway's movie has an economical way with death. Darby's father, two minor villains, even Campbell, all die quickly, almost casually, without ceremony – not in slow-motion ballet nor mourned by an intrusive orchestra. Ballard's beautiful, sensitive, photography of Colorado and California places the story in a different terrain to most Westerns.

For Richard Schickel, "John Wayne has discovered what's funny about the character he has always played and gives us a rich double vision of himself. He is himself and he is himself playing himself – an exuberant put-on that seems to delight him as much as it does us."

Nowhere is that better captured than in the final scene where, reprimanded by Matty for being "too old and fat to be jumping horses", Wayne doffs his hat, says "Well, come and see a fat old man sometime", jumps the fence and rides away across the snowy mountains. It is a bittersweet finale. Funny, because Cogburn – and Wayne – remain joyously ornery. Yet sad because, like Matty, we know Cogburn is riding off to more missions, more villains, until, one day, he fills his hand too slowly with lead and dies.

The Duke goes gloriously, stirringly, over the top in *True Grit*, playing himself and parodying himself at the same time.

137

Unforgiven

dir Clint Eastwood, 1992, US, 131m
cast Clint Eastwood, Gene Hackman, Morgan Freeman,
Richard Harris, Jaimz Woolvett, Saul Rubinek
cin Jack N. Green *m* Lennie Niehaus

"What I like about *Unforgiven* is that every killing in it has a reper-cussion." **Clint Eastwood**'s remark immediately identifies the differ-ence between this, his last great Western, and the spaghetti Westerns in which he made his fame.

Clint as bounty hunter William Munny – unforgiven, by himself, for his life of violence?

Unforgiven starts with a drunken, violent attack on a prostitute (**David Webb Peoples'** screenplay, finished in 1976, was called *The Cut Whore Killings*) but it is the refusal of sheriff Little Bill (**Gene Hackman**) to take the offence seriously that has disastrous repercussions.

The sadistic public whipping of a dandy gunslinger (**Richard Harris**), the humiliating death of a bounty hunter (**Morgan Freeman**) and, finally, Little Bill's own death at the hands of ageing gunfighter William Munny (Eastwood) all spring from Little Bill's casual act of minor injustice. Dying, Little Bill moans that he doesn't deserve his fate, only to be told by Munny: "Deserve's got nothing to do with it."

Many critics hailed *Unforgiven* as a revisionist Western, and this is partially true – Eastwood does set out to make amends for past "sins", in terms of casual violence and the genre's presentation of women. But the movie might be better described as an über-Western. The generous time given to supporting players like Freeman and Harris recalls the generosity of a great John Ford Western. Munny's life – as the ex-gunfighter half-civilized by his dead wife and turned into an incompetent farmer – internalizes the conflict between guns and advancing civilization, often symbolized by women, that runs through many great Westerns. Munny, incredibly incompetent when first returning to the life of violence, ultimately dispenses justice with terminator-on-horseback efficiency.

The moral issues are as muddy as the streets in Big Whiskey. Munny is the hero – because Clint is almost always the hero – even though there is much not to admire about his character. In the end, he may be the hero because he learns that his time, like Shane's, is past and his job is to fade away. Equally, though sheriff Little Bill is usually seen as the villain – and his arrogance is the catalyst for the violence that follows – he is building a house, an obvious symbol that unlike almost anyone else in the town he is trying, however imperfectly, to make Big Whiskey a community.

Unforgiven is set at a time when the Old West is dying – a point eloquently made in the opening shot of a house, a tree and a man at a graveside – and has a drained, wintry look, appropriate to the historical moment and to Munny's – Eastwood's? – season of life. Lawmen and gunslingers are, at this point in the West's history, exceptional enough to be pursued by pulp writers. But the gap between emerging pulp myth and messy, haunting reality is exposed when Munny recalls shooting a drover through the mouth: "He didn't do anything to deserve getting shot, at least, nothing I could remember when sober."

The probable repercussion of that killing is that Munny, even as he settles down to run a dry goods store in California with the brothel's madam, remains unforgiven – by himself.

Vera Cruz

dir Robert Aldrich, 1954, US, 94m
cast Gary Cooper, Burt Lancaster, Denise Darcel, Cesar Romero, Sarita Montiel
cin Ernest Laszlo *m* Hugo Friedhofer

Gary Cooper took the role of an ex-Confederate colonel in partnership – and conflict – with **Burt Lancaster**'s mercenary against the advice of Clark Gable who, after seeing Lancaster in *From Here To Eternity* (1953), told Coop: "That young fella will wipe you off the map."

Luckily Coop ignored Gable, enabling Aldrich to make what was, for its time, an extraordinarily cynical and humorous Western. The modern tone may explain the hostile verdict of Anglo-American critics on its release, typified by the *New York Times*'s Bosley Crowther who labelled it a "big, noisy, badly photographed hodgepodge of outdoor melodrama". François Truffaut, whose detailed structural analysis of the movie is one of the highlights of his *My Life In Films*, praised it as a "John Huston movie that succeeds", acknowledging the film's Huston-like mix of strong plot, cynical attitude and vivid action. History has tended to agree with Truffaut.

The premise is simplicity itself: two adventurers – Coop's more honourable than Lancaster's – caught up in the Mexican revolution try to double-cross each other over a hoard of gold. But as Truffaut shows, the movie is a "dazzling exercise in story construction", with the key themes – encirclement by the Mexican troops, the stealing of the loot and a partner saving the other's life – repeated twice. What starts off as an exercise in rip-roaring cynicism ends, a little more conventionally, with Cooper, inspired by his love for an idealistic young Mexican girl, forced to kill his partner so the gold can aid the revolutionaries.

Aldrich had a gift for staging action sequences and the film rattles along so quickly you forgive the occasional excess (though you do wonder whether the beautiful countess – **Denise Darcel** – whom the pals are escorting needs slapping around quite so often). The pairing of Lancaster's selfish charmer and Coop's essentially dignified hero makes this feel more than a well-crafted mechanical exercise.

The humour and clever story construction impressed a young Italian moviemaker called **Sergio Leone** who briefly worked alongside Aldrich on the epic *Sodom And Gomorrah* (1962). The cynical tone, the bounty hunter motif, the motivation (greed), the double-crosses and betrayals, even the film's habit of interrupting Lancaster's curses with trumpet fanfares, would all inspire him. Indeed, *Vera Cruz* is probably the Hollywood movie which most influenced spaghetti Westerns.

The film's Mexican setting was a backdrop that Sturges, Leone, Sergio Corbucci and Sam Peckinpah profitably exploited in the 1960s. Aldrich didn't profit in the same way – his portrayal of Mexican characters caused riots in Mexican cinemas. But his *Vera Cruz* helped give the Western a new lease of life.

The Virginian

dir Victor Fleming, 1929, US, 91m, b/w
cast Gary Cooper, Walter Huston, Richard Arlen, Mary Brian, Helen Ware, Chester Conklin
cin J. Roy Hunt, Edward Cronjager *m* Karl Hajos

When **Gary Cooper** played **Owen Wister**'s Virginian as a lean, elegant, romantic, fundamentally decent, laconic loner in this Victor Fleming movie he wasn't just giving the definitive performance as one of the great heroes of Western fiction, he was, in a very real sense, defining the Western movie hero.

Wister's hero – a man with no name long before Clint chewed on a cheroot – wasn't from Virginia by accident; the designation was supposed to convey a certain social status. The author saw his character as a direct descendant of the chivalrous knights of old. **Victor Fleming** understood the fairytale quality of Wister's novel which is one reason why his film – the first sound adaptation of the book after two silent versions, the first directed by Cecil B. DeMille – is so superior to the 1946 remake starring Joel McCrea.

Newly arrived schoolmarm Molly Wood (Mary Brian) attracts both the Virginian and his pal Steve (Richard Arlen), but inevitably it's Coop she falls for. Their budding romance is disturbed by the evil Trampas (Walter Huston), and by Steve who joins Trampas's gang of rustlers, is captured by a posse and lynched – rough justice which the Virginian is forced to supervise. Shocked, Molly spurns the Virginian, but forgives him when he is wounded. But Trampas still wants the Virginian to leave town and is out gunning for the hero.

The Virginian is a hard movie to judge afresh because so many of its conceits and scenarios soon became integral to the Western: the tall, handsome, shy hero, reluctantly confronting the outlaw; the ugly, uncouth villain in black; the sexually pure and morally innocent schoolmarm/wife-to-be; the tragic friendship between hero and friend led astray; the walkdown to the gunfight; the cattle drive.

The film's matter-of-fact approval of the necessity of lynching – taken from the novel where Wister relies on sophistry to distinguish "good" lynchings of rustlers from "bad" lynchings of Southern negroes – makes for harrowing viewing. Wister's – and the film's – stance that you can judge a lynching by the quality of the people pulling the rope hasn't dated well.

Fleming's *The Virginian* was so successful that it was reissued in 1935 by popular demand, but oddly it didn't usher in a golden age of great Westerns. The stock situations and characters it presented would, instead, be exploited for the next decade mainly in B Westerns, though it would be an obvious source for Cooper's most famous Western, *High Noon* (1952).

Warlock

dir **Edward Dmytryk, 1959, US, 122m**
cast **Richard Widmark, Henry Fonda, Anthony Quinn, Dorothy Malone, Dolores Michaels, Wallace Ford**
cin **Joseph MacDonald** *m* **Leigh Harline**

Imagine the town in *High Noon* (1952) if Gary Cooper had fled. That is the parlous state Warlock is in as this movie starts, quivering in fear of the San Pablo gang, whose pleasure it is to shoot barbers, humiliate sheriffs, rustle cattle and massacre Mexicans. Tired of cowering, the townsfolk hire a marshal, Clay Blaisdell (**Henry Fonda**), who rides into Warlock with his crippled, loyal sidekick Tom Morgan (**Anthony Quinn**).

So far, so conventional. But *Warlock* is no ordinary town-taming Western. It is as clear as the filmmakers could make it in the 1950s that Quinn's lame gambler/gunfighter is in love with Fonda's marshal, "the only man who looked at me and didn't just see a cripple". Why there's even talk of the satin sheets they have brought to town! When the marshal suggests he'll marry and settle in Warlock, Quinn's psychological breakdown triggers an inevitable shoot-out with Fonda who, traumatized by the necessity of killing his old friend, kicks the walking stick away from a lame jabbering judge.

But the real conflict – the shoot-out that seems inevitable yet never happens – is between Fonda's marshal and **Richard Widmark**'s deputy sheriff, Johnny Gannon. Widmark once belonged to the San Pablo gang but, haunted by their massacre of Mexicans who rustled the wrong cattle, he turned to liquor. When that doesn't deaden his guilt, he volunteers to become deputy sheriff, drawing him into likely conflict with Fonda.

Widmark's defection is seen by many as justifying director **Edward Dmytryk**'s decision to testify before Congress against the Communists. Even without that interpretation, the symmetry is remarkably neat. Widmark's character, one of the Western's oldest stereotypes, is the "good" bad man who, to survive, must face Fonda's "bad" good man.

For Fonda, Blaisdell is the exact midpoint between the quiet heroics of Wyatt Earp in *My Darling Clementine* (1946) and the flashy villainy of Frank in *Once Upon A Time In The West* (1968). Fonda's Blaisdell is much closer to the real Earp than Ford's hero: a brave, efficient gunfighter, with a highly personal sense of right and wrong, who brings his own saloon to whichever town he is taming and whose best friend is a sometime pimp.

Charismatic, yet menacing, Blaisdell tames the town, defies a lynch mob, attracts the lustful attentions of the repressed Dolores Michaels, shoots Johnny's bad brother Billy, reluctantly, in a fair fight and is forced to kill his friend. Finally, after giving Quinn as near a Viking funeral as he can manage in a two-bit town out West, he spurns Michaels' offer of marriage – and the opportunity to shoot Widmark – riding out of town to his next mission.

A deliberate inversion of *My Darling Clementine*, *Warlock* is a surprisingly sour Western, as unflattering in its portrayal of the townsfolk (who await a gunfight "like little boys waiting for the circus parade") as *High Noon*, with strong undertones of homoeroticism and Greek myth.

Leone often said he had the idea of casting Fonda in *Once Upon A Time In The West* after seeing his brittle martinet in *Fort Apache* (1948). But Blaisdell is the more likely inspiration. Leone's scriptwriter Luciano Vincenzoni says: "[*Warlock*] was Leone's favourite. He had it imprinted in his head."

The Wild Bunch

dir Sam Peckinpah, 1969, US, 145m
cast William Holden, Ernest Borgnine, Robert Ryan, Warren Oates, Edmond O'Brien, Ben Johnson
cin Lucien Ballard *m* Jerry Fielding

Released in sharp contrast the same year as *Butch Cassidy And The Sundance Kid* and *True Grit*, **Sam Peckinpah's** revolutionary, gloomily romantic masterpiece burst on the scene, to be met with horror and awe in equal measure.

The admiration was for the realism and vitality in a film in which you could taste the dust. The horror was in reaction to the extreme violence and beautiful bloodshed that took the Western into new, extreme territory. The story is set in 1912 when **William Holden's** past-it outlaw and his gang head for Mexico to make one last dirty haul, hunted by betrayed ex-partner **Robert Ryan**. But they are just as much in flight from the 20th century, automobiles, flying machines and machine guns symbolizing the finish of the West they understand.

Mexico is convulsed with revolution. But it retains an old-time playground allure for the out-of-time, misogynist brutes. For they are all savage killers, and Peckinpah audaciously, compellingly discovers their depths and humanity, leading them inexorably to a mad, suicidal final bow. There are extraordinary and extraordinarily cruel images. Young children laugh watching a writhing scorpion devoured by ants. Screaming horses plunge off a dynamited bridge.

When Holden, Borgnine, Oates and Johnson – in a nihilistic fit of uncharacteristic altruism – return to reclaim their captive comrade (Jaime Sanchez's Angel) they watch in slow-motion shock as his throat is cut. There follows a long, heart-stopping pause as the Bunch, guns drawn, and the mob surrounding them fall silent and frozen, every one fearful and fully aware before all hell breaks loose. Holden is shot in the back by a woman and wheels to blow her away.

The Peckinpah myth is so loud – and *The Wild Bunch* such a visceral experience – that it's easy to miss the craft. Yet filmmaker Paul Schrader says "No one has mastered the art of multi-camera

The Wild Bunch inspired horror and awe among their adversaries, as well as among critics and filmgoers.

multi-speed editing like Peckinpah, even today. He would have five or six cameras going at different speeds and know how it was all going to cut together." That craft is most obvious in the film's sensational finale. But *The Wild Bunch* wouldn't be the tour de force it is without Peckinpah's astonishing, obsessive, attention to detail. L.Q. Jones, a member of his stock company, recalls that Peckinpah threatened to fire a crew member because one character had eight beans on his plate in a close-up and, in a long shot in the same scene, thirteen beans.

The Wild Bunch is all one in the gut for the clean-cut, mythic Fordian hero. But a film that ends in demented, despairing laughter (Ryan's) proved an authentic, influential cultural statement – a Western that tried to deal with the legacy of the Vietnam War and force the audience to confront their own lust for violence.

The Icons: Western legends

Clint Eastwood's third outing as The Man With No Name in Sergio Leone's *The Good, The Bad And The Ugly* made Hollywood finally take notice.

The Icons:
Western legends

Some actors and directors – and even the odd composer and stunt man – have defined our image of the West, shaping the Western genre itself, and leaving their mark on cinema and on popular culture. Here we tip our hats to the truly iconic figures, from Robert Aldrich to Yosemite Sam.

Robert Aldrich

1918–83

In 1957 Robert Aldrich was listed as one of the seven great creators of the cinema by the Belgian Club du Livre de Cinéma. For a man who had directed his first film only in 1953, he was in exalted company, alongside Buñuel, Huston, De Sica and Renoir. His reputation has fluctuated since but today he is honoured as the creator of two truly remarkable post-war Westerns: *Vera Cruz* (1954) and *Ulzana's Raid* (1972).

Born to a wealthy family, Aldrich served a lengthy apprenticeship as assistant or second unit director, before making his directorial debut in 1953 with a baseball movie. In 1954 he made two strong Westerns. *Apache*, starring **Burt Lancaster** and Jean Peters as blue-eyed Apaches, marked a significant step forward in Hollywood's treatment of Native Americans but, compromised by studio interference, it was not as ground-breaking as *Vera Cruz*. More than any other single Western, this cynical tale of mercenaries and macho one-upmanship, pairing **Gary Cooper** and Burt Lancaster, laid the basis for the spaghetti Western while anticipating the amoral violent West of Peckinpah's *The Wild Bunch* (1969).

His next Western, *The Last Sunset* (1961), was a Freud-on-the-range saga touching on incest, Indians and suicide that didn't entirely convince, despite an astonishing performance from Carol Lynley as the young frontier girl. *Four For Texas* (1963) was a comedy Western in which Dean Martin and Frank Sinatra were outshone by the mammary marvels of Anita Ekberg and Ursula Andress. Perhaps disillusioned, Aldrich then shunned Westerns for eight years, returning with his masterpiece *Ulzana's Raid*, a violent, shocking, gritty Western, rich with allusion to the Vietnam War.

After such uncompromising magnificence, the gentle Western comedy of *The Frisco Kid* (1979) was doomed to fail. Though Gene Wilder did his best, Aldrich had bowed out of the genre in a bizarrely anti-climactic manner. But then, as a director, he had often been too busy for his own good. If Aldrich had made just *Apache*, *Vera Cruz* and *Ulzana's Raid*, he would be regarded as one of the Western's true masters.

Ulzana's Raid
dir Robert Aldrich, 1972, US, 103m

Ulzana's Raid is no *Soldier Blue*-style one-sided exposé, but instead, thanks to Alan Sharp's script, a dark, violent portrait of a brutal cat-and-mouse conflict between cavalry and Indians in which even the landscape seems cruel. Burt Lancaster is McIntosh, the scout who, though sympathetic to the Apaches' plight, helps the cavalry track down Ulzana and his renegades. For some, the film is as much a portrait of America's racial divide as a post-liberal, Vietnam Western.

Gene Autry
1907–98

For a man who couldn't ride, act, tie a lasso or shoot, Gene Autry had a surprisingly glorious career as the first definitive singing cowboy, the kind of character that Curly Bonner was modelled on in Peckinpah's *Junior Bonner* (1972).

"America's Favourite Cowboy", as he was once dubbed, was born in Texas in 1907. With help from **Will Rogers**, he broke the movies in 1934, and began churning out musical Westerns. Most of the true milestones in his career are to do with sales of his records – he is alleged to be the first artist ever to sell a million copies of a record – not his movies.

His million-seller was "Silver-Haired Daddy Of Mine". He first sang it on screen in a 1935 film called *Phantom Empire* in which he galloped between Radio Ranch and a strange underground civilization. Not all of Autry's Westerns – he made over 100 – were that original.

The most critically rated – if that's not overstating the case – is *Tumbling Tumbleweeds* (1935), his first film for Republic. Like many of his films, it had no respect for historical accuracy: in this case, he uses a modern record player to trap the villains; in other films, cars, radios and aeroplanes would make anachronistic appearances. But he wore a white hat, was kind to women – apart from when he sang to them – and was darn patriotic to boot.

Reviled by many critics, yet hugely successful, Autry smoothed the path for the likes of **Roy Rogers**, **Tex Ritter** and other singing cowboys. His style hasn't aged well – Ritter is easier to listen to, warmer and less monotonous. Rogers, though a virtual duplicate of Autry, surpassed his master by occasionally starring in bigger Westerns, notably *Son Of Paleface* (1952). But if Autry hadn't ridden onto a set on his trusty steed Champion, Rogers, Ritter & co. might never have made it.

Budd Boetticher
1916–2001

Quentin Tarantino named Michael Madsen's fallen swordfighter in *Kill Bill* (2003) Budd in tribute to Budd Boetticher, the cinema snob's favourite Western director, still criminally under-rated by the masses. The French adopted him in the 1950s, while Leone, Bogdanovich and Tarantino have all paid homage. This is no more than Boetticher deserves. He made seven great, unusual, economical, enigmatic, minutely detailed Westerns. If they have a message, it is, as Jim Kitses says in *Horizons West* (named after a Boetticher film), "Everybody loses", though this dark pessimism is softened, somewhat, by a sense of life's absurdity.

Boetticher fell in love with bullfighting while in Mexico and, in 1941, offered technical advice on Rouben Mamoulian's matador movie *Blood And Sand*. After a decade of B movies, in 1951 he made *The Bullfighter And The Lady*, an Oscar-nominated autobiographical film that had 37 minutes cut by producer **John Wayne** because he thought the male bonding scenes made the actors "look like poofs".

Boetticher persevered. In 1952 he made three decent B Westerns: *The Cimarron Kid* (making a star of Audie Murphy), *Bronco Buster* and *Horizons West*. In 1953 *Seminole* and especially *The Man From The Alamo* (with Glenn Ford wrongly accused of cowardice) were better still.

His meisterwork – and they can be judged almost as one movie – is the cycle of seven films he made with **Randolph Scott**. Starting in 1956 with *Seven Men From Now*, the Ranown films (named after Scott's production company) included *The Tall T* (1957), *Decision At Sundown* (1957), *Buchanan Rides Alone* (1958), *Westbound* (1959), *Ride Lonesome* (1959) and *Comanche Station* (1960). Five were co-written with direc-tor-in-the-making Burt Kennedy.

Boetticher brilliantly used Scott's wooden-ness to express stoic indifference to danger as he rode, alone, through the West, often determined to exact a revenge he knew was futile. Though remarkably consistent in structure, plot, theme, use of landscape and running length (three of the Boetticher/Scott/Kennedy collaborations are 78 minutes), the films do vary in tone – from the elegiac but optimistic *Ride Lonesome* and the sometimes farcical *Buchanan Rides Alone* to the bitterly ironic *The Tall T* and the sour and dark *Decision At Sundown*. They vary in quality, too: *Decision At Sundown* and *Westbound*, neither writ-ten by Kennedy, are the weakest, while Boetticher felt *Seven Men From Now* was the best.

Critic Andrew Sarris captured the essence of the Ranown Westerns, describing them as "con-structed partly as allegorical Odysseys and partly as floating poker games where every character takes turns at bluffing about his hand until the final showdown". So why are they not better known? Perhaps, as Kitses says, it is because they

Budd Boetticher's favourite Westerns

For such an iconoclastic director, Budd Boetticher's selection of his favourite Westerns is surprisingly orthodox, though he has the chutzpah to rank his *Seven Men From Now* above *High Noon* and *Shane*.

1 *Treasure Of The Sierra Madre* (1948)

2 *Red River* (1948)

3 *The Wild Bunch* (1969)

4 *Seven Men From Now* (1956)

5 *High Noon* (1952)

6 *Shane* (1953)

7 *Rio Bravo* (1959)

Source: *Variety Book Of Movie Lists*

are too sane, too unpretentious, too unshowy to dazzle in a market driven by "pathological characters, dystopic visions and bravura action".

Their overall excellence earned Boetticher a shot at big-budget Westerns, but he turned down the chance to direct Wayne and in 1960 went to Mexico with his then wife **Debra Paget** to make another bullfighting movie, which eventually emerged as *Arruza* (1972). In the next eight years, Paget left him, he was jailed, committed to an asylum, and went broke. He returned to Hollywood – and the Western – in 1969 with the half-decent *A Time For Dying*, starring Audie Murphy. More Westerns with Murphy were planned but the star died in a plane crash. In an unsatisfactory epilogue to Boetticher's Western career, he scripted *Two Mules For Sister Sara* (1970) but was deemed too out of touch – by the producer not star Clint Eastwood – to direct it. At only 54, he found himself in professional exile.

In old age, Boetticher relished the rediscovery of his Ranown films which had, he said once, "taken Randolph Scott and shoved him up John Wayne's ass". Presumably, the greatest B-movie director in Hollywood history had never forgiven the Duke for calling him "Narse" – short for Narcissus.

William Boyd

1895–1972

Even Boyd's widow called him "Hoppy", he was so inextricably linked to the Western hero, **Hopalong Cassidy**, who he had made his life's work. In 1948 he sold his ranch to buy the rights to the character, a pioneering move that made him a millionaire. Boyd was so famous as Hoppy that he turned down the part of Moses

Hopalong Cassidy was a "Galahad of the range" who hated villains, varmints and grammatical errors.

in Cecil B. de Mille's *The Ten Commandments* (1956), fearing audiences would expect him to ride down from the burning bush on his trusty steed Topper.

Boyd, though slightly more versatile than his Hoppy movies suggest, had no great range as an actor and was happy to be defined by his version of Clarence E. Mulford's pulp fiction hero. He turned Hoppy, *Time* magazine noted, "into a veritable Galahad of the range", who never smoked, drank, kissed girls or drew his gun before the villain. "I played down the violence, tried to make Hoppy an admirable character and insisted on grammatical English", said Boyd. This rare blend of virtue, comedy and grammar was popular enough for the character to lead 66 movies and 52 episodes of the TV show.

Boyd had quit school in Oklahoma when his parents died and, when he arrived in Hollywood in 1919, his hair was already grey. In 1935, he was offered the role of a villain in *Hop-along Cassidy* (the hyphen was, despite Boyd's grammatical perfectionism, later dropped). **James Gleason**, due to play the limping hero, pulled out so Boyd inherited the part. In this film, Hoppy had a few rough edges, but Boyd would sandpaper these away – and drop the limp. Hoppy sat on his ranch, waiting for heroines, villains and troubled neighbours to come to him (partly because of Boyd's barely adequate horsemanship), but viewers knew the bad guys would lose and Hoppy, invariably clad in black, would always come out smiling.

The first movie popularized one of the great Western formulas, the trio Western, with a youngster for romantic interest and a grizzled veteran for comic relief, though aficionados often prefer the unusually sombre *Three Men From Texas* (1940). From 1937 to 1943, Boyd was the second most popular Western star but, in 1943, producer Harry Sherman gave up

on the formula. After buying the rights, Boyd made twelve more movies himself, although budget cuts meant that later films were often largely shot indoors. He also produced a much-screened *Hopalong Cassidy* TV series in 1952. He was 57 by then and soon yielded the small screen to younger stars. Today, there is still an official Hopalong Cassidy fan club, while the movies and TV episodes are being re-released on DVD.

Three Men From Texas
dir Lesley Selander, 1940, US, 70m

In this superior trio B Western, Boyd's Hopalong actually leaves his ranch. Boyd apprehends Andy Clyde, a braggart cook, and takes him back to California where Russell Hayden is trying to bring law and order to a community terrorized by mean saloon proprietor Morris Ankrum. After a bullet in the shoulder stops Hayden's solo heroics, the three unite to capture Ankrum and his gang of cut-throats. With more plot, more tension and a darker tone than many Hopalong adventures, this is probably the strongest film in the series.

Yakima Canutt

1895–1986

"I spent weeks studying the way Yakima Canutt walked and talked", **John Wayne** recalled. "He was a real cowhand. The angrier he got, the lower his voice, the slower his tempo."

For Wayne, who, as one stunt man said, "sat about as easily in the saddle as a bag of walnuts", Canutt was an invaluable role model. Unlike the Duke, Canutt valued his independence enough not to last long on John Ford's sets – not that it harmed his career.

Canutt called himself Yakima after the town where, just after World War I, he became famous as a rodeo rider. In Hollywood, his voice was

Whip crack away! Yak Canutt, stunt man extraordinaire, brings his pizzazz and professionalism to *Stagecoach*.

too distorted by illness for him to be a leading man but he was involved in over 230 Westerns, choreographing the brawl (positioning the camera at angles to the fighters so the crucial punch seemed to land squarely on the jaw), starring in many scary stunts and inspiring fake cowboys like Wayne. The Duke didn't just learn how to walk and talk from Yak, he learned how to swirl his gun too.

Often, in Western scripts from the 1930s, the writer wouldn't bother detailing a stunt, they would just write "Action by Yak Canutt" in the screenplay. He was awarded a special Oscar in 1966. He is best known today, not for his influence on Wayne, but for his pass under a moving stagecoach in the John Wayne/Ford movie *Stagecoach* in 1939.

James Coburn
1928–2002

As knife-throwing Britt in Sturges' *The Magnificent Seven* (1960) James Coburn was the most intriguing presence in the movie although he had only eleven lines. His laconic charisma served the Western well in the 1960s and 70s.

Coburn always wanted to be an actor but, after studying under Stella Adler, it took him until the late 1950s to make it in Hollywood. His first breakthrough came with a supporting role in **Budd Boetticher**'s *Ride Lonesome* (1959), followed by his movie-stealing performance in *The Magnificent Seven*.

Sam Peckinpah spotted him and cast him in his magnificent ruin *Major Dundee* (1964). In

William A. Graham's strange comedy Western *Waterhole Number 3* (1967), Coburn's character, with memorable political incorrectness, defined rape as "assault with a friendly weapon". He was put to better use in Leone's Mexican Revolutionary Western *Duck, You Sucker* (1971), his underplaying a welcome relief from Rod Steiger's theatrics.

Reunited with Peckinpah as Garrett in *Pat Garrett And Billy The Kid* (1973), Coburn was simply definitive as the ageing, reflective man of action, reluctantly impelled to shoot his old friend. Working for an egocentric, self-doubting, alcoholic genius like Peckinpah wasn't easy but Coburn made use of the experience, basing his Oscar-winning turn as a drunken, fearsome father in *Affliction* (1997) on his memories of the director.

He never made a Western quite as good as *Pat Garrett* – or matched his nonchalant brilliance in the role – but he was more than watchable in Richard Brooks' re-examination of the Western myth *Bite The Bullet* (1975). He couldn't save Andrew V. McLaglen's *The Last Hard Men* (1976) from predictability. Plagued by illness, he didn't make another Western until 1990, when he played John Chisum in the rambling, but not uninteresting, revisionist Western *Young Guns II*.

When he died, the obituaries often started "*Our Man Flint* actor…", but when he listed his four great roles he didn't choose the super-spy spoof, preferring two Peckinpah roles – Pat Garrett and Steiner, the hero of Peckinpah's war movie *Cross Of Iron* (1977) – the character he had modelled on Peckinpah in *Affliction* and his knife-throwing hero in *The Magnificent Seven*. "Some you do for love, some you do for money", he said, explaining how he chose parts. His Westerns usually look like he made them for love.

Gary Cooper
1901–61

As Pauline Kael noted, Gary Cooper had the kind of look that made you want to give him power of attorney. Charles Laughton said of him: "We act, he is." That sense of integrity and authenticity made Coop one of the greatest Western icons. Hollywood is still looking for a replacement, with both **Clint Eastwood** and **Kevin Costner** cursed with the tag "the new Gary Cooper".

Coop's pre-eminence is greater testament to his onscreen image than to the quality of his Westerns. He appeared in over thirty (counting the silents) but only a handful are regarded as true classics of the genre: *The Virginian* (1929), *The Plainsman* (1936), *The Westerner* (1940), *High Noon* (1952), *Vera Cruz* (1954) and *Man Of The West* (1958).

He had one advantage over rivals: he'd worked on his father's ranch in Montana, learning to ride, feeding 450 cattle and shovelling manure at 40 degrees below. He started out in the movies as a $10 extra cowboy in the 1920s, rising to star in a series of silent Westerns before making his mark in *The Virginian*. His turn as Owen Wister's Western hero was especially notable for the laconic speech which, riffed by a thousand impressionists, later became a cliché.

In 1936 Cooper played another great Western hero, Wild Bill Hickok, in *The Plainsman*, memorable for a scene in which, even hung upside down and smoked by the Sioux, he refuses to overact. The best of Coop's heroes were subtly, quietly drawn, played so low-key that co-stars often found him wooden – until they saw the rushes. George Burns used to joke that Coop was out-acted by a wooden Indian but **Burt**

The best lines in the West

For a genre whose heroes are reputed to say just yup or nope, the Western has had some classic lines. Here is a small selection.

"If you wanna call me that, smile." Gary Cooper, *The Virginian* (1929)

"Never liked seein' strangers. Maybe it's because no stranger ever good-newsed me." Walter Brennan, *Red River* (1948)

"There's no livin' with a killing." Alan Ladd, *Shane* (1953)

"You're not only wrong, you're wrong at the top of your voice." Spencer Tracy, *Bad Day At Black Rock* (1954)

"There are some things a man can't ride around." Pernell Roberts, *Ride Lonesome* (1959). Or, as John Wayne said in *Stagecoach* (1939): "There are some things a man can't just run away from."

"All I want is to enter my house justified." Joel McCrea, *Ride The High Country* (1962)

"People scare better when they're dying." Henry Fonda, *Once Upon A Time In The West* (1968)

"Fill your hands, you son of a bitch!" John Wayne, *True Grit* (1969)

"If they move, kill 'em." William Holden, *The Wild Bunch* (1969)

"You've got to remember that these are just simple farmers. These are people of the land. The common clay of the new West. You know ... morons." Gene Wilder, *Blazing Saddles* (1974)

"You gonna do something? Or are you just gonna stand there and bleed?" Kurt Russell, *Tombstone* (1993)

missed Method actors as "a bunch of goofballs", but their mentor Lee Strasberg proclaimed Cooper a natural Method actor.

In 1940 he showed genuine comic flair in William Wyler's *The Westerner*, as the drifter who pleads for his life with Walter Brennan's Judge Roy Bean, though he hated the film. Three years later, he made the Spanish Civil War "Western" *For Whom The Bell Tolls*, written for him by his friend **Ernest Hemingway**. He sent his "Nope, yup" image up nicely in the comedy Western *Along Came Jones* (1945) and was convincing as the aloof, embittered, hero in Raoul Walsh's Florida Western *Distant Drums*, released in 1951, the same year he dropped out of the list of the top ten box-office attractions.

High Noon (1952) rode to his rescue. His portrayal of gaunt, grimly determined, yet scared, sheriff Will Kane is often wrongly attributed to a duodenal ulcer, rather than acting. Even if his career was fading, it took guts to play such an unusual variation on the stereotypical sheriff.

Sensing the Western could nourish his image, he stayed with the genre for André De Toth's *Springfield Rifle* and, in 1954, teamed up with Robert Aldrich and Lancaster in the sublime *Vera Cruz*. His final two Westerns were unusual. In Anthony Mann's grim, violent *Man Of The West*, he plays the kind of tormented hero James Stewart had perfected for the director. Fans didn't warm to Coop as a reformed outlaw, though the film was a masterpiece. He rode out of the genre in Delmer Daves' *The Hanging Tree* (1959) as the burnt-out doctor revived by caring for Maria Schell.

Today, Coop pops up in the most surprising places. In 1969 the French novelist and moviemaker Romain Gary published a comic novel about an American fleeing America called *Adieu Gary Cooper*. In *The Sopranos*, mobster

Lancaster, on the set of *Vera Cruz*, tried to upstage him with fancy gunplay and had to admit defeat. For Coop, less was more. He dis-

Tony mused on the fate of Gary Cooper in his first therapy session. The star was, the poet Carl Sandburg said, "one of the most beloved illiterates this country has ever known". Playwright Clifford Odets probably summed up Coop – and his screen image – better: "He had an old-fashioned politeness but he said nothing casually."

The Hanging Tree
dir Delmer Daves, 1959, US, 106m

The Hanging Tree is a complex Western, thick with melodrama, which makes stunning dramatic use of space, alludes to André Gide's *La symphonie pastorale* and anticipates the amoral West of Leone. Cooper gives a classic performance as the haunted doctor who rides into a mountain mining town, tends to Maria Schell, the temporarily blinded victim of a stagecoach robbery, and is drawn into confrontation with Karl Malden's sleazeball. The plot's holes are largely obscured by the quality of the acting, especially from the touching, mysterious Schell.

Sergio Corbucci

1927–90

In 1995 the end credits of Jim Wynorski's Western *Hard Bounty* thanked "the two Sergios" – Leone and Sollima, masters of the spaghetti Western. Wynorski later admitted "it was supposed to be the three Sergios [honouring Corbucci too] – but there was a mix up".

The omission was not untypical. The career of Sergio Corbucci was long conflated with his brother Bruno's in certain reputable film directories. But this former film critic – who learned his trade at the Cinecittà studios making low-budget Hollywood retreads like *Goliath And The Island Of Vampires* (1961) – made thirteen Westerns.

None of his movies are as famous as Leone's Dollars trilogy because Corbucci never truly cracked the American market. He once famously

said that while Ford had the Duke, and Leone had Clint, he had **Franco Nero**. Yet he used Nero well, especially in *Django* (1966), such a cult smash in Europe that it inspired over 50 unofficial sequels, imitations and spin-offs. Even Corbucci felt obliged to return to the theme, co-writing *Django 2: il grande ritorno* (*Django Strikes Again*) in 1987.

Many of Corbucci's early Westerns – *Massacro al Grande Canyon* (*Massacre At Grand Canyon*, 1965), *Minnesota Clay* (1965), *Navajo Joe* (1966, starring Burt Reynolds) and *Johnny Oro* (*Ringo And His Golden Pistol*, 1966) – were watchable, unspectacular, yet occasionally surprising. For a filmmaker who worked with the great **Roberto Rossellini**, Corbucci was strangely content to rely on arresting imagery, gags, a strong sense of style, graphic visual clichés, an obsession with religious satire, and a willingness to steal from/ pay homage to other directors. Corbucci called his films Zapata Westerns – "proletarian fables in which the heroes are on the left and the bad guys on the right". In truth, he was too undisciplined to be that dogmatic – and his films are all the better for it.

Il mercenario (*The Mercenary*, 1968) and, better still, *Il grande silenzio* (*The Great Silence*, 1969), in which the familiar deserts are replaced by snowy wastes and the hero is called Silence, show Corbucci at his best. But, although *Il mercenario* was a relative success in America, *Il grande silenzio* was not released in cinemas there, a failure that restricted Corbucci's freedom and budgets on subsequent movies.

In 1970 he made *Companeros* – a film marked by strange symbolism and some fine action sequences – and the unusual, depressing *Gli specialisti* (*The Specialists*), with Johnny Hallyday, probably the finest Western polemic against hippies ever made. Thereafter, most of his Westerns chiefly served to prove the law of diminishing returns. Yet his legacy has endured. To watch *Il grande silenzio* for the first time is to discover scenes, ideas and props that turn up in the **Clint Eastwood** movies *Hang 'Em High* (1968), *Joe Kidd* (1972) and *Unforgiven* (1992), and in *Reservoir Dogs* (1991).

 Il grande silenzio (The Great Silence)
dir Sergio Corbucci, 1966, It, 95m

Jean-Louis Trintignant is a mute gunfighter who, on behalf of a trapped outlaw gang and a vengeful widow, must confront bounty hunters led by sadistic Klaus Kinski. This is more politicized than most Leone Westerns: the outlaws stole to survive and only have a price on their heads courtesy of Luigi Pistilli's venal homicidal banker. Leone's Westerns are cynically, violently exhilarating, whereas *Il grande silenzio* is a haunting, sad film, its bleakness underpinned by the well-shot snowy landscapes – the Pyrenees doubling beautifully for the Utah mountains – and accentuated by Ennio Morricone's mournful score.

Kirk Douglas

1916–

A boy born Issur Danielovich Demsky, into a Russian-Jewish family in a New York ghetto, was always going to have his own take on a phenomenon as American as the Western. Though best known as the crucified rebellious slave in *Spartacus* (1960), Kirk Douglas brought an intensity and originality to his Westerns which gave something unique to the genre.

He moseyed into the Western in Walsh's *Along The Great Divide* (1951), one of two of his films which he recommends none of his fans should watch – the other being his next Western, the lumberjack tale *The Big Trees* (1952). He had his finger amputated in Hawks's *The Big Sky* (1952), though Hawks complained "He isn't

nearly as good as Wayne". The physical suffering continued in **King Vidor**'s *Man Without A Star* (1955), in which he was whipped with barbed wire, although at least on this occasion the pain didn't seem so sadistically irrelevant.

That film marked the start of an astonishing Western winning streak for Douglas. In the next seven years, he starred in three celebrated Westerns: his eye-catching melodramatics suited the role of doomed Doc Holliday, lightening up Sturges' epic *Gunfight At The OK Corral* (1957); he was a joy as the unstable gunman who falls, unknowingly, for his daughter in Aldrich's Freudian Western *The Last Sunset* (1961); and he was superb in *Lonely Are The Brave* (1962), his favourite of his own movies. In between, he made two more good adult Westerns: *Last Train From Gun Hill* (1959), Sturges' *3.10 To Yuma* revamp, and *The Indian Fighter* (1955), **André De Toth**'s beautiful, erotically charged wagon train Western.

Perhaps fearing typecasting, Douglas stayed off the range until 1967, when he starred in Andrew McLaglen's slightly clichéd *The Way West* alongside Mitchum and Widmark and, more entertainingly, in *The War Wagon*, where he appeared wearing only a gun belt. His next two Westerns – *There Was A Crooked Man* (1970), opposite Henry Fonda) and *A Gunfight* (1971), alongside Johnny Cash) – though original and well played, didn't quite come off.

He directed and starred in two 1970s Westerns. *Scalawag* (1973), an attempt to Westernize *Treasure Island* with music, was a tad ambitious for his directorial debut. The more accomplished *Posse* (1975) used the Western to comment on Nixon and Watergate. In *The Man From Snowy River* (1982), given a beard, an axe, a whiskey bottle and a wooden leg, he gleefully accepted the invitation to overact.

Douglas never made a Western with Ford, Mann, Peckinpah or Leone (and only one with Hawks) and starred in just one classic traditional Western (*Gunfight At The OK Corral*). Yet, from 1955 to 1975, the Western would have been duller – and less diverse – without him.

Posse
dir Kirk Douglas, 1975, US, 93m

Many Western traditionalists hated Douglas's attempt to explore Richard Nixon's disgrace in a Western. But Douglas is in intelligently restrained form as ambitious US marshal Howard Nightingale. In an attempt to futher his political career, he hires a super-posse to help him capture an outlaw (Bruce Dern, in a movie-stealing performance) but his plan backfires. The reversal of the genre's standard good guy/bad guy roles is a little too neat but this likeable, cynical, Western is much better than detractors suggest.

Clint Eastwood

1930–

After knocking around as a lumberjack, soldier and handsomely lanky small-time actor before his success as ramrod Rowdy Yates in TV's cattle-drive odyssey *Rawhide*, Clint Eastwood was underwhelmed when offered a low-budget Western to be shot in Spain by an unknown Italian director. But he took the job, little realizing **Sergio Leone**'s *A Fistful Of Dollars* (1964) would create the spaghetti Western and make him a supercool international icon.

Eastwood's enigmatic drifter in Leone's landmark trilogy (*For A Few Dollars More* and *The Good, The Bad And The Ugly* swiftly followed) put him on the A-list in Hollywood, where he steadily mined the vein Leone had opened, playing laconic and ruthless tough guys of few words. *Coogan's Bluff* (1968) – in which Eastwood's Arizona lawman shows the NYPD how it's done – began his

influential collaboration with **Don Siegel**, with whom he would make five pictures including the unusual Civil War drama *The Beguiled* (1971) and iconoclastic cop phenomenon *Dirty Harry* (1972).

If he starred in some Leonealike Westerns – *Hang 'Em High* (1968) and *Joe Kidd* (1972) – when he took up directing, forming Malpaso Productions, he proved himself a craftsman of intelligence and no little wit. To Eastwood fell the task of keeping the Western alive and interesting in the bleak years of the 1970s and 80s. His

Our man Clint: Eastwood almost single-handedly kept the Western alive in the lean times of the 1970s and 80s.

commanding charisma overcame the supposed unfashionability of genre films like *High Plains Drifter* (1973), *The Outlaw Josey Wales* (1976) and his *Shane* revamp *Pale Rider* (1985), which took $60 million in the US. Both *High Plains Drifter* and *The Outlaw Josey Wales* were initially damned for their violence but are now recognized as Westerns of real merit, reflecting the genius of an actor and filmmaker who had grown up on the genre and knew its clichés, structures and iconography inside out. His affection for the Wild West – and its showbiz trappings – shines through the gentle comedy of *Bronco Billy* (1980).

Eastwood sealed his reputation as the majestic eminence of American film with his farewell Western, the great *Unforgiven* (1992), poignantly dedicated to his two "teachers", Siegel and Leone. Well into his 70s Eastwood continued to reign as the kind of American hero still universally admired: independent, steadfast, honest, an artist characterized by seeming artlessness.

Bronco Billy
dir Clint Eastwood, 1980, US, 119m

You could think of this as *The Outlaw Josey Wales* with gentle comedy replacing the carnage. In *Bronco Billy*, Clint is a loner who resents company yet somehow finds himself surrounded by a troupe of oddballs and no-hopers as he fulfils a long-nursed dream to launch his own Wild West show. Some of the Clintisms are familiar from his tougher movies – he saves Sondra Locke from sexual assault for the fourth film in a row – but, overall, this has just enough edge, wit and tone to make the cutesiness palatable. This is one of Eastwood's favourite films.

Henry Fonda
1905–82

"I thought about groceries." That's what Henry Fonda told his daughter Jane when she asked

Henry Fonda was a star who always kept part of himself in reserve – from the audience, the camera and his family.

him how he'd prepared for a harrowing scene. She was understandably mystified but then her father has long perplexed relatives, colleagues and critics.

Fonda's quiet moral authority made him a natural to play presidents real (in *Young Mr Lincoln*, 1939) and imaginary (in *Fail-Safe*, 1964), but three Westerns prove his range was wider than our collective memory might suggest. In *My Darling Clementine* (1946), his portrait of Wyatt Earp as a quiet, almost shy, gunslinger turned sheriff is so evocative that the image of him reclining on his porch is more powerful than the gun play. In **Edward Dmytryk**'s dark *Warlock* (1959) he is both hero and villain as the marshal for hire. Nine years later, in *Once Upon A Time In The West*, he shoots a child in one of the most shocking sequences in the Western's history.

Handsome and versatile, Fonda made so many types of films that he wasn't particularly thought of as a Westerner. His first Western was **Henry King**'s *Jesse James* (1939), in which he starred as the hero's down-to-earth brother. He reprised the role in Fritz Lang's creditable sequel *The Return Of Frank James* (1940). But the culmination of his early career was embodying rural nobility in three pictures for **John Ford** in 1939–40 (*Young Mr Lincoln*, *Drums Along The Mohawk* and *The Grapes Of Wrath*) and William Wellman's *The Ox-Bow Incident* (1943). It took guts to make *The Ox-Bow Incident*, a powerful indictment of vigilantes and lynch mobs. There is a story that he was haunted by a lynching he saw as a child, and the subject recurs in *Young Mr Lincoln* and *Warlock*.

In a 40-year on-off career in the Western, Fonda worked for such great directors as John Ford, Anthony Mann and Sergio Leone. Though his name is synonymous with Ford's, the director only used Fonda to full advantage in two Westerns: *Drums Along The Mohawk* and *My Darling Clementine*. By the time Ford made *Fort Apache* (1948), the director had transferred his interest to Wayne and cast Fonda as the martinet. Fonda had come to regard Ford as "a great director but a cruel son of a bitch" and the director may have found the Duke more pliable.

After being – his son Peter has suggested – greylisted for his liberal views in the 1950s, Fonda rediscovered the Western near the end of the decade, and the genre would be good to him for the next fifteen years.

He was impressive as the embittered bounty hunter in Mann's good, didactic *The Tin Star* (1957) and charismatically ambiguous in the brilliant *Warlock*. He shone in two comedy Westerns: as an ageing cowboy in *The Rounders* (1964) and the stricken gambler in *A Big Hand For The Little Lady* (1966).

In 1968, he played the bad guy twice. First, in the underrated *Firecreek*, opposite old pal **Jimmy Stewart**, and then, to devastating effect, in Leone's *Once Upon A Time In The West*. Leone had tried to cast Fonda, his favourite actor from childhood, in all his Westerns, and finally succeeded, brilliantly casting Fonda against type in the star's last truly great Western. Neither *The Cheyenne Social Club* (1970) nor the bitter, funny *There Was A Crooked Man* (1970) could match that. His stately performance in Tonino Valerii's spaghetti spoof *My Name Is Nobody* (1973) was a fitting postscript to his Western career.

There was a reserve about Fonda, an implication of conflicts and emotions kept barely in check, a distance in the blue eyes, a toughness behind the smile, that almost always made him interesting to watch. Because he never seemed as comfortably familiar as, say, John Wayne, he could convincingly portray many more shades of heroism and villainy than almost any other leading Western star.

The Rounders
dir Burt Kennedy, 1964, US, 85m

With two middle-aged cowboys – Henry Fonda and Glenn Ford – who long to open a bar in Tahiti, *The Rounders* is an obvious precursor of Kennedy's more commercially successful *Support Your Local Sheriff* (1969) in which James Garner dreams of retiring to Australia. Whereas the more famous comedy feels like a broadly played sitcom, *The Rounders* is a lot of unpretentious fun, helped immeasurably by Fonda and Ford as two diametrically opposed cowpokes, united by a common fantasy.

Glenn Ford

1916–

Glenn Ford is an easy actor to underrate. Unshowy, understated, inconspicuously handsome, he somehow made, as David Thomson suggested, genial, relaxed sincerity interesting. He had a precise sense of what worked for him – he was often shot showing only the left side of his face, the right having been kicked by a horse – and, as a Western star, he knew his trade. He could draw in 0.4 seconds, faster than **John Wayne** or *Gunsmoke* star **James Arness**.

Ford drifted into show business and, after a stop-start rise, interrupted by World War II, ended up in Westerns. As a Western icon, his golden era began with *The Man From Colorado* in 1948 and effectively ended, a decade later, with the comic *The Sheepman*. He was often cast as a young cowboy who gets into trouble or as a loner wrongly accused but not all his performances were so steely – he could play comedy too. Even in the 1950s, studios exploited his craft and quiet charisma to disguise the routine nature of such films as *The Redhead And The Cowboy* (1951), *The Secret Of Convict Lake* (1951) and even, though he's superb in it, *The Violent Men* (1955).

Because it is his more heroic Westerns that are usually rerun on TV, his range is often overlooked. In the outlandish, gripping *Lust For Gold* (1949), he gives one of his best performances, making his prospector reprehensible, mad, yet not entirely unsympathetic. His turn as the tyrannical judge suffering from what we now call posttraumatic stress disorder in Henry Levin's dark, psychological Western *The Man From Colorado* (1947) is just as compelling.

He stuck closer to the reluctant hero type in **Budd Boetticher's** *The Man From The Alamo* (1953) but the movie – and his portrayal of the man shunned for alleged cowardice – is of real quality. Between 1956 and 1958, he starred in more quality Westerns than some stars managed in a lifetime. In three of these gems – *Jubal*, *3.10 To Yuma* and *Cowboy* – he was directed by Delmer Daves.

3.10 To Yuma is so good that *Jubal*, a Western reworking of *Othello*, and *Cowboy*, a fish-out-of-water Western loosely modelled on Frank Harris's notoriously unreliable memoirs, are often overlooked. *The Fastest Gun Alive* (1956) is much better than its formulaic title while *The Sheepman* is genuinely funny. Just when it seemed Ford could do no wrong, he starred in *Cimarron* (1960). Tarnished as the star of this lavish, flaccid remake, his career – and reputation – never fully recovered, and from then on he languished in mainly dull horse operas. The pick of his later Westerns are Burt Kennedy's comic *The Rounders* (1965) and *Santee* (1973), a good, if flawed, revenge Western.

The Sheepman
dir George Marshall, 1958, US, 91m

One of the funniest comedy Westerns of the 1950s, *The Sheepman* benefits from a fine screenplay – by William Bowers and James Edward Grant – and from Ford's deadpan delivery as the farmer whose decision to settle down with a flock of sheep he has won at cards almost ignites a range war in cattle country. Shirley MacLaine offers strong support. Watch out, too, for Slim Pickens as the sheriff who goes fishing every time there's a spot of trouble.

John Ford

1894–1973

If John Ford – born Sean Aloysius O'Feeney – cannot be credited with inventing the Western he is justly revered for adding immeasurably to the genre's vocabulary, depth and artistry. A master storyteller, he turned history into legend, creating a mythology for America. Although he worked in many genres and received an unequalled four Academy Awards for direction of non-Westerns and two more for wartime documentaries, he famously introduced himself: "I'm John Ford. I make Westerns."

At 18 Ford joined his actor–writer–director brother Francis in Hollywood as propman, stunt double and assistant to his sibling mentor. A director by 21, he made scores of silent films, mainly Westerns, 26 of them starring his friend **Harry**

John Ford on the set of *The Man Who Shot Liberty Valance* with two of the genre's greatest icons, James Stewart and John Wayne.

Carey. His railroad epic *The Iron Horse* (1924) was a landmark Western, introducing many elements that became staples. During his forty years helming sound pictures Ford became internationally renowned as a master of world cinema, the most American in personal vision and visual style.

His films were distinguished by beautiful compositions, thrilling action and rich contrasts – between frontier and civilization, sweeping landscape and intimate human drama. Among his signature works his 1939 productions *Stagecoach* and *Drums Along The Mohawk*, his lyrical Wyatt Earp film *My Darling Clementine* (1946), the Cavalry trilogy of *Fort Apache* (1948), *She Wore A Yellow Ribbon* (1949) and *Rio Grande* (1950), *The Searchers* (1956) and *The Man Who Shot Liberty Valance* (1962) all vie for places in people's personal top tens. He also made the definitive wagon train movie, the often neglected *Wagon Master* (1950). Even David Thomson, who rails against Ford in his biographical dictionary of film, calls *The Searchers* a "riveting, tragic, and complex experience, a movie in which Ford gives up many of his false certainties and a story filled with disturbing, half-buried thoughts of race and failure".

Ford's so-called "stock company" of regular players – which included **Ward Bond, Victor McLaglen, Harry Carey Jr** and **Ben Johnson** – hold a special place in Western devotees' affections. And the panoramic setting for many of his films, spectacular Monument Valley on the Arizona–Utah border, is universally recognized as "Ford Country" – why else was Sergio Leone so keen to film part of *Once Upon A Time In The West* there?

Ford's Westerns grew darker and more complex as he aged. As Martin Scorsese notes, you can trace the evolution through three Ford/Wayne heroes: "The character of the hero becomes richer, more complex, with each decade. The Ringo Kid of *Stagecoach* grows first into the benevolent father figure of *She Wore A Yellow Ribbon*, then Ford transforms him into Ethan Edwards, the misfit of *The Searchers* … John Wayne's heroic persona has turned dark and obsessive."

For some, Ford's Westerns didn't just darken, they deteriorated after *The Searchers*. Sometimes, it is easy to forget that directors are human. Ford's astonishing longevity in Hollywood – his movies spanned half a century – had its price and that price was fatigue, emotional, physical and artistic, visible in such late, still valid, works as *Cheyenne Autumn* (1964).

In his career Ford touched on most of the Western's major themes, drew on the traditions of the dime novel and Frederick Jackson Turner's frontier historiography and, in his best films, showed an unmatched flair for combining the intimate and the epic in a single moment.

Even Hawks admitted that Ford made better Westerns than he did. But Ford's influence is global. **Akira Kurosawa** admitted that Ford – along with Frank Capra and William Wyler – was one of his three favourite directors and said "the grammar of the Western" had infused his own movies. In turn, Kurosawa's work would be reinvented by Leone, another Ford aficionado, whose rise would coincide with the master's retirement. Even François Truffaut, who as a critic had viciously slammed many of Ford's movies, recanted when he started making his own films, noting that "with a kind of royal leisure, John Ford knew how to make the public laugh or cry. What he didn't know how to do was bore them."

Rio Grande
dir John Ford, 1950, US, 105m, b/w

Reconciliation – as a prelude to the building of a new ideal community/society – is the thrust of the conclusion to

Ford's gallant 7th Cavalry chronicles. In the aftermath of the Civil War and the break-up of captain John Wayne's marriage to reproachful belle Maureen O'Hara, the need to stick together in pursuit of marauding Apaches unites individuals. Thematically reconciliation represents North and South; at the personal level it delicately negotiates the strained relationship between the hardened father and his newly recruited son. *Rio Grande* is also memorable for Ben Johnson's spectacular stunt riding and folk songs from the Sons of the Pioneers.

William S. Hart

1864–1946

Is the fade-out of silent cowboy star William S. Hart's career the point at which the Western began to lose its way? For some purists, the eclipse of Hart's more authentic West by **Tom Mix**'s circus showmanship led, disastrously, to the formulaic oaters that have blighted the genre.

A stage actor who moved to Hollywood in disgust at the "burlesque manner" in which the West was filmed, Hart starred in, wrote and directed his own films, presenting a romanticized, yet authentic, version of the West that captured the public's imagination. *Motion Picture Classic* magazine neatly summed up his shtick in one dismissive review, saying: "Hart is once again a kindly bad man who once again encounters regeneration and a cutie." Though Hart was a pillar of rectitude, he had a lived-in world weariness that

anticipated the twilight years of Gary Cooper and Randolph Scott.

At his best Hart gave Hollywood its first classic Westerns. His films showed a clear vision of the West – sharpened by his friendships with cowboys and lawmen like **Wyatt Earp** and **Bill Tilghman** – and a deep understanding of the Western as a story form. *Hell's Hinges* (1916), much admired by French author Jean Cocteau, was the blueprint for countless town-taming Westerns, while *The Toll Gate* (1920) anticipated, in its creation of archetypes, such later classics as *Shane* (1953). But he liked to moralize, grew egotistical (criticizing Owen Wister's *The Virginian* for being false to "cowboy life as I

William S. Hart, seen here in *The Gun Fighter* (1917), coined many Western clichés, defining the influential archetype of the reformed outlaw.

knew it", even though he knew less about cowboy life than Wister) and lapsed into self-parody in such turkeys as *Singer Jim McKee* (1924). He also made the frankly racialist *The Aryan* (1916), in which his hero's "fall" is symbolized by his loss of racial identity.

In the Jazz Age, Hart's moralizing seemed old-fashioned, but he refused to heed Paramount's warnings to change his films or watch his appeal wane. In 1925 he starred in *Tumbleweeds*, which belatedly made concessions to popular taste – it was a truly epic Western, not a small-scale melodrama, and he rode with a sidekick, not alone. But it was a movie of real quality, with a land rush scene likened to the work of Sergei Eisenstein. One of the film's minor innovations – Hart riding straight up in the saddle – was adopted by **John Wayne** and many others. But the film was badly distributed and, disillusioned, he retired to his ranch.

Today Hart is almost forgotten, yet so many of the plots, costumes, devices and trappings we take for granted in Westerns started with him. He is, however, remembered as the model for the statue of "The Range Rider of the Yellowstone" which marks the cattle range frontier in Billings, Montana.

Hell's Hinges
dir Charles Swickard, William S. Hart, 1916, US, 55m, b/w

A golden silent, worth watching for one iconic scene: when Hart's reformed hired gun reads the Bible for the first time, while smoking, with a whiskey at hand. Hart's meisterwork is a landmark, developing some of the genre's greatest themes and myths: the opposition of civilization and savagery; the redemption of man in the wilderness and/or through the love of a good woman; and the archetype of a strong, masculine hero, capable of violence, who ultimately discovers a strong moral sense.

Howard Hawks
1896–1977

Howard Hawks never shaped the Western as much, say, as he influenced screwball comedy but he made one of the greatest ever Westerns, *Red River* (1948), proving, decisively, that John Wayne really could act.

Hawks once famously said "A good movie is three good scenes and no bad scenes." Such homespun wisdom didn't fool French filmmakers like **François Truffaut** who revered him but, combined with what was, for some intellectuals, a worrying versatility, it led to Hawks initially being damned as a "good all-rounder".

Fuelled by the kind of self-confidence that comes from being the apple of a doting, wealthy, grandfather's eye, Hawks broke into the movies as a propman in the 1910s. He directed eight silents but the talkies – and dialogue – made him as a director. He excelled in gangster movies, screwball comedies, action/adventure films and, though he came to the genre late, Westerns.

The Western suited Hawks's themes – male friendship, professional heroes who get the job done, usually learning the value of teamwork on the way – and his style of filmmaking. He had a precise sense of structure, a straightforward way with a story, and was a careful craftsman. French director Jacques Rivette said of Hawks's Western *The Big Sky* (1952): "The smooth orderly succession of shots has a rhythm like a pulsing body. Each shot has a functional beauty, like a neck or an ankle."

His first Western was *Viva Villa* (1934) which he started but handed over to director Jack Conway. Doing the kind of favour his Western heroes often did for each other, he had refused to testify against a drunken actor who had urinated over a military parade. In 1935 Hawks made a star out of **Walter Brennan** in the Gold Rush Western drama *Barbary Coast*. Other genres then preoccupied him though he worked, uncredited, appalled, on *The Outlaw* (1943).

In *Red River*, an epic reworking of *Mutiny On The Bounty* that is subtler and more darkly complex than its source, he gave the genre some of its definitive cattle drive scenes. His next Western, *The Big Sky*, was his most homoerotic, an epic tale of a troupe of men, led by **Kirk Douglas**, journeying through hostile territory along the Missouri River. Described by Hawks as "a love story between two men", *The Big Sky* was compelling, even with twenty minutes cut for release.

Rio Bravo (1959), provoked, he insisted, by his disgust at *High Noon* (1952), was his first major take on the trio Western – with John Wayne in the lead, Dean Martin as a drunk, and Ricky Nelson as the brave but green youngster. His next – and last – two Westerns, *El Dorado* (1967) and *Rio Lobo* (1970), were variations on that theme, both also starring Wayne. Hawks admitted he made them, almost as a holding operation, while he tried to figure out where Hollywood filmmaking was going. Westerns, he said, didn't change much.

El Dorado is a true gem, helped by Robert Mitchum's brilliance as the drunken sheriff. But in *Rio Lobo* the formula looked tired and the recycling of scenes – such as the good guys barricading themselves in the sheriff's office to wait for help – too obvious.

By the 1970s, word of his brilliance had begun to spread beyond France. He has been lauded by the likes of Peter Bogdanovich and **Quentin Tarantino** – who once cited *Rio Bravo* as his favourite movie. Hawks didn't shape the Western like Ford but he twice reinvented the genre's greatest star, pushing Wayne towards the

Rollin', rollin', rollin': the iconic songs

- **"Blazing Saddles"**

"He rode a blazing saddle, he wore a shining star..." Mel Brooks wanted to hire a singer who could spoof Frankie Laine. Imagine his surprise when Frankie turned up for an audition. The parodic theme is as memorable as the genuine articles.

- **"Do not forsake me, oh my darlin'"**

Frankie Laine had the hit but Tex Ritter sang this Dimitri Tiomkin/Ned Washington theme mournfully, ominously and manfully throughout *High Noon*.

- **"3.10 to Yuma"**

Frankie Laine sang this powerful theme originally, but it was beautifully covered in 1967 by British folk chanteuse Sandy Denny, who made the most of the melancholy, melodramatic lyrics.

- **"The Good, The Bad And The Ugly"**

Arguably the most memorable theme Ennio Morricone ever wrote, covered all the way to the top of the charts by Hugo Montenegro, this is still passed on through the power of whistling.

- **"Tumblin' Tumbleweeds"**

A hardy perennial, as monotonous, yet inspiring, as a ride on the range, "Tumbling Tumbleweeds" has appeared in the soundtrack to over twenty movies – from John Ford's *Rio Grande* (1950) to *The Big Lebowski* (1998).

glory of *The Searchers*, and then, in *Rio Bravo*, giving the Duke a blueprint for the kind of movie that would, in the star's declining years, entertain millions.

Hawks never, he said proudly, made a movie that made a statement, but his best work is infused with a very American brand of optimism.

Ben Johnson

1918–96

A champion rodeo star, Ben Johnson started out in Hollywood looking after horses on **Howard Hughes'** *The Outlaw* (1941). Tall, handsome, slow-drawling, he graduated into a likeable and effective character actor who couldn't, however, carry an A-list picture by himself and was too often underused as a villain or sidekick.

A particular favourite of Ford's and Peckinpah's, his impressive resumé spans such classics as *Red River* (1948) and *She Wore A Yellow Ribbon* (1949), subtler psychological Westerns like *Shane* (1953), experimental failures like *One-Eyed Jacks* (1961) and such powerful revisionist works as *The Wild Bunch* (1969). Even he seemed hard put to define his appeal, saying "Everyone in town's a better actor than I am but no one else can play Ben Johnson."

Ironically, although he played in more than fifty Westerns, he won his only Oscar as Sam the Lion, the cinema owner in Peter Bogdanovich's *The Last Picture Show* (1971), after insisting that the director took some of the cursing out of his lines.

Sergio Leone

1929–89

No movie genre is as quintessentially American as the Western. Yet the top two films in the Internet Movie Database's poll of the greatest Westerns – *The Good, The Bad And The Ugly* (1966) and *Once Upon A Time In The West* (1968) – were both made by an Italian, Sergio Leone.

To some critics, Leone's Westerns – as Italian or European Westerns – had no authentic roots and were the satirical, violent, phoney, commercially driven works of a gifted cineaste. It's obvious that Leone had studied and assimilated imagery, dialogue, technique, plots and themes from directors as diverse as Ford, Walsh, Zinnemann, Boetticher, Kurosawa, Aldrich, Fuller and Ray. (He always cited Chaplin and George Stevens as key influences.) But the game of hunt the influence doesn't "explain" Leone's Westerns. Their roots are rich and complex, drawing on his love of Western lore, his study of American history and Sicilian puppet theatre, and his love/hate relationship with the America that defeated – and liberated – his Italy.

Leone was born into the cinema, the son of a silent movie actress and a silent movie director. He assisted or ran the second unit on a host of movies, including *Ben-Hur* (1959), before earning his keep writing, and directing "pepla" – fake Hollywood sword and sandal epics, made in Italy.

While organizing chariot races, he was dreaming of gunfights and, when Italian producers lost faith in pepla and switched to Westerns, encouraged by the success of German adaptations of **Karl May** novels, Leone seized his chance. His first, *A Fistful Of Dollars* (1964), cost $200,000 and grossed over $8 million in the US and Italy. With a running time of 97 minutes, *Fistful* rattled along. He understood the impatience contemporary audiences felt with the standard Western because he shared it: rather than open with a gunfight and then build up to a violent finale, he scattered his set pieces throughout, changing the pacing of the Western for good.

Leone's first Western introduced a new star, Eastwood, and a new style. He paid homage to – and corrected – the Western, creating a world that was brutal, absurd, realistic, yet at the same time surrealistic, cartoonish and operatic, the

Sergio Leone revived the Western, but his best genre films were fuelled by a love/hate relationship with America and American culture.

weirdness accentuated by **Ennio Morricone's** strange, brilliant soundtrack. In his four indisputably great Westerns – the Dollars trilogy and *Once Upon A Time In The West* – there was a perfect fit between genre and director.

Eastwood and Leone parted after the trilogy, which finally gave Leone the chance to cast Fonda and invert the iconography of the Western with the brutal opening of *Once Upon A Time In*

The West. An artistic triumph, it took just $1 million in the US. With everyone from Eastwood to Elvis Presley starring in spaghetti clones, Leone found it hard to capitalize on his film's critical success.

Some critics claim Leone hated the Western. Even an admirer like Roger Ebert concluded that *The Good, The Bad And The Ugly* "builds on the rubbish of Western movie clichés, using style to elevate dreck into art". But these Westerns are not just postmodern exercises in style. "Ford sees the problem from a Christian point of view," Leone said once, "his protagonists look forward to a rosy future, whereas I see the history of the West as the reign of violence." This change of emphasis, **Sam Peckinpah** admitted, made movies like *The Wild Bunch* (1969) possible.

Leone's obsessive quotation of great American movies is part of an inquiry into what it meant, in the 20th century, to live with America, and the image of America. To an Italian boy who had worshipped American icons like Gary Cooper – and then encountered the "energetic, deceptive" GIs in their Jeeps – this inquiry was as much personal as intellectual.

He only directed one other Western, the flawed, intriguing Mexican Revolutionary tale *Duck, You Sucker* (1971). Leone's last hurrah in the genre was *My Name Is Nobody* (1973), a strange blend of Italian and American Westerns, again starring Fonda, which he supervised with director **Tonino Valerii**. Yet his achievement as a Western director is monumental. At his funeral, a German fan brandished a placard which read: "John Ford is nothing."

 A Fistful Of Dollars/ Per un pugno di dollari

dir Sergio Leone, 1964, It, 100m

A shameless, bravura retelling of Akira Kurosawa's sardonic 1961 samurai classic *Yojimbo* (a source Leone belatedly acknowledged), *A Fistful Of Dollars* flies in the face of Fordian tradition as Eastwood's mercenary drifter blows into town. Dusty, serape-clad, with a smouldering cheroot – which Eastwood hated using – clenched in his mouth, the laconic anti-hero accepts the pay of both warring sides carving up the town's land, pitiful assets and women. Found out and subjected to a beating, he pays everyone back in a systematically sadistic shoot-'em-up, shot, like the film, with what *Variety* called "James Bondian vigour".

Joel McCrea
1905–90

In 1981, when Maureen Stapleton won the best supporting actress Oscar for her role in Warren Beatty's *Reds*, she waved the statuette and said: "This is for Joel McCrea." Beatty could be seen mouthing in disbelief, "Joel McCrea?" But Stapleton had never made any secret of the fact that it was her childhood crush on McCrea that led her to act.

David Thomson describes McCrea as a "sweet, modest man, not in the least starry, shy about his own sierra-like handsomeness but with a rare gentleness, a knack of listening to women and a knack of underplaying key moments". Today, McCrea is better known as the star of Preston Sturges' hilarious satire *Sullivan's Travels* (1941) but in the 1940s and 50s, he was one of the Western genre's most bankable stars.

McCrea started out as a stunt double, benefited from the advent of talkies and was a versatile leading man until, in 1946, he played the titular hero in *The Virginian* and made almost nothing but Westerns for the next sixteen years. The switch reflected his tall, rugged good looks and his own interests – he became a rancher in the 1940s. Like **Randolph Scott**, he had presence, integrity and the ability to extract the maximum effect from minimal dialogue but his onscreen persona was several degrees warmer than that of his laconic co-star in *Ride The High Country* (1962).

The titles of his films suggest a certain formulaic repetitiveness (*Cattle Drive, Cattle Empire, The Oklahoman*) but he made some decent Westerns. His golden run started with *Ramrod* (1947), one of the best noir Westerns, and continued with *Colorado Territory* (1949), Raoul Walsh's Western retread of his gangster movie *High Sierra* (1941).

In 1955 McCrea shone in two Jacques Tourneur films: as the heroic judge in the atmospheric *Stranger On Horseback*, which almost doesn't feel like a Western, and as Wyatt Earp in the compelling *Wichita*, which featured a cameo from Sam Peckinpah, who directed the dialogue.

Peckinpah memorably pitted McCrea against Scott in his nostalgic classic *Ride The High Country*. McCrea fits the role of the ageing former sheriff so snugly it's hard to believe he was originally cast as the Oregon Kid, a former lawman now intent on stealing gold. Luckily, McCrea and Scott both wanted to swap roles. McCrea's death scene seemed terribly apt, a farewell from a star who, though he'd starred in his share of noirish Westerns, symbolized a more honourable kind of West than Hollywood, as the 1960s wore on, cared to portray. He had represented a quiet kind of decency soon deemed obsolete as the Western – and the society that it reflected, albeit in distorted fashion – changed for ever.

Wichita
dir Jacques Tourneur, 1955, US, 81m

Joel McCrea is a perfect fit for the well-worn role of Wyatt Earp's quiet gunslinger elected to clean up Wichita. Jacques Tourneur's direction defines the conflict in spaces: indoor/private vs. outdoor/public. Images of a small boy accidentally shot while peeping from a window and a wife shot through her front door are shocking reminders that the casualties weren't always "professionals". The movie draws on real events – but the historical hero was not Earp but a Judge Tucker. Earp appropriated the story with the help of Paul Lake, his hagiographer, a technical adviser on this film.

Anthony Mann
1906–67

In 1958 Jean-Luc Godard effused about Anthony Mann's *Man Of The West*, "Every shot shows Mann is reinventing the Western." Today, only a few cineastes have heard of him. Only the release of *Open Range* (2003) – the Kevin Costner Western that pays an obvious visual debt to Mann – has hinted at a re-evaluation of one of the least celebrated, most talented, Western directors of the 1950s, the genre's golden decade.

Anton Emil Bundesman started out in Hollywood working alongside **Preston Sturges** on *Sullivan's Travels* (1941). He went on to direct some notable B-movie noirs and, in a series of brutal, subtle, intelligent Westerns, introduced a noirish emphasis on characters haunted, wounded or threatened by the past. His work was characterized by a gift for matching landscape and character so precisely that the terrain seemed, at times, to shape the action. He said once, "If you're going to tell a story, instead of telling an intellectual story – which by necessity requires a tremendous amount of words – pick one that has pictorial qualities to start with." For Scorsese, "The Western allowed for elaborate psychological, even Freudian, dramas. While **John Ford** only alluded to the dark side, Anthony Mann dwelled in it."

He launched his Western career in 1950 with two contrasting films, *Devil's Doorway*, a bitter re-evaluation of the Native American's plight, and *The Furies*, a family Western whose conflict anticipated the *King Lear* elements in *Man Of The West* and Mann's unrealized dream of filming the Shakespearean tragedy as a Western.

In the next ten years he made a further nine Westerns, five with **Jimmy Stewart**: *Winchester '73* (1950), *Bend Of The River* (1951), *The Naked Spur* (1952), *The Far Country* (1954) and *The Man From Laramie* (1956). He reinvented Stewart and, as Godard noted, looked set to reinvent the genre. Four of the Stewart Westerns (the exception is the not quite as good *The Far Country*) and *Man*

In *The Man From Laramie* Anthony Mann juxtaposes character and landscape to emphasize his hero's vulnerability.

Of The West, Mann's startling collaboration with Gary Cooper, represent his finest work. But all his Westerns, even the studio-wrecked *Cimarron* (1960), have some interest.

Two of Mann's later Westerns – *The Last Frontier* (1955) and *The Tin Star* (1957) – are almost as fascinating as the Cooper/Stewart films. *The Last Frontier*, marred by knockabout comedy and a ludicrous happy ending, makes fine use of Victor Mature and Anne Bancroft as

it questions the "civilizing" of the West. In *The Tin Star*, with **Henry Fonda**'s bounty hunter aiding **Anthony Perkins**' inexperienced sheriff, the embittered old hand learns as many truths as the tyro in a story told as much through imagery as by dialogue. After *Cimarron*'s failure, he turned to the epic, though the Western's influence is obvious in *El Cid* (1961). When he died in 1967, his reputation, for a while, seemed to have died with him.

His Westerns don't have the range of Ford's, but his dark vision, original imagery and focus on the human psyche's latent desires and obsessions anticipated the glories of Leone and Eastwood as Western filmmakers.

Devil's Doorway
dir Anthony Mann, 1950, US, 84m, b/w

An astonishingly radical Western for its day, Mann's take on the fate of the Native American is far less optimistic than the same year's *Broken Arrow* and was, not coincidentally, much less commercially successful. Robert Taylor is on top form as the Shoshone who, decorated for bravery fighting for the Union at Gettysburg, returns to his homeland and dies, in army uniform, defending his people's rights against sheepherders and the US cavalry. The film's stark dismissal of liberal platitudes endures better than many woollier Westerns from this era.

Lee Marvin

1924–87

"If I have any appeal at all, it's to the fellow who takes out the garbage", Lee Marvin said once. He was doing himself a serious disservice. He may have started out as a villain for hire but he became, as the novelist George Pelecanos put it, "our greatest silent screen actor who happened to be working in the era of sound".

Marvin always maintained that his best acting was done in the Marines in World War II, pretending not to be scared in battle in Asia. That knowledge of, as his director John Boorman said, "the depth of our capacity for cruelty and evil" informed the heavies he played in such films as *Gun Fury* (1953), *The Stranger Wore A Gun* (1953), *Bad Day At Black Rock* (1954), *Seven Men From Now* (1956) and *The Comacheros* (1961), as well as his showy, whip-cracking villain in *The Man Who Shot Liberty Valance* (1962).

He won an Oscar for his dual turn in the classic comedy Western *Cat Ballou* (1965). He tried to give half the credit to his horse, and became, probably to his own surprise, a star. He cemented his new status, starring as a mercenary alongside Burt Lancaster in **Richard Brooks'** fine Western *The Professionals* (1966), mumbling his way through the musical Western *Paint Your Wagon* (1969) and shining in the superb *Monte Walsh* (1970). He was less assured in **Stuart Rosenberg**'s *Pocket Money* (1972) and in **Richard Fleischer**'s *The Spikes Gang* (1974) but then so were the movies. His final Western, *The Great Scout And Cathouse Thursday* (1976), dismissed by one reviewer as "coarse, crass and calamitous", is worth watching mainly for Marvin's battle of wits with Oliver Reed.

That marked the end of a strange career in Westerns, blighted by poor quality control and too many movies where you can almost see Marvin calculating the size of his paycheck.

Cat Ballou
dir Elliot Silverstein, 1965, US, 96m

Jane Fonda, Lee Marvin (as both a gunslinger with a drink problem and an outlaw with a nose problem) and the Greek chorus of minstrels Nat King Cole and Stubby Kaye make Elliot Silverstein's comic, musical, parody Western, derived from Roy Chanslor's novel, a charming gem. Catherine Ballou (Fonda) hires gunfighter Kid Shelleen (Marvin) to avenge her father's murder but, realizing he is too drunk, takes up gunslinging herself, inspiring the Kid to face his twin/nemesis Harry Strawn (Marvin) who had the tip of his nose bitten off in a gunfight.

Robert Mitchum

1917–97

When Walter Brennan, the veteran character actor and Old West enthusiast, saw Robert

Robert Mitchum said he had two acting styles – with or without a horse. But his quiet, brooding physical presence gave his many Westerns a distinct flavour.

Mitchum on the set of Robert Wise's noir Western *Blood On The Moon* (1948), he said: "That is the goddamndest realest cowboy I've ever seen."

Mitchum had the bulky physique and easy grace of a cowboy and, on screen, laconic came even more naturally to him than to **Gary Cooper**. His wry detachment implied he had seen the worst life had to offer and was quietly convinced more of the same was on the way. Roughly a third of his major movies were Westerns – he once said he had two acting styles, "with and without a horse" – and they were among his best, most unusual, pictures.

A onetime hobo, soldier of fortune and convict (jailed for possessing marijuana), Mitchum regarded the movie business as a magic carpet, choosing roles for the money and the locations. Unlike many male stars, he had a physical presence that suggested he really could wrestle a bull, lasso a runaway horse or throw a knockout punch. "The three toughest guys in the movie business", said Budd Boetticher, "were Jack Palance, Bob Ryan and Mitchum. And Mitchum was the toughest."

The Western discovered him. In the 1940s, he was a supporting presence in Hopalong Cassidy movies. In 1945, his turn as a vengeance-seeking cowboy in the Zane Grey horse opera *West Of The Pecos* served notice of a star in the making.

His cynical, sensual charm made him a natural for the dark, intriguing, amoral world of film noir and he was at his best in two noir Westerns: *Pursued* (1947) and *Blood On The Moon*. He didn't make a truly bad Western in the 1950s. **Nicholas Ray's**

The Lusty Men (1952), arguably the best rodeo Western, and *The Wonderful Country* (1959), with Mitchum as the conflicted half-breed hero, were the standouts. In **Otto Preminger**'s *River Of No Return* (1954), Mitchum was a fine foil for **Marilyn Monroe**. Less innovative than *The Wonderful Country*, *Bandido* (1956) was another Mexican Western, anticipating *The Magnificent Seven* (1960) and *Duck, You Sucker* (1971), in which the role of an outwardly cynical gun runner who ends up fighting for the little guy seemed made for him.

He turned down *The Misfits* (1960) because he feared working with **John Huston** would kill him (he had a point: the movie may have killed his replacement Clark Gable) and didn't return to the saddle until the late 1960s. Then, in rapid succession, he starred in *El Dorado* ("as John Wayne's leading lady", he quipped), *The Way West*, *Villa Rides*, *5 Card Stud*, *Young Billy Young* and *The Good Guys And The Bad Guys*. *El Dorado* (1966) was the standout. The rest are colourful, action-packed, entertaining – yet slightly disappointing.

Only in the 1970s did critics begin to truly appreciate Mitchum. He could, as David Lean noted, "just by being there, make almost any other actor look like a hole in the screen". To the Western, Mitchum brought a quietly subversive presence, which made his best films – *Pursued*, *Blood On The Moon* and *The Wonderful Country* – feel like no other Hollywood Westerns. In two movies – *The Lusty Men* and *El Dorado* – he gave near-definitive studies of dignified, worn out, broken down heroes. In 1993, when George P. Cosmatos made *Tombstone*, Mitchum was the perfect narrator. If he never became as central to the Western as his friend John Wayne, he was, as Brennan had pointed out, believable, in a business where too many actors were merely plausible.

The Lusty Men
dir Nicholas Ray, 1952, US, 113m, b/w

In his first Western, Nicholas Ray brings a richness and complexity to what could have been a routine oater. Mitchum is the former rodeo star, struggling to settle down, who mentors Arthur Kennedy in the skills of the trade. Success turns Kennedy's head but, despite his drinking and womanizing, wife Susan Hayward refuses to leave him for Mitchum. With Horace McCoy, who wrote *They Shoot Horses Don't They?*, on script duty, *The Lusty Men* beautifully captures the scarred misfits and outsiders Ray was drawn to and the dusty rodeo towns, dilapidated ranches and trailer camps they lived in.

Tom Mix
1880–1940

Tom Mix rode into stardom and drove out of it. In 1906 he was hired by the Selig studio to look after horses on set. He was even more persuasive with horses than with women and, by 1910, this former Texas Ranger and rodeo champion was acting in his own movies, the first Hollywood star who really looked good on a horse and the inspiration for the likes of **John Wayne** and **Ronald Reagan**. He was the perfect Jazz Age cowboy, starring in Westerns that were a high-speed melange of horse tricks, fist-fights, comedy and chases.

Mix's life was shrouded in myth and media speculation. He hadn't fought in the Spanish–American War when he was 18, and probably never was a marshal in Oklahoma. But he did do his own stunts, eschewed realism for a circus showman's ideal of what the West should have been like and, in hundreds of movies (too few of which survive), was a clean-living, flashily dressed, good-humoured, good-looking superman on a horse. What Mix did, possibly without realizing, was define the template for B Westerns.

Tom Mix in *The Great K And A Train Robbery* (1926). The Western's first superhero, Mix was kind to women, horses and his tailor but mean to villains when he had to be.

The Last Trail — gave him his biggest smashes. But in 1928 a blip in box-office takings for Westerns persuaded Fox to drop him. After several low-budget silents — and duty as a pallbearer at **Wyatt Earp**'s funeral in 1929 — he returned with nine talkies for Universal in 1932–33. The best of these — *Destry Rides Again* (not the James Stewart movie) and *The Rider Of Death Valley* — were among his finest films but he wasn't as relaxed in talkies and was no longer as agile. In 1935 he rode off into the sunset — as far as Hollywood was concerned — to the circus. He died in a car crash in 1940.

The ravine where he died in Arizona was named The Tom Mix Wash but that isn't the end of his strange posthumous fame. The radio show he started in 1933 carried on until 1950. In 1975 Darryl Ponicsan's entertaining novel *Tom Mix Died For Your Sins* inspired a minor revival in the Mix cult, and the radio show returned briefly. In 1988 the tale of his friendship with Earp inspired Blake Edwards' *Sunset*, in which Mix is played by a badly miscast **Bruce Willis**. In the Mexican Western comedy *Mi Querido Tom Mix* (1991), the heroine dreams Mix will liven up her drab life. And the relative merits of Mix and William S. Hart are debated by the train robbers in Richard Linklater's *The Newton Boys* (1998).

When Selig folded in 1917, Mix moved to Fox where, at his peak, he was earning $17,500 a week. From 1920 to 1927, he starred in a remarkable number of quality Westerns including *The Untamed*, *Sky High*, *Soft Boiled* and *North Of Hudson Bay* (directed by John Ford). Four Zane Grey adaptations — *The Lone Star Ranger*, *Riders Of The Purple Sage*, *The Rainbow Trail* and

Mix's surviving films often run on Turner Classic Movies, he was one of the inspirations for Alan Moore's comic-book hero Tom Strong and you can now buy 36 brands of Tom Mix Stetsons at various online emporiums. Not bad for a star who hasn't made a movie in more than seventy years.

Ennio Morricone

1928–

No composer has had such a profound impact on the Western as Leone's old schoolmate Ennio Morricone. Yet his work with Leone has overshadowed almost all of his other scores so that, today, he is typecast as the music man for spaghetti Westerns.

Morricone started writing film scores in the early 1960s, and even wrote derivative soundtracks for a couple of precursors to the spaghetti Western. But it was working with Leone that made him. Before their collaboration, the typical Western score had been a sweeping orchestral affair. But Morricone – like Leone – was a minimalist when it came to sounds in movies. He preferred strong themes played on a few instruments. Certain sounds – jangling guitars, a lone, often female, voice, a flute, a Jew's harp, a whistled theme – became trademarks as Morricone sought to write music that felt as if it were coming from within the scenes on the screen. He made innovative use of character signatures: the haunting, wailing harmonica in *Once Upon A Time In The West* (1968) didn't just introduce **Charles Bronson**'s character, it added to the tension. At other times, his scores were slyly humorous, mocking the characters or providing an ironic contrast to the action.

The "Dollars" movies were made so fast that Morricone didn't have time to write the music before shooting, as he and Leone had hoped, but that was how they created the score for *Once Upon A Time In The West*. Because Leone used post-synchronized sound, the music could be played on set while scenes were being shot, helping set the mood and inspiring some of the extraordinarily precise matching of sound and action. The relationship between sound and vision wasn't always about iconic tunes: in the opening of the film, it is the minimal use of noise which makes the effect so powerful.

Morricone was a master at building up tension musically, a talent Leone, who carefully monitored the highs and lows of his own narratives, soon came to appreciate. Like Leone, Morricone was a master allusionist, blending pop, Italian opera, Japanese samurai and Hollywood Western while acknowledging the influence of Bach and Stravinsky.

Though he collaborated most closely with Leone, Morricone worked for many other Italian Western directors at the same time, producing, for example, a haunting score for Corbucci's *Il grande silenzio* (1968). By 1971, when Leone made his Mexican Western *Duck, You Sucker*, the composer was confident enough to pen a funny, self-mocking score. He repeated the trick, more broadly, for the comedy spaghetti Western *A Genius, Two Partners And A Dupe* (1975).

Although it was Westerns that made his name, Morricone's range was much wider than that: out of more than 500 films and TV series, only about 30 were Westerns. He began composing for Hollywood in the late 1960s but, with the notable exception of *Two Mules For Sister Sara* (1969), didn't get to score American Westerns. This was partly because America had almost stopped making them, but also because the genre's directors wouldn't hire him for fear of being accused of plagiarism. It was an odd, ironic twist for a man who, in 1962, had re-scored the theme for the dependable TV Western *The Virginian*.

It is obvious, however, from the soundtracks of most Hollywood Westerns made from 1970 onwards that directors and composers have listened to Morricone and taken notice. And so, if you listen to the music of *Kill Bill 2* (2004), has Tarantino.

Warren Oates

1928–82

A lanky, laconic actor with a cock-eyed grin and a versatile scowl, Warren Oates may be the only Western icon to have co-starred with Sam Peckinpah, Henry Fonda, Rin Tin Tin and Dennis Hopper. A firm cult favourite, best known for his role in Peckinpah's *Bring Me The Head Of Alfredo Garcia* (1974), Oates died of a heart attack at 53, ending a long, slow, climb to stardom.

Kentucky born, a former US marine and hat-check boy, Oates looked too unusual – with beady eyes, snaggled teeth and receding hair – to be a conventional Western hero. He started out in the genre as a villain in the 1950s US TV series *Have Gun Will Travel* (after a minor role in a *Rin Tin Tin* episode) but it was as one of the depraved Hammond brothers, notorious for their liberal definition of conjugal rights, that he caught the eye in Peckinpah's *Ride The High Country* (1962). In the 1960s his offbeat onscreen persona was used to good effect by Peckinpah (in *Major Dundee*, 1964) and **Monte Hellman** (in his existentialist Western *The Shooting*, 1967). He was more accomplished being enigmatic or slimy than as a white-hat in the dreadful sequel *Return Of The Seven* (1967).

The success of *The Wild Bunch* (1969) cemented his popularity as one of the Western's most left-field leading players, and he was called on by **Peter Fonda** for *The Hired Hand* (1971) and by James Frawley to play alongside Dennis Hopper in *Kid Blue* (1973). Hellman hired him again for *China 9, Liberty 37* (1978).

If Oates never became a star in the mould of John Wayne or Gary Cooper, he used his gift as an actor to give himself a shot at some of the most intriguing leading roles. As he admitted once, he was almost the antithesis of the Duke: "My image of the Western man is John Wayne and I'm just a little shit. In a Western role, the man has to be bigger than life, bigger than the screen." Oates wasn't bigger than the screen, but he was usually interesting to watch on it.

China 9, Liberty 37 (Amore, piomto e furore)
dir Monte Hellman, 1978, It, 102m

Often regarded as the final spaghetti Western, this was to be the last Western for both Oates and Monte Hellman. Fabio Testi is hired to kill Warren Oates so the railroad can seize his land but finds he likes Oates too much to kill him – though when Oates's sexually frustrated wife Jenny Agutter thinks she's killed him, he's happy to run off with her. Punctuated with bizarre moments, *China 9, Liberty 37* – the title refers to a road sign pointing to Texas towns – is not as accomplished as *The Shooting*, but it's gritty, violent and infused with an eroticism that borders on pornography.

Jack Palance

1919–

Few actors have made such a vivid debut in the Western as Jack Palance. He gave one of the genre's definitive studies in villainy as Wilson, the hired gun in *Shane* (1953), a role that made full use of his taut, menacing face, the legacy of

"Wilson was fast!": Western villains who made our blood run cold

• **Robert Ryan as Ben Vandergroat in** *The Naked Spur* **(1952)**

If the Academy gave Oscars for goading, Robert Ryan would have had a cabinet full. In *The Naked Spur* and *Bad Day At Black Rock* (1954) he is utterly magnificent as the cynical, eloquent villain who always threatens to steal the initiative and the scene. His sinister chuckling charm is crucial to *The Naked Spur*, a perfect counter for Jimmy Stewart's tormented hero.

• **Jack Palance as Wilson in** *Shane* **(1953)**

As Wilson, the lethal, doomed gunfighter in *Shane*, Jack Palance can sneer an opponent into fatal errors. With his twisted wire physique, we first see Wilson riding into town on a horse that's too small for him, exuding awkward menace. Standing with his hand waiting impatiently by his holster, he has a deadly poise. Even in the final gunfight, he looks simply gleeful as he gives the two-word reply – "prove it" – that he knows will trigger hostilities.

• **Henry Fonda as Frank in** *Once Upon A Time In The West* **(1968)**

Seldom have a pair of blue eyes so set the tone for a movie. Fonda's baby blues look more empty than innocent as he kills a child to protect his identity.

• **Robert Duvall as Jesse James in** *The Great Northfield Minnesota Raid* **(1971)**

Gone is Jesse James, the cowboy Robin Hood. In his place we have Duvall's grim, cold-blooded, yet not utterly charmless, homicidal psychopath with a terrible haircut.

• **Kris Kristofferson as Charlie Wade in** *Lone Star* **(1996)**

Kristofferson's bigoted "bribes and bullets" lawman doesn't have much screen time – it is his murder the new sheriff has to solve – but even in flashback he's so memorably vicious that he haunts the movie.

---

plastic surgery after wartime injury. He would later parody the part in an Oscar-winning turn in Billy Crystal's comedy *City Slickers* (1991).

The son of Ukrainian immigrants – born Vladimir Palahniuk in Pennsylvania – Palance is one of the Western's most enduring bad guys, though he has sometimes impressed in more sympathetic roles, notably as a gunfighter trying to settle down in *The Lonely Man* (1957) and *Monte Walsh* (1970). He can be flamboyantly menacing but is at his most disturbingly effective when restrained, bringing an air of barely contained violence to such roles as Toriano, Charlton Heston's adversary in *Arrowhead* (1953).

After his initial success in the Western, Palance played villains in film noir and melodrama. **Richard Brooks'** fine Western *The Professionals* called Palance back to the genre in 1966, and he gave one of his best performances as the bandit who isn't as bad as the heroes are led to believe. Over the next decade, he would star in a remarkable number of American and European Westerns. His first spaghetti Western was Corbucci's *Il mercenario* (*The Mercenary*, 1968), in which his white-suited villain dies with blood spouting from his carnation. In Corbucci's *Companeros* (1970) he was delightfully – and, for once, appropriately – over the top as the once-crucified villain with a wooden hand. He was almost as outrageous as the parson who leads his sons into rape and pillage in Henry Levin's shoddy *The Desperadoes* (1969), ably personified Southern bigotry in *The McMasters* (1970) but was at his finest opposite **Lee Marvin** in the melancholy *Monte Walsh*.

Quality control – over scripts, more than performances – became an issue for Palance. He was too good for most of the Westerns he was cast in over the next eighteen years. None of them quite match *Monte Walsh* but *Chato's Land* (1972) and *Diamante Lobo* (1976) are worth watching.

His performance as Curly, the scary trail boss in *City Slickers*, led to one of the funniest Oscar acceptance speeches ever. Halting for words as he clutched his statuette, Palance improvised by doing push-ups. Even he couldn't save the sequel *City Slickers II: The Legend Of Curly's Gold* (1994). But his resurgence continued with a role in *Buffalo Girls* (1995), the acclaimed TV adaptation of Larry McMurtry's novel, a fitting way to bow out of a genre he had graced for more than forty years.

Sam Peckinpah

1925–84

"He was a genius for about four hours then he was gone" is James Coburn's telling recollection of working with Sam Peckinpah, arguably the most controversial director in the West. Coburn had fonder memories of the wayward genius than **Maureen O'Hara**, who recalled "how uncomfortable I felt watching him waste the day away relentlessly scratching his crotch", and **Charlton Heston**, who admitted: "Sam is the

only person I've physically threatened on set."

Peckinpah directed only seven true Westerns and his reputation in the genre rests on *Ride The High Country* (1962), *The Wild Bunch* (1969) and *Pat Garrett And Billy The Kid* (1973). Actor Robert Culp, speaking at Peckinpah's funeral in 1984, said: "The miracle of Sam was that he got any of them [the movies] done at all … Rather than say 'I wish he'd done one or two more', let's just thank that incredible, savage, iron, burning will that he got them made."

Peckinpah grew up closest to his grandfather, a judge, congressman and deadly shot. He drifted into the theatre and the movies, playing a bank teller in the **Joel McCrea** Western *Wichita* (1955). He made his reputation in TV as the creator of the series *The Rifleman* and *The Westerner*, before, to O'Hara's chagrin, being asked to direct *The Deadly Companions* (1961). Often dismissed – even by Peckinpah – as routine, his debut is a genuinely intriguing psychological Western, overlooked because it doesn't suit the director's mythology. In 1962, he paired McCrea and Scott in the magnificent *Ride The High Country*, which anticipates the ageing gunfighter theme of *The Wild Bunch* and the regretful tone of *Pat Garrett*.

On his next Western, *Major Dundee* (1964), Heston threatened to run him through with a sabre, but the studio did Peckinpah more harm, cutting the film so clumsily it became a magnificent ruin. Left unemployable, he bided his time writing *The Glory Guys* (1965) and *Villa Rides* (1968) before making his comeback movie *The Wild Bunch*.

On release, the movie polarized opinion with its violent attempt to reinvent the Western. In the decades since, its tale of – to quote David Thomson – "violently talented men hired for a job that is loaded with compromise, corruption and double-cross" seems as much a parable about filmmaking in Hollywood as a story about doomed, desperate gunfighters.

His next movie, the gentle comedy Western *The Ballad Of Cable Hogue* (1970), was a real departure, though it returned to the theme of a hero rendered obsolete by progress. The subtle, underrated rodeo picture *Junior Bonner* (1972), with **Steve McQueen**, was overshadowed by the next year's *Pat Garrett*, a great mournful Western released against Peckinpah's will by MGM.

That was his last undisputed great Western. For some, *Bring Me The Head Of Alfredo Garcia* (1974) is a fine Western; for others, it's a grim, horrific, brilliant thriller. Either way, it bombed on release, pigeonholing Peckinpah as Bloody Sam. As Hollywood discovered the pleasures of *Jaws* and *Star Wars*, Peckinpah would wonder: "Is there a place in this world for me anymore?" Like his gunfighter heroes, he had outlived his usefulness. When he died, he was making music videos for Julian Lennon.

Since his death, Peckinpah's reputation has fluctuated. The charge of misogyny has stuck. As Pauline Kael noted, he has only two notable female characters in his films – a young bride (in *Ride The High Country*) and a slut (in *Straw Dogs*, 1971). Others have accused him of self-indulgence and incoherence. But his best Westerns still move, appal and intrigue.

Peckinpah had a true sense of film, a pessimistic vision that infused his finest work, and a unique perspective on the West. But the confrontations he courted to motivate himself ultimately defeated him. Kael, again, summed him up rather nicely: "Lord, he was clever, demonically intuitive, and he had such self-dramatizing brio. Though the competition is keen, he's perhaps the greatest martyr/ham in Hollywood history."

The Ballad Of Cable Hogue
dir Sam Peckinpah, 1970, US, 121m

The failure of this movie, in which the titular hero and a prostitute think they have made a life for themselves in the desert only to have their paradise ruined by the coming of the automobile, hurt Peckinpah even harder than the poor box-office takings for *The Wild Bunch*. As Stella Stevens, who plays the prostitute Hildy, noted, the movie "wasn't released, it was flushed". After the violent energy of *The Wild Bunch*, this gentle, lyrical ode to the dying of the West bemused Peckinpah's new fans. The love scenes between Stevens and Robards have all the emotional resonance of a greetings card but the film has a Felliniesque dreamy imagery and is full of what Alex Cox called "the wonderful sadness" that infused Peckinpah's great work.

Robert Ryan
1909–73

He never had the ticket-selling clout to be a headline star like **Clark Gable**, but after watching a film featuring Robert Ryan, his was often the performance you remembered most. He was, as the actor and filmmaker John Houseman said, "a disturbing mixture of anger and tenderness who had reached stardom by playing mostly brutal, neurotic roles that were at complete variance with his true character".

Craggy, gruff and virile, Ryan made his name playing villains in film noir, but in 1948 his grim, cold-blooded portrait of the Sundance Kid in *Return Of The Bad Man* lit up what was otherwise a standard Randolph Scott Western. Ultimately, as an actor, Ryan would find it hard to land parts big enough for his talent, but in the 1950s he became one of the Western's most charismatic bad guys.

He had obvious physical assets as a villain. His lanky physique could seem surprisingly threatening, his distinctive rasping voice gave his dialogue a bitter authority and he could be more menacing with a look than other actors with a gun. Yet he infused his best bad guys with a sense of secret hurt and intense bitter emotion that made him all the more watchable.

His memorably megalomanical ex-Confederate officer in Budd Boetticher's *Horizons West* (1952) was a preview of glories to come. He was just as impressive for **John Sturges** (in *Bad Day At Black Rock*, 1954, and as Ike Clanton in *Hour Of The Gun*, 1967), **Anthony Mann** (in *The Naked Spur*, 1952) and **André De Toth** (in *Day Of The Outlaw*, 1959, in which he duels with outlaw leader Burl Ives). If anything, Ryan could be too good – in *Bad Day At Black Rock*, he is more complex than the film has time for.

He could play heroes – as he showed in Burt Kennedy's proto-New Age Western *The Canadians* (1961) and Robert D. Webb's *The Proud Ones* (1956). But his fine performance in the latter, as a brave yet vulnerable sheriff, hampered by disability, was wasted in a modest movie. After that, Ryan's star waned, but his career revived in the late 1960s, with three Westerns: Richard Brooks' *The Professionals* (1966), *Hour Of The Gun* and the glorious farewell that was his turn as Thornton in *The Wild Bunch* (1969). He was ill by then but his tall, gaunt, grey presence perfectly captured his character's spiritual depletion.

Randolph Scott

1898–1987

The Western saved Randolph Scott – and almost swallowed him. To moviegoers who don't like the genre, his fame rests, almost solely, on his alleged affair with flatmate **Cary Grant**. But in Westerns, his iconic status is reflected in *Blazing Saddles* when Cleavon Little says to the townsfolk, who have just refused his request for help, "You'd do it for Randolph Scott." The townsfolk then take off their hats and whisper reverently "Randolph Scott!" before singing a chorus of "Randolph Scott".

Scott graduated to Westerns via romantic movies, comedies, musicals and war films, but then concentrated, from 1946 until his last film in 1962, pretty exclusively on the genre. He made so many, at such a pace – 35 between 1940 and 1955 – that many were bound to be routine. But he impressed in Fritz Lang's Cain and Abel themed epic *Western Union* (1941) and in André De Toth's *Man In The Saddle* (1951). His beautifully judged performance in *Carson City* (1952), also for De Toth, hinted at splendours to come. Some of his best work supported other movies – his satisfying turn in *The Bounty Hunter* (1954, De Toth again) was second billing to *Dragnet*.

Tall, light and handsome, with piercing blue eyes, Scott always seemed most at home in Westerns. By the 1950s, though physically still in prime condition, his face had acquired a weary weatherbeaten quality which brought gravitas to the laconic, fatalistic, self-reliant persona which was central to the seven movies he made with **Budd Boetticher**. These movies – *Seven Men From Now, Decision At Sundown, The Tall T, Buchanan Rides Alone, Ride Lonesome, Westbound* and *Comanche Station* (and Peckinpah's fine *Ride The High Country*) – made Scott's reputation.

The Boetticher films were critically ignored on release but are now recognized as one of the Western's crowning glories. Only an actor with Scott's sure sense of his range and skills could have so convincingly portrayed Boetticher's slightly archaic hero in these bittersweet Westerns, creating a persona that reminded French critic André Bazin of **William S. Hart**. Scott only won the

Randolph Scott brought a weatherbeaten gravitas to his role as a heroic loner in Budd Boetticher's *The Tall T.*

role in *Seven Men From Now* because **John Wayne**, who was originally going to make it, thought he'd be cheap. "Let's use Randolph Scott", the Duke told Boetticher. "He's through."

Scott, who read the *Wall Street Journal* between takes, was a multi-millionaire and, after the brilliant farewell of *Ride The High Country* (1962), hung up his spurs. Yet his image lives on. He was

ironically celebrated in the 1973 US hit single "Whatever Happened To Randolph Scott?" by the Statler Brothers. What happened is that the real Scott died old and rich, while the on-screen icon is still "ridin' the trail alone", as the song put it, in our memory and on television, and inspiring stars and directors from Eastwood and Leone to Tarantino.

Barbara Stanwyck

1907–90

"When she was good, she was very, very good. And when she was bad she was terrific" was how Walter Matthau described Barbara Stanwyck. Though no Western role quite matched her glittering medusa in the noir classic *Double Indemnity* (1944), Stanwyck was the genre's greatest matriarch. The theme to Sam Fuller's *Forty Guns* (1957) described her character as a "high-riding woman with a whip" and, as such, she was more of a threat to the patriarchal norm of the celluloid West than dear, gorgeous **Maureen O'Hara**.

Stanwyck epitomized the wisecracking, cynical, tough, feisty, yet sexy, frontier woman of the West in such films as *Cattle Queen Of Montana* (1954), *The Maverick Queen* (1956) and *Forty Guns*. In a male-dominated, macho genre, she was one of the few actresses who could carry a Western on her own.

Stanwyck – born Ruby Stevens in Brooklyn, New York – had a knack for making melodrama convincing, possibly because her own life was so full of it. Orphaned as an infant, she was raised by an older sister who was a dancer. Ruby drifted into the same world and, legend has it, found her stage name on a poster for a movie called *Barbara Frietchie* starring an actress called Jane Stanwyck.

In her first major Western, George Stevens' *Annie Oakley* (1935), she was fresh, believable and sparky in the title role. She was less notable in Cecil B. De Mille's railroad epic *Union Pacific* (1939), but in *California* (1946), which starts with her being run out of town for immorality, her cynical saloon queen nods to triumphs to come.

The 1950s were her golden decade for Westerns. She excelled as the vicious, jealous Electra figure in **Anthony Mann**'s pseudo-Freudian Western *The Furies* (1950), though the movie left some cold. She was reunited with *Double Indemnity* co-star Fred MacMurray for *The Moonlighter* (1953), a tepid Western that has, however, more recently gained some feminist cred for Stanwyck's bringing her bank-robbing old beau MacMurray to justice.

Stanwyck perfected her sassy matriarch in Allan Dwan's *Cattle Queen Of Montana*, soaring above the script and co-star **Ronald Reagan**. As an outlaw who gives young studs the runaround, even she couldn't stop *The Maverick Queen* seeming like a cheap clone of *Johnny Guitar* (1954). But she was glorious in Sam Fuller's *Forty Guns*. After that final brilliance, she drifted into semi-retirement before reigning again – as a more sympathetic kind of matriarch – in the 1960s TV Western *The Big Valley*.

Stanwyck had always wanted to play Westerns and to introduce more realistic female characters. "Some producers think women just kept house and raised children in those days," she said once, "but if you read history, they did a lot more than that." Stanwyck fulfilled her goal, managing ranches, toting guns and riding in jeans and buckskin – all, traditionally, the prerogatives of the male hero. No wonder some enthusiasts see her Western heroines as precursors of Xena the warrior princess.

Forty Guns
dir Sam Fuller, 1957, US, 80m, b/w

Stanwyck never posed a greater threat to Western codes than as Jessica Drummond, the rancher backed by forty mercenaries, torn between protecting her wastrel brother and her love for the town's new marshal (Barry Sullivan). Clad in black, her face hard yet delicate, Stanwyck is lean, mean and magnificent in a deliciously lurid tale that Douglas Sirk would have been proud of. Told, at one point, that she looks upset, Stanwyck replies: "I was born upset!" The innuendoes upset the censors – especially when Stanwyck asks if she can feel the marshal's pistol.

James Stewart

1908–97

Despite a degree in architecture from Princeton and a theatre background, Jimmy Stewart had a drawling country-boy manner. His most iconic line of dialogue was "Aw shucks", he was pigeon-holed as "Mr American Pie", and he never took acting lessons (he insisted "I don't act, I react"), yet he brought a miraculous variety of shadings and interpretations to what is, in memory, a very precisely defined persona. Once he became a true star, he could never play a real villain, but he used his natural charm to lead us into the dark, troubled heart of some very odd heroes.

In his gangly youthful stardom, he conveyed earnest idealism in such gems of Americana as *Mr Smith Goes To Washington* (1939) and his first major Western, *Destry Rides Again* (1939), in which he is simply flawless as the pacifist sheriff. But Stewart – like his good friend Henry Fonda – used the Western to reinvent himself. His troubled, suffering loners in a series of superior Westerns of the 1950s and 60s gave the homespun charm an edge of almost pathological intensity.

The roll began with **Anthony Mann**'s revenge shoot-'em-up *Winchester '73* (1950), the first of eight films they made together. He went native with the Apache in the then-radical Indian Western *Broken Arrow* (1950). Then, under Mann's direction, Stewart was the outlaw in need of redemption in *Bend Of The River* (1952), the neurotic bounty hunter in *The Naked Spur*

(1953), the cattleman trying to escape his past in *The Far Country* (1955) and the brutalized avenger in *The Man From Laramie* (1955).

After *The Man From Laramie*, Mann and Stewart parted, but they had re-established Stewart at the box office and redefined his character as, noted critic David Thomson, "a tougher, more pained and selfish man, who was often made to suffer and put to a broad test of courage and wounding".

After going through the motions in *Night Passage* (1957), at long last he teamed up with John Ford, creating the classic *The Man Who Shot Liberty Valance* (1962) – in which Stewart is contrasted with **John Wayne** – the less impressive *Two Rode Together* (1961) and a satirical Wyatt Earp in *Cheyenne Autumn* (1964). But the quality of his Westerns had begun to vary. His chemistry with Maureen O'Hara made Andrew McLaglen's sub-Fordian *The Rare Breed* (1966) more fun than it deserved to be, just as his rapport with Fonda made Gene Kelly's *The Cheyenne Social Club* (1970) seem funnier than the script. His reluctant sheriff in *Firecreek* (1968) was compelling and, for once, free of mannerism, providing a striking contrast to Henry Fonda's villain.

It was fitting that two very different giants of the genre met up at the end of their respective careers for *The Shootist* (1976), in which Stewart's doc tells Wayne he's dying. Asked about their contrasting appeals, Stewart once said: "Maybe what it is is that people identify with me, but dream of being John Wayne."

Winchester '73
dir Anthony Mann, 1950, US, 92m, b/w

Luckily director Fritz Lang quit, enabling Mann and Stewart to start their collaboration. Stewart must defeat his evil brother and get his Winchester '73 rifle back. The episodic story – as the rifle changes hands – enables Mann to tour

John Sturges always got the maximum out of Kirk Douglas – famously in *Gunfight At The OK Corral* and, as seen here, in *Last Train From Gun Hill.*

the genre, throwing in cavalry, Indians and Indian traders, while the jagged landscape suits the dark psychological tale of vengeance. *Winchester '73* is lavishly cast: Shelley Winters, Dan Duryea, Rock Hudson, Tony Curtis and John McIntire all feature, though Stewart's surprisingly intense hero stands out.

John Sturges

1911–92

The work of John Sturges is long overdue for the kind of rehabilitation that has so benefitted Douglas Sirk. But even the French, determined celluloid iconoclasts, have lost their early enthusiasm for Sturges' oeuvre. As a director, he may have no critical reputation whatsoever, but he made two of the most famous Westerns ever (*Gunfight At The OK Corral*, 1957, and *The Magnificent Seven*, 1960), as well as *Bad Day At Black Rock* (1954), a classic contemporary Western of the McCarthy era.

Sturges entered films young. As a wartime Air Corps captain he directed and edited 45 documentaries. This served him well back in Hollywood, where he proved solid at delivering taut, tense action in such unfairly neglected Westerns as *The Walking Hills* (1949, starring **Randolph Scott**), the entertaining Civil War drama *Escape From Fort Bravo* (1953, starring **William Holden**) and the intense *Last Train From Gun Hill* (1959).

Westerns suited Sturges' strengths: a clean uncluttered style, an eye for effective and evocative compositions, and a knack for getting the most out of actors. His finest grand action sequences – the Indian attacks in *Escape From Fort Bravo* and *The Law And Jake Wade* (1958), the closing battle in *The Magnificent Seven* and the shoot-out in *OK Corral* – have a sureness of touch that many of today's action-movie makers could learn from.

From 1949 to his retirement in 1973, he made thirteen Westerns, as well as helping out uncredited on Robert Parrish's subversive 1958 Western *Saddle The Wind*. Three of these are very good or great: *Bad Day At Black Rock* (1954), a great noir thriller/Western; *Gunfight At The OK Corral*, an important hit that revived studio interest in Westerns; and *The Magnificent Seven*, simply top-class entertainment.

Sturges is often pigeonholed as a craftsman but his films have a stronger political content than, say, Howard Hawks's. His Westerns often expose the unpleasant realities obscured by the West's heroic mythology. Racism is confronted in *Bad Day*, *The Magnificent Seven*, *Last Train From Gun Hill* and his last contribution to the genre, the little-known European Western *Valdez The Half-Breed* (1973). Elsewhere Sturges touches on military martinets (in *Escape From Fort Bravo*), rape and murder (starkly depicted in the opening of *Last Train From Gun Hill*), while his *Hour Of The Gun* (1967) is an impressive, revisionist continuation of Earp's story. Making *Bad Day* in Hollywood in 1954 – in a community still infected by anti-Communist hysteria – took some guts.

Of his lesser-known Westerns, *The Law And Jake Wade*, *Backlash* (1956, a Freudian/Oedipal saga with **Richard Widmark** as the neurotic hero) and *Hour Of The Gun* have real merit. The most uninteresting Western he ever made is *Joe Kidd* (1972), a flavourless spaghetti Western starring Clint Eastwood, but then, some suggest, he was hitting the bottle by then. Sturges didn't have the vision of a Ford, Peckinpah or Leone, and he was only as good as his scripts, but his best films have stood the test of time.

The Law And Jake Wade
dir John Sturges, 1958, US, 86m

For some, this is Sturges' best Western. Beautifully shot by Robert Surtees, with a strong cast and an intriguing story, *The Law And Jake Wade* generates as much genuine tension as *Gunfight At The OK Corral*. Robert Taylor is Jake Wade, a reformed outlaw whose life was once saved by his old partner Holister (Richard Widmark). Hearing Widmark is to be hanged, Taylor saves him. But Widmark promptly kidnaps Taylor to help him find the loot from their last robbery. Taylor proves he's still seriously underrated as an actor but Widmark steals the honours as the wily villain.

Raoul Walsh
1887–1980

Albert Edward Walsh's idea of comedy may have been, as the wisecrack went, to burn down a whorehouse, but, lame humour aside, his contribution to the Western is immense. Raoul – as he styled himself, partly in honour of his mother's Spanish blood – perfected and almost defined the migration Western, discovered **John Wayne** nearly a decade before **John Ford** and acted as a role model for the Irish–American director.

Born in New York in 1887, Walsh started out as an actor, starring as John Wilkes Booth in **D.W. Griffith**'s *The Birth Of A Nation* (1915). But in 1929 he lost an eye in an accident on set and had to retreat permanently behind the camera, having already directed such masterpieces as *The Thief Of Baghdad* (1924).

In 1930 he made *The Big Trail*, an epic migration Western that introduced wide-screen projection and, more importantly, a new star called – after much debate – John Wayne. The movie might, if Fox hadn't been teetering towards bank-

Walsh and Ford

It is hard to think of a director as independently minded as **John Ford** having a role model. But John Wayne's biographer Garry Wills draws enough parallels to make you wonder.

Let's start with the eye-patch. Walsh wore his after losing an eye in 1929; Ford adopted one later, to protect his eyes from lights, and to flip down to signify to a visitor that an audience was over. Ford "discovered" **John Wayne** in 1939 with *Stagecoach* but Walsh persuaded the actor to change his name and gave him his first lead in a major Western – *The Big Trail*, a ship of fools Western that anticipated Ford's classic – in 1930. Ford made great play of his uncredited, masked role as a Klansman in **D.W. Griffith**'s *The Birth Of A Nation* – and boasted of his encounters with the film's legendary director – but Walsh had a more significant role, without a mask, as John Wilkes Booth, and had been tasked with negotiating with Pancho Villa for another of Griffith's productions. Finally, while Ford claimed to have been a cowboy out West, Walsh was the one who really rode herds in New Mexico.

Harry Carey Jr said that "Walsh was the kind of guy Ford admired" – a man's man, wit and adventurer who arrived on set every day with a different gorgeous blonde. None of this negates, or even qualifies, Ford's greatness as a filmmaker but it is an intriguing reminder that even icons have idols of their own.

dwelling on the story of Quantrill's renegades, became Republic's biggest box-office hit but is best remembered for a stunt in which four men and a team of horses leap off a bluff into a lake.

Walsh then made *They Died With Their Boots On* (1941), the definitive traditional treatment of George Custer with **Errol Flynn** as the dashing officer. Flynn's performance has worn surprisingly well – even the reviewer for *The Onion* praised "the new world of doubt behind the mask of Flynn's self-confidence".

From the late 1940s on, Walsh increasingly relied on the Western. Two noirish Westerns stood out – *Pursued* (1947) and *Colorado Territory* (1949) – while *Along The Great Divide* (1951), starring **Kirk Douglas**, has divided critics. In 1953, he made the compelling, low-budget *Gun Fury*, in which a bride-to-be is kidnapped by Philip Carey's psychotic outlaw. *The Tall Men* (1955) was a step up, opening, tellingly, with Clark Gable spotting a corpse hanging from a tree and saying to Cameron Mitchell: "Looks like we're near civilization." His comedy Western *The Sheriff Of Fractured Jaw* (1959), in which Kenneth Moore roams the West like Bertie Wooster, remonstrating with gun-toting cowboys, is, mostly, subtler than a fire in a brothel. His final Western – and last film – *A Distant Trumpet*, released in 1964, was an intelligent cavalry Western, beautifully shot and scored, scuppered by having Troy Donahue as the male lead.

Walsh was so versatile – and some of his gangster movies, such as *White Heat* (1949), so great – that his contribution to the Western is overlooked. But he discovered the Duke, inspired Ford and **Sergio Leone** (who, told by Walsh the Western was finished, proved him wrong), and never made a really poor Western, usually living up to his oft-quoted credo: "Cinema is action, action, action, but it must all be in the same direction."

ruptcy, have made the Duke a megastar. Walsh noted: "I discovered what is probably the world's greatest box-office star and a great American."

Gangsters preoccupied Walsh for the next decade but, in 1940, he was reunited with Wayne, fresh from the triumph of *Stagecoach* (1939), in a Western called *Dark Command*. The film,

John Wayne

1907–79

Born Marion Michael Morrison, John Wayne bestrides the Western genre, a bow-legged colossus in jeans.

Despite his good looks, college football star physique, friendship with "Pappy" Ford and early success in *The Big Trail* (1930), the young Wayne toiled in B oaters and serials like *The Three Mesquiteers* for ten years before Ford gave him a shot in *Stagecoach* (1939). The instant Wayne's Ringo Kid appears on the trail it is apparent we are in the presence of a star as big as Monument Valley. He would remain one for forty years, and one of the mightiest box-office

John Wayne, Ronald Reagan and George W. Bush

By 1980, disillusioned, disenchanted America wanted something simple to believe in. As Gil Scott-Heron put it in his seminal monologue *B Movie*, "nostalgia, that's what we want … a time when the movies were in black and white and so was everything else … a time when the US cavalry always rode in to save the day at the last moment … they were looking for John Wayne, but since John Wayne was no longer available they settled for Ronald Reagan."

Reagan assured ordinary Americans that the simple certainties of good guys in white hats and bad guys in black still applied. He was often erroneously dubbed a B-movie cowboy – he starred in just six Westerns – but his campaign made the image work for him. A famous campaign poster, "Bedtime For Brezhnev", showed a cowboy Reagan facing down the Soviet leader.

Unlike **Theodore Roosevelt**, who was tagged "The Cowboy President", Reagan knew little about cowboy life. But he traded on the cowboy's heroic image, as personified by John Wayne, who won a Congressional medal for bravery even though, like Reagan and **George W. Bush**, he had never proved his valour in real combat. The myth of Wayne's heroism was so entrenched in the American imagination that soldiers in Vietnam suffered from "John Wayne Syndrome" in which they endured mental agonies for not living up to the superhuman standards of his movies.

The Reagan/Wayne linkage was most explicit at the 1984 Republican convention when clips of the Duke introduced a film celebrating Reagan's life and presidency. It made good political sense for Reagan to wrap himself in Wayne's rhetoric – almost like borrowing charisma – and describe himself, after Wayne's death, as a close friend.

The Duke's example didn't bring moral certitude to foreign policy. While the conflict with the Soviets was dubbed a classic Western duel between good and bad, in central America and Iran, Reagan's administration sided with the kind of villains and vigilantes the Duke would have run out of town.

Unlike Reagan, George W. Bush isn't a fake cowboy, though the cowboy image has been polished – with endless photo-opportunities down on the ranch – by spin doctors keen to position this rich, patrician easterner as a man of the people. George Lakoff, a linguist at the University of California, has even suggested that Bush has changed the way he talks in public to sound as clipped and tough as John Wayne. Sounds absurd, but if you watch tapes of Bush debating during his campaign for Texas governor in 1994, he sounds more articulate than he has been, off-the-cuff, as president.

Those who didn't vote for Bush often use "cowboy" as a pejorative term – or deride him as a phony cowboy – but the image plays well with his hardcore fans who buy George W. Bush sheriff T-shirts. The easiest decision Bush has made in his presidency was probably to sign a proclamation in May 2005 designating 22 July as National Cowboy Day.

draws of all, with almost 250 pictures under his belt.

Above all Wayne embodied the Frontier Legend, his persona reflecting America's cherished self-image: independent, strong and true. Asked what distinguished him from other cowboy stars he replied "John Ford". But it was **Howard Hawks** who provided a turning point, eliciting a revelatory performance from him in *Red River* (1948). After seeing it, a startled Ford used him more challengingly, their collaboration peaking in the 1956 masterpiece *The Searchers*.

Wayne had always moved with the confidence and daring of a singer, but he learned to look imposing on a horse, to talk less – and more slowly – and to act less. His costume – the placket-front shirt with its buttoned panel – was part of the aura. Even his chest seemed fortified. Until 1970 he rarely suffered on screen. Even cast alongside Fonda and Mitchum, he dominated the screen. Mark Rydell used this persona to shocking effect in *The Cowboys* (1972), killing Wayne's superhero horribly.

In his greatest Westerns, Wayne was remote, stubborn, lonely yet romantic. But he was at his most iconic in what we might call his "Get off your horse and drink your milk" phase, from *Rio Bravo* (1959) to *True Grit* (1969). A benevolent superman who strode into command of screen and movie, his heroism was unquestioned, his triumph unqualified in these repetitive, entertaining Westerns, in which he was often likeable, funny and warm.

A severely underrated actor – critics were too often blinded by the mediocrity of his most formulaic roles or deterred by his right-wing political stance – a vehement proponent of Midwestern values and a hellacious, hard-drinking man's man, his walk, his talk and his

catchphrases entered popular mythology. His final role as the dying gunman in **Don Siegel's** *The Shootist* (1976) was a perfect, elegiac farewell. American writer Joan Didion said: "He determined forever the shape of certain of our dreams."

More than a star, Wayne was an institution, awarded an Oscar for his indomitable "fat old man" in Henry Hathaway's *True Grit* and, by special act of US Congress, a gold medal inscribed simply "John Wayne, American".

Truly he became inseparable from his tall-in-the-saddle roles. In the late stages of his battle with "The Big C", winking at a journalist who spotted him washing down medication with mescal, he growled: "Goddamn! I'm the stuff men are made of."

Richard Widmark, who co-starred with him in *The Alamo* (1960), caught Wayne's contribution to the genre best when he said: "To me, John Wayne is Westerns."

Big Jake
dir George Sherman, 1971, US, 109m

It's hard to believe a Western this good can be so neglected. Unusual, funny and violent, it rings several changes on the Duke's formula. His arrival on screen is much delayed as rancher Maureen O'Hara muses how best to reclaim her kidnapped grandchild, concluding: "It is going to be a very harsh, unpleasant kind of business and will require an extremely harsh, unpleasant kind of man." Wayne is just such a man. The film has a biographical richness, unobtrusive echoes of Homer's *Odyssey*, and an unusual showdown, choreographed by Harry Carey Jr.

Richard Widmark
1914–

Richard Widmark had tremendous breadth as an actor – going from giggling psychos who killed little old ladies in film noirs to one of the heroes of the Alamo without appearing stretched – but he wasn't a complete chameleon. In his best performances there was always a flavour of his personality, not as overpowering as, say, the essence of John Wayne, but definitely present. He had an unusual face. The cheekbones looked like they'd been squeezed, the blue eyes could seem disproportionately large and his white teeth could look surprisingly sinister when he sneered. He was a dependable actor who parlayed his professionalism into stardom.

He learnt to ride – after a struggle – on his first Western, **William Wellman**'s *Yellow Sky* (1948), a kind of cowboy *Treasure Of The Sierra Madre*, in which he is deranged by his lust for gold. By the time he returned to the saddle, he had fought and won the right to play more than just sneering villains and he was quietly heroic as the survivor of an ambush in **John Sturges**' *Backlash* (1956), compelling in *The Last Wagon* (1956) and, sneer back in place, a fine foil for Robert Taylor in *The Law And Jake Wade* (1958).

The Western that really defined Widmark as one of the genre's icons was *Warlock* (1959) in which, as a reformed gang member, he perfected his image as the quiet, unshowy hero, grudgingly accepting the need to do good. That critical success elevated him to the big league. He was suddenly playing opposite **John Wayne** (in *The Alamo*, 1960, his Jim Bowie one of the best things in the movie) and for **John Ford** (excelling in *Two Rode Together*, 1961, and *Cheyenne Autumn*, 1964). As the American Western declined in the late 1960s, he found it harder to get the right roles – neither *Alvarez Kelly* (1967) nor *The Way West* (1968) really clicked – but he was superb in two elegiac end-of-the-West movies, *Death Of A Gunfighter*

Richard Widmark, seen here in *Cheyenne Autumn*, could be deranged, heroic, melancholy and plain bad, but somehow a flavour of the man always came through.

(1969) and *When The Legends Die* (1972). In the former, Widmark is a sheriff whose time has passed while, in the latter, his dissolute drunken old rodeo pro sparks beautifully off Fredric Forrest's tyro in a superbly constructed picture.

Those two elegies marked the end of Widmark's time in the saddle, though he would later make a few TV Westerns. It was his peculiar misfortune to have risen to the top in the American Western in the early 1960s, at the very point when it had started to lose its way.

The Last Wagon
dir Delmer Daves, 1956, US, 99m

The Last Wagon is a compelling, ambiguous Western. Widmark is a trapper, raised by Indians, who, having killed the murderers of his Indian wife and child, is escorted to trial. When Indians attack the wagon train he's travelling with, the survivors, many overtly racist, turn to him. Widmark is so good you hardly notice the contradictions piling up (for example, the anti-racist theme sits oddly alongside standard action sequences of Indian attacks). The film is justly famed for bold, symbolic use of landscape. Sadly, Daves wasn't allowed to be as bold with the too-pat denouement.

Yosemite Sam

A furry little bundle of irascibility, Yosemite Sam was invented by Michael Maltese, modelled on director Friz Freleng and, invariably, opposed by Bugs Bunny.

All moustache, gun barrels and hilarious rambunctious declarations ("I'm the roughest, toughest hombre west of the Rio Grande and I don't mean Mahatma Gandhi", he shouts in *Bugs Bunny Rides Again*, 1948), Yosemite Sam was easily the greatest cartoon cowboy.

He made his official debut in 1945, returned to the screen in 1948 and thereafter made one or two cartoons a year until 1964. He sometimes rode off the range to become a pirate, but invariably returned to lose another battle of wits – in which he was always unarmed – with Bugs. Like most of the other famous Looney Tunes, he had a supporting role in *Who Framed Roger Rabbit?* (1988). He was at his most influential in the late 1960s and 70s when he was more convincing – and amusing – than many villains in big-screen Westerns.

The Stock Company:
Western archetypes

The US cavalry were always on time and occasionally, as in John Ford's classic *Fort Apache*, ahead of themselves when they rushed into battle.

The Stock Company:
Western archetypes

Pulp writer Frank Gruber says there are seven essential Western plots:

1 The Union Pacific story (the railroad/stagecoach comes to town or wagon train adventures)
2 The ranch story (conflict between ranchers or ranchers vs. others)
3 The empire story (an epic version of the ranch story)
4 The revenge story
5 The cavalry and Indians story
6 The outlaw story
7 The marshal story.

Gruber's list, though not all-encompassing, explains why the Western's stock company is large enough to populate Tombstone. Here we look at some of the archetypes – the black-hatted bad guy, white-hatted lawman, virginal school-marm, crazed Indian warrior, New Age chief, comic sidekick and tart with a heart – who have ridden into town most often.

Badges

The tin star is such a sacred symbol of a lawman's authority that when Coop chucked his in the dust in *High Noon* (1952), it was shockingly subversive.

The wearing, taking or discarding of a tin star is a significant moment in a Western, so crucial that many titles spin off it: *Man Without A Star*

(1955), *The Silver Star* (1955), *The Tin Star* (1957) and the superior B Western *The Badge Of Marshal Brennan* (1957), to name but four.

The John Cunningham story that inspired *High Noon* was called *The Tin Star*; the title and themes would later inspire the Anthony Mann Western of that name. Coop's dusty finale was referenced in Charles F. Haas's imaginatively titled B Western *Star In The Dust* (1956), *Warlock* (1959) and *Lone Star* (1995), but it's just one of many badge references in *High Noon*. Coop removes his badge at the start, anticipating wedded bliss and a new marshal; his ambitious deputy Lloyd Bridges takes his badge off when Coop snubs his aspirations; and Coop carries a deputy's badge on his fruitless search for citizens brave enough to be deputized.

Cooper's marshal insists he's the same man with or without a badge. That isn't true of Sam Peckinpah's **Pat Garrett**. When Billy the Kid asks Garrett how it feels to wear a badge, Garrett replies, "It feels like times have changed", signifying his new role, the end of their friendship and the start of their fatal contest.

In *For A Few Dollars More* (1965), **Clint Eastwood** asks the sheriff: "Isn't a sheriff supposed to be loyal, courageous and, above all, honest?" When the sheriff agrees, Eastwood removes the badge, saying: "Think you people need a new sheriff." Clint reworks the gag in *High Plains Drifter* (1972), pinning the sheriff's badge on Mordecai, the midget town jester, saying "'Bout time this town had a new sheriff." When the mayor calls him a runt, Mordecai crows: "I'm not a runt any more, I'm the new sheriff!"

The arbitrariness perfectly catches the random way in which, across the real West, badges were stuck on people who may, only a few days ago, have been outlaws. Desperate times led to some desperate recruitment. After a wild youth – and an arrest for horse-stealing – **Bill Tilghman** became one of the West's straightest lawmen. One of the first things he did when appointed marshal of Dodge City in 1884 was make a badge out of two gold $20 pieces.

The Tin Star
dir Anthony Mann, 1957, US, 93m, b/w

Greed, hate, violence, racism, decency – it's all here in Anthony Mann's underrated Western. Henry Fonda underplays beautifully as the embittered bounty hunter who thinks he's teaching tyro sheriff Anthony Perkins but finds he has much to learn too. Perkins looks slightly out of place out West but Mann makes that work to his advantage as he lets the characters and imagery carry the story. This is *High Noon* without the civics lesson.

Bounty hunters

In *Garden Of Evil* (1954), Cameron Mitchell's bounty hunter sneers: "I've killed better men than you just for a living." Coop, betraying the traditional Westerner's scorn for mercenaries, replies: "I'm gonna make you kill a man to his face." Peckinpah echoes that contempt in *The Wild Bunch* (1969), when Strother Martin and L.Q. Jones dig gold teeth out of their victims.

The private eye is beloved in Hollywood but his Western equivalent was largely ignored or derided until the 1950s. In that decade, **Anthony Mann** built two Westerns around the figure of a traumatized or endangered bounty hunter – *The Naked Spur* (1952) and *The Tin Star* (1957) – and Randolph Scott was twice a mercenary: for André De Toth in *The Bounty Hunter* (1954) and Budd Boetticher in *Ride Lonesome* (1959). In these films, however, the profession was temporary, symbolizing the character's personal confusion.

Then in 1965 came *For A Few Dollars More*, with its famous caption: "Where life had no value, death sometimes had its price. That is why the bounty killers appeared." Leone's tale of two bounty hunters explicitly referenced De Toth's movie and *The Tin Star*. In the 1960s, bounty hunters like Clint or **Charles Bronson** in *Once Upon A Time In The West* (1968) were the charismatic heroes of an alienated era, even when demonized. Klaus Kinski's mad, bad Loco is one of the delights of Sergio Corbucci's *Il grande silenzio* (1969), as he stoops to pick up bounty corpses stashed in the snow.

In *The Outlaw Josey Wales* (1976), however, Eastwood portrayed bounty hunters as scum, a *volte face* that wouldn't have shocked Dan Duryea's character in the 1965 B Western *The Bounty Killer*. He lectures the locals: "Do you know why I'm a bounty hunter? Because you good people pay me to do it. You can't do your own dirty work, but you can't wait to spit on the man who does it for you!" Duryea's frustration might have been eased by *Unforgiven* (1992), in which Eastwood's Will Munny — geddit? — blends Leone's and Mann's interpretations of the archetype.

The stereotype has led to the unhistorical assumption that the real West was full of bounty hunters. But Bill O'Neal, in *The Pimlico Encyclopaedia Of Western Gunfighters*, has concluded that only three of the 255 gunfighters in his study made a living as bounty hunters. It was far more common for a proficient Westerner to hire his gun out temporarily to a party in a dispute.

Buffalo

There were probably 25 million buffalo (or American bison) on the Western plains before the white man arrived. On horseback from the seventeenth century, Native Americans followed the herds, making them a life-support system. The Blackfoot extracted 88 commodities from the buffalo, including food, cups and needles. But disease and settlers diminished the herds, and the railroad's arrival exacerbated matters. The tracks destroyed the range, the trains scared the herds and hired hunters slaughtered them for food and to sell the hides back east. Some 4.4 million were killed between 1872 and 1874. By 1890 there were just 750 left. Even **Buffalo Bill**, named for his expertise in shooting the beasts, called for their preservation.

The slaughter was marked in a Dick Foran singing cowboy epic *Treachery Rides The Range* (1936), a Three Stooges comedy Western, *The Outlaws Is Coming* (1965), and Richard Brooks' *The Last Hunt* (1955). After conservation efforts, North America's buffalo herd is now around 350,000, so this iconic beast is alive and grazing.

The Last Hunt
dir Richard Brooks, 1955, US, 98m

For a romantic matinee idol, Robert Taylor made pretty gritty Westerns and played some seriously bad dudes. In this fine, original Western, he is a crazed buffalo hunter who kills for fun, not need, but ultimately gets so spooked by the creatures he turns violently on his brother Stewart Grainger and Debra Paget, his beautiful Indian captive.

Cattle

Branding 'em, fording rivers with 'em, searching for strays after the stampede — where would Westerns be without beef on the hoof? Cows were once almost as important to white Westerners as the buffalo was to the Native American. The creation of the cattle trails, pioneered with the

Once Howard Hawks had staged the ultimate cattle drive in *Red River*, no other filmmaker dared to compete.

Chisholm Trail in 1867, signalled a boom that soon had the beasts spreading across Colorado, Montana and Wyoming, enriching many. The trails were a truly epic enterprise: from 1867 to 1871, 1.5 million head of cattle moved up the Chisholm Trail.

This era inspired the great cattle drive movie *Red River* (1948), which features the immortal "Yee Haw!" scene, when **John Wayne** orders "Take 'em to Missouri, Matt", and an epic stampede when a cowpoke fatally spooks 9000 head into a bellowing blur of hooves and horns. At times like this, it's easy to see why Wayne growls, in Mark Rydell's *The Cowboys* (1972), "The cow is nothing but trouble tied up in a leather bag."

Filming such moments wasn't cheap. When *Lonesome Dove* was made for TV, writer Bill Wittliff was asked to excise the cattle to save money. He replied: "This is a story about cowboys taking their first trail herd to Montana. It'd be a little awkward without the cattle." But few directors have emulated *Red River*'s sweep, either due to cost or from a recognition that, as a cattle drive movie, it is very hard to top. The film influenced Mann's *The Far Country* (1954), which condemned Stewart's "hero" for selling to the highest bidder, regardless of the cost to society. **Delmer Daves'** *Cowboy* (1958) took the deconstruction further, with a bleak, comic take on the business, while Dick Richards' *The Culpepper Cattle Co.* (1972) "exposed" the emptiness of the cattle drive myth with added grimness.

By the late 1880s, over-stocking, range wars (like the Johnson County War) and blizzards had stilled the epic trails. Smaller trails petered out in the 1900s, as most cowboys became ranch hands. The age of consolidation, incorporation and scientific improvement that followed inspired few films, most notably **Andrew McLaglen**'s frankly average *The Rare Breed* (1966), in which Maureen O'Hara introduces the Hereford cow to the West.

Cattle barons

If, like Richard Nixon, you revere the leathery 1970 John Wayne version of **John Chisum**, you probably see the cattle baron as an ornery, but decent, entrepreneurial hero. If, like Sam Peckinpah, you see him as a symbol of "every goddamn landowner who wants to put a fence around this country", Barry Sullivan's sinister background presence as Chisum in *Pat Garrett And Billy The Kid* (1973) may seem more persuasive.

Chisum — believed in real life to have ordered the massacre of Native Americans "suspected" of cattle stealing — illustrates the ambiguity surrounding the Western cattle baron. On the good side, you have gallants like **Hopalong Cassidy** and father figures like the Duke's Chisum; on the other, you have an appalling gallery of despots, megalomaniacs, racists and perverts. That ambiguity even permeates the great *Red River* (1948), in which John Wayne is driven to the point of collapse but — such is the scale of his endeavour — seems as much anguished, romantic and heroic as unhealthily obsessed.

The cattle business financed the opening of the West but after 1870, when some started fencing off land, barons were no longer simply heroic pioneers. Real cattle barons were often either foreign — typically British — or financed by British money. After some boosterish publicity in 1881 in James S. Brisbin's self-help guide *The Beef Bonanza: How To Get Rich On The Plains*, the cattle business was a minor gold rush. But the bigger barons formed themselves into livestock associations that often acted like cartels, denying land to wannabe barons, stopping cowboys running their own herds (a stance that led to the Texan cowboy strike of 1883) and stopping farmers using free grass.

It was as rich, complacent, land-hogging dinosaurs that, from the late 1940s, cattle barons featured in Hollywood Westerns. From *Duel In The Sun* (1946) to *Rio Bravo* (1959), the baron was a tyrannical patriarch, often in Freudian conflict with his family and in ruinous dispute with small ranchers and farmers. The idea that "the farmer and the cowhand should be friends" was largely confined to the score of *Oklahoma!* (1955).

Some barons – like Wayne in *Red River* – redeemed themselves. Others – Donald Crisp in *The Man From Laramie* (1955) – were Lear figures. The most eloquently villainous was *Shane*'s Rufus Ryker, who made the Cattlemen's Association's case before dying. A fad for cattle baronesses – often played by Barbara Stanwyck – didn't improve ethics much.

Wayne's *Chisum* – which Nixon saw as a parable of how law came to America – built on the benevolence of TV ranchers like *Bonanza*'s Ben Cartwright, but it was Peckinpah's sinister Chisum who set the tone for the 1970s' villainous quasi-Nixonian barons, nastily epitomized by Jason Robards in *Comes A Horseman* (1978). Their violent monopoly capitalism couldn't stop homesteaders inheriting the West. Yet the idea that owning cattle made you someone of substance remains. Even in an unusual contemporary Western like *Lone Star* (1995), one character dismisses another, saying "He's all hat and no cattle."

🎬 Chisum
dir Andrew McLaglen, 1970, US, 110m

A big, splashy celebration of the cattle baron as a heroic capitalist who stands up for the little guy – even though, as played by John Wayne, he's physically and financially a big guy – *Chisum* extols the virtues of benevolent dictatorship. Wayne's good cattle baron Chisum confronts the evil capitalist Murphy (Forrest Tucker), with help from Pat Garrett and Billy the Kid as Andrew McLaglen's feelgood fantasy manipulates history to produce a good, formulaic Western.

Comic sidekicks

The grizzled, orthodontically challenged, catch-phrase-spouting sidekick, supplying easy laughs or eccentric colour, is a stereotype which can be traced back to Don Quixote's **Sancho Panza**.

The most famous Western sidekicks were **Walter Brennan**, **Andy Devine** (the driver in *Stagecoach*, 1939) and **George "Gabby" Hayes**. Brennan and Devine had damaged vocal cords, their distinctive voices helping them make more impact with few words. Hayes, overcoming the handicap of normal vocal cords, had his speechifying spoofed as "authentic frontier gibberish" in *Blazing Saddles* (1974).

With the Western market volatile in the 1960s, casting two top stars in one film seemed good insurance, so grizzly comic coots enjoyed less screen time. One of the last great sidekick turns was Jack Elam's town character in the *Support Your Local Sheriff/Gunfighter* films (1968/71).

Cowboys

Myth makers have seldom worked with less promising material than the poorly paid, overworked, badly fed, sleep-deprived, imperilled American cowboy whose freedom, often romanticized as wanderlust, boiled down to the right to roam the West seeking work. Their heyday lasted from the 1860s to the 1890s. Just as real cowboys became ranch-bound, the mythologized cowboy emerged as a heroic, glamorized archetype that, in a nation recovering from civil war, was conveniently unifying and distinctively American.

The cowboy was a truly cinematic hero with a horse, a cheap, iconic prop (a gun), a distinctive costume and the right to ride in and out of anywhere – as they do at the beginning and end of most Westerns – with no back story needed.

The cowboy persona was a collaborative enterprise – with Bronco Billy Anderson, William S. Hart, Tom Mix, John Wayne, Gary Cooper, Randolph Scott, Robert Mitchum and Clint Eastwood the most significant contributors – but Wayne and Scott symbolize two contrasting celluloid cowboy traditions.

Randolph Scott, like Gary Cooper, is believably human. Strong, silent, fallible, with a hard-earned, desperately sustained integrity, these cowboys don't shoot lightly and only triumph after considerable agony. Realism is not an especially useful yardstick in judging Westerns but it's easy to imagine that cowboys like Scott rode the West. With Cooper's death in 1961 – and Scott's retirement in 1962 – this kind of cowboy largely rode off into the sunset, leaving the celluloid range free for the superheroic **John Wayne**.

The glorification of the mythic cowboy was almost inversely proportional to the marginalization of the real cowboy in American society. The best estimates suggest there are fewer than 10,000 working cowboys in America today – of which a third work in rodeos, circuses and shows – and their lives are more accurately reflected in *Will Penny* (1967) than in any of Wayne's formula 1960s Westerns.

Eastwood initially seemed the Duke's complete antithesis: a brutal, cynical warrior, more gunfighter than cowboy. But in *The Outlaw Josey Wales* (1976) he revealed a courage, a plain-speaking laconic humour, a reluctant determination to do the right thing and, ultimately, a surprising warmth that was reminiscent of Wayne. Once thawed, he never fully returned to the freezer.

Will Penny
dir Tom Gries, 1967, US, 108m

Move over Moses. Charlton Heston's best performance on screen is as the restless cowpuncher embroiled with Donald Sutherland's scenery-chewing marauding preacher, who is briefly saved by Joan Hackett but can't wed her because he grimly recognizes, "I'm a cowboy, I've been one all my life." Not fantastically original, *Will Penny* is an absorbing, accurate, quietly revisionist Western.

Death

"Killing used to be fun and games in Apacheland," said Sam Peckinpah, "you fired a shot and three Indians fell. That began to change when Jack Palance shot Elisha Cook Jr in *Shane*."

The Western was, for decades, strangely shamefaced about its characters' violent ends. In the 1930s and 40s, a grimace, a clutch at the abdomen, a quick fall forward signified death. One glorious exception was *The Ox-Bow Incident* (1943), in which the three lynched innocent men literally cast awful shadows across the screen. *Shane* (1953) pointed to grim reality but it was the films of Leone and Peckinpah that challenged the traditional Western way of death.

Leone increased the quantity of deaths, aiming for fatal action every ten minutes, and flouted the rules. The shooting of a child would have been shocking in *Once Upon A Time In The West* (1968) even if **Henry Fonda** hadn't fired the gun. Peckinpah changed the quality of death with his gorily romantic, slow-mo "ballets of death" in *The Wild Bunch* (1969). Ironically, his most moving death scene was **Slim Pickens'** low-key exit in *Pat Garrett And Billy The Kid* (1973), the tragic futility underscored by Katy Jurado's tears and the distant strains of "Knockin' On Heaven's Door".

Sam Peckinpah changed the quantity and quality of death in a Western, perfecting the slow-mo balletic death.

Jim Jarmusch, in his mysterious Western *Dead Man* (1995), stretches death to the ultimate: his hero Blake has a bullet lodged so close to his heart that he is effectively dead in the saddle and must just accept the fact.

Funerals

John Ford is the acknowledged master of the Western funeral, arranging them with deliberate precision. Early in *The Searchers* (1956), as Ford's favourite hymn "Shall We Gather At The River?"

is sung, the mourners are clustered slightly to the left, with a wagon on the right, giving a diagonal shot up the hill to the grave. For Ford, funerals are a symbol of community. So when Wayne's Ethan Edwards says "Put an amen to it" and turns away from the mourners, it is striking evidence of his estrangement. **Robert Altman**'s *McCabe & Mrs Miller* (1971) referenced Ford's iconic funerals, though the hymns are sung by whores.

The importance of a Christian burial in what feels, at times, like a godless wilderness is reflected in *The Stalking Moon* (1968), in which Gregory Peck's scout risks Indian attack to bury massacred travellers.

When not attending funerals, Ford's heroes often, like Wayne's Nathan Brittles in *She Wore A Yellow Ribbon*, talk to the gravestone of a family member or, like Henry Fonda's Lincoln in *Young Mr Lincoln*, address the grave of their first love.

The Western funeral that influenced Leone most was Torrey's burial in *Shane* (1953), with the deceased's dog groaning at his master's coffin – a roughly hewn affair that was the model for the McBains' coffins in *Once Upon A Time In The West* (1968). The most shocking coffin in a Western is the one dragged by the hero at the start of **Sergio Corbucci**'s *Django* (1966). Peckinpah uses a coffin more subtly in *Pat Garrett And Billy The Kid* (1973). In a cameo, he is making a coffin for a child and, metaphorically, for the Old West's heroes and the Western itself.

In *She Wore A Yellow Ribbon*, as in most John Ford Westerns, funerals were symbols of community, only shunned by outsiders.

Gunfighters

"A gun is a tool, Marian, as good or as bad as the man using it." So Shane says, and he proves his point in the bloody final gunfight.

In 1917, when **William S. Hart** made *The Gunfighter*, the gunfighter myth was already shaping perceptions of the West, fuelled by vastly inflated tales of violent shoot–outs and gunfighters' prowess. (It is hard, for instance, to prove that Billy the Kid killed more than four men, though legend credited him with 21, "not including Mexicans".) The most notorious gunfighters often fought with a grievance – against the cattle barons' monopoly of power, a real-estate grab or the reconstruction of the South – that was understood by many ordinary Westerners, who saw them as social bandits, not mercenary murderers. There were even, though you would hardly know from Hollywood Westerns, black gunfighters like Texan **Cherokee Bill**, hung in 1896 after thirteen alleged murders.

In *Shane* (1953), Stevens distilled two halves of the stereotype: the "good" bad man – Shane – whose deadly expertise is a last resort and Wilson, plain bad, living by the gun. The fact that Shane was once "Wilson" – a point underlined when a homesteader says gunfighting is

In *Shane*, Jack Palance's smirking hired gun Wilson is so fast he can savour his victim's terror.

just murder – makes the final confrontation more powerful.

Wilson is a lean, cold-eyed, powerful sadist, who likes his coffee black, like his hats and gloves, and is fast enough to briefly hold his gun on an opponent, savouring his victim's horrified astonishment, before blowing him into the mud. For Shane, the gun is a burden; for Wilson, it is relished as a musician might delight in his violin.

Gunfighters became so common in 1960s Westerns that writers went to desperate lengths to distinguish them, creating blind, epileptic, mute or priestly shooters. Those who survived the last reel had one thing in common: godlike proficiency with a gun.

Man With The Gun
dir Richard Wilson, 1955, US, 83m, b/w

Orson Welles's disciple Richard Wilson brings Wellesian foreboding to this sombre tale of a brooding gunslinger (Robert Mitchum) who must clean up the town to win back his estranged wife (Jan Sterling). With a sadism and elegiac tone that anticipates the glory that would be Peckinpah, *Man With The Gun* is a good noir Western.

Gunfights

No image is as powerfully linked to the Western as the "walkdown" where two holstered cowboys, armed with six-guns, pace towards each other down a dusty street.

The walkdown was popularized in **Owen Wister**'s novel *The Virginian*, which drew on a real walkdown between **Wild Bill Hickok** and **Dave Tutt** on 21 July 1865 in Springfield, Missouri. The argument was trivial – over a watch – the outcome deadly. The two men approached each other across the square. At fifty yards, they drew. Tutt fired and missed. Hickok

shot Tutt through the heart, turned to the dead man's friends and said: "Aren't you satisfied, gentlemen?"

The courtly confrontation recalled jousting knights, but most gunfights were messy, unheroic affairs. In the 587 gunfights described in Bill O' Neal's encyclopaedia of gunfighters the norm is a duel where men fire madly, repeatedly, but miss or wound an opponent only lightly.

Yet Hickok's walkdown became part of Hollywood's Western code: in Michael Winner's *Lawman* (1970), even Robert Ryan's cowardly sheriff exclaims: "I hate backshooters!"

The age of chivalry ended in the 1960s. In Italian Westerns the gundown was as common as the gunfight (Sergio Sollima even made two Westerns called *The Big Gundown 1* and *2*). In *The Wild Bunch* (1969), the ageing gunfighters – even with a Gatling gun – ultimately shoot against ridiculous odds. And in Peckinpah's last great Western, the showdown between Pat Garrett and Billy the Kid is an execution, not a contest.

Woman They Almost Lynched
dir Allan Dwan, 1953, US, 90m, b/w

This famously features a rare all-woman gun duel between sexy leather-trousered villainess Audrey Totter and the beautiful, virtuous Joan Leslie. An able cast – Brian Donlevy is Totter's infamous husband Quantrill – an unusual story and Dwan's deft touch make for a superior B Western.

A Gunfight
dir Lamont Johnson, 1970, US, 89m

The idea of gunfights being staged for entertainment wasn't invented by Sam Raimi in *The Quick And The Dead* (1995). It was at the heart of this offbeat Western in which Kirk Douglas and Johnny Cash agree to stage a gunfight, and charge admission, so the victor can start a new life. Cash and Douglas are in fine form in a Western that, ultimately, is too original for director Lamont Johnson to handle.

Guns

"Fill your hands, you son of a bitch!" When Wayne's Rooster Cogburn issued this challenge in *True Grit* (1969), his hands were already full. In one was a Colt 45 "Peacemaker", in the other a 16-shot Winchester repeater rifle.

From the man with no surname (Shane) to the man with no name at all, everyone had a Colt 45 Peacemaker, usually slung on the right hip in a tied-down, quick-draw holster. It never misfired, rarely required maintenance, seldom needed reloading but curiously often contained more than six bullets and was accurate enough to shoot the gun from the hand of the man in the black hat at 50 yards.

Samuel Colt patented the first practical multiple-shot pistol in 1837, but, in 1847, launched the six-shot Walker Colt 44. Measuring 15 inches from butt end to barrel tip and weighing four and a half pounds (think two bags of sugar), the Walker Colt was a handgun only if you had very large hands. But it had real firepower. Colt's marginally smaller and lighter Dragoon 44 became standard issue in the Civil War.

The Walker and Dragoon Colts were "horse pistols" rather than sidearms. **Clint Eastwood**, wielding a rare pair of Walkers in *The Outlaw Josey Wales* (1976), pulls off a great gunfighter trick – the border roll, where the gun is presented butt first, apparently peaceably, but with the index finger curled around the trigger guard to allow it to be twirled back the right way round. This is hard enough to do with a normal-sized gun, let alone a Walker.

The first real handgun was Colt's lighter Navy 36, made in 1851, which could be carried on the body and was used by Jesse James and Bill Hickok. Both the Navy 36 and the Army Colt 44 were, like the Walker and Dragoon, "cap and ball" revolvers.

Each chamber of the cylinder had to be laboriously loaded with gunpowder, lead ball and percussion cap. Reloading took an age; in wind and rain, or on horseback, it was practically impossible, so those who lived by their pistols carried more than one.

Westerners didn't all carry Colts. The 1858 model Remington revolver was a better gun, more robustly built, less prone to falling apart, faster to reload, with a rudimentary safety "notch" that stopped the gun going off if dropped. Watch the big shoot-out in *Pale Rider* (1985) for a rare glimpse of a fast-reloading 1858 Remington. The Remington was supplanted as the professional's favourite when Smith & Wesson launched the first big-bore metallic-cartridge-firing revolver in 1870, the outstandingly accurate Model 3 "American", popular with showbiz sharpshooter **Annie Oakley**, armed robber **Cole Younger** and desperado **John Wesley Hardin**.

Colt launched the Single Action Army 45 six-shooter in 1873. The "Frontier" model, a short-barrelled version rechambered to take the same 44 cartridge as the Winchester rifle, is the gun we know as the 45 Peacemaker, even though it was really a 44 and the Peacemaker tag arrived years later. The fact that it was as rare as hen's teeth until the late 1870s hasn't deterred movie props departments from using it wherever and whenever.

Hats

You can tell a lot – though not everything – about a Western character by the colour of his hat. In a B Western, the guy in the white hat, the hero, will defeat the black-hatted baddie. The same coding applies to Shane (white-hatted) and Wilson (black-hatted). But, in a rare burst of originality, loveable **Hopalong Cassidy** wears a black hat, as, confusingly, does Marshal Kane in *High Noon* (1952). In *Red River* (1948), John Wayne's cattle baron initially wears a white hat but, by trail's end, has donned a black one. Villains in white hats are scarce – a rare famous example being Paul Newman's Billy the Kid in *The Left Handed Gun* (1958).

Horse soldiers

The cavalry charge is so embedded in the Western that, in the Three Stooges comedy *Out*

West (1947), a colonel declares: "Son, never in the history of motion pictures has the US Cavalry ever been late."

The thin blue line protecting settlers was predominantly infantry, but the US Cavalry – especially the 7th Cavalry, notorious from Little Bighorn – usually ride to the rescue on celluloid. And wherever they rode, Ford notes in *She Wore A Yellow Ribbon* (1949), "that place became the United States".

Mythology has overridden such inconvenient historical reality as the fact that, between 1867 and 1891, over 80,000 troopers deserted. Similarly, Westerns have largely ignored the US cavalry's

John Ford defined the cavalry Western in *Fort Apache* but his heroes were soldiers and reluctant commanders, not West Point martinets.

ethnic diversity. In 1866 Congress authorized two black cavalry regiments, but their story has remained largely offscreen, though Ford tried to compensate for such omissions by casting Woody Strode as the hero of *Sergeant Rutledge* (1960) and John "Bud" Cardos had a stab at telling the black regiments' story in *The Red, White And Black* (1970).

Westerns are surprisingly ambivalent about traditional military virtues. Ford's ideal cavalry are rough, ready, democratic, very Irish in the lower ranks and reliant on skills learned out West and not, like **Henry Fonda**'s martinet in *Fort Apache* (1948), at West Point. They seek, not martial glory, but a peace in which civilization can be built.

Ford defined – then challenged – the cavalry Western, mocking the cavalry in *The Searchers* (1956). In *Two Rode Together* (1961), horse soldiers are bemused bystanders, while in *Cheyenne Autumn* (1964) Fonda's martinet has mutated into Karl Malden's Nazi by any other name.

By 1969, when Wayne staged his final cavalry charge in Andrew McLaglen's *Undefeated*, the heroic rescue was a dead cliché. Revisionist Westerns like *Little Big Man* (1970) and *Soldier Blue* (1970) presented the US Cavalry as a crazed, genocidal force. James Frawley's wry *Kid Blue* (1973) seems like an ironic epitaph for the cavalry Western, with Dennis Hopper rescued at the last moment by an Indian horse charge.

They Died With Their Boots On
dir Raoul Walsh, 1941, US, 140m, b/w

A stirring, glamorized, entertaining biopic of Custer, with fine action sequences, and a hero perfectly suited to Errol Flynn's persona. Despite the heroic gloss, the script has thoughtful moments, notably when an officer tells Custer/Flynn: "The only real Americans in this merry old parish are on the other side of that ridge with feathers in their hair."

Injuns

"I learned something that day," says **James Stewart** after encountering Apaches in *Broken Arrow* (1950), "Apache women cried over their sons." It's a mark of the Western's blinkered attitudes that, in the 1950s, this was a radical idea.

Till then, the Western's stance could almost have been summed up by Montana Congressman James Cavanaugh's line: "I have never in my life seen a good Indian, except when I saw a dead Indian." The exploration and conquering of the West was seen – in movies and society – as a heroic, essential, nation-building enterprise. The savagery, broken promises and racist arrogance of the war against the Indians didn't unduly trouble the American conscience until the 1950s. When **Henry Fonda** said, in *Drums Along The Mohawk* (1939), "I don't think we'll have any trouble with the Indians, we've always treated them fair", no irony was intended.

Though most Westerns dwell on the war's tragic finale in the 1870s to 1890s, the real damage had been done by then. There were only 400,000 Indians left in North America by 1840, compared with some 10 million in the 1490s.

Native Americans were invariably depicted as faceless barbaric hordes whose habit of attacking peaceable settlers excused America's genocidal response, though there were some surprising exceptions to the general contempt. In 1925 George B. Seitz filmed Zane Grey's Western *The Vanishing American*, in which tribal leader Richard Dix isn't punished for an interracial romance.

As adversaries, the Apache had the most melodramatic charisma – 47 Westerns mention Apache in their titles. They fought a bitter war against seventeenth-century Spanish colonists. Some folk memory of that may have shaped

Cheyenne Autumn, Ford's Native American Western, was undermined by Navajo extras smuggling jokes into their dialogue.

their screen image as cruel, fierce, unknowable, hollering, torturing savages. For many years, only a few portrayals – Jeff Chandler's Cochise (in *Broken Arrow*) and Burt Lancaster (in *Apache*, 1954) – broke the savage stereotype.

Movies like *Broken Arrow*, *Devil's Doorway*, *Apache* and *Taza, Son Of Cochise* started to change that in the 1950s, though such liberalism had limits. *Broken Arrow* honours Cochise for wanting peace, but marginalizes Geronimo as a "bad Indian". In Ford's *Two Rode Together* (1961), the Geronimo figure Stonecalf is killed, a cavalryman noting: "There was no reasoning with hotheads like Stonecalf, his death is most timely."

Even Ford atoned for earlier excesses with the monumental *Cheyenne Autumn* (1964), but the Navajo extras aren't speaking Cheyenne – they're telling jokes in their native tongue.

By 1970 the Western had come full circle, with *Little Big Man*, *Soldier Blue*'s slow-mo carnage and *A Man Called Horse* all, with varying success, taking the Native American viewpoint. *A Man Called Horse* was sincere, though the Sioux – who hold Richard Harris prisoner – never hung captives from hooks by their pectorals. *Little Big Man* did more to destroy stereotypes, though – like *Dances With Wolves* – it created new politically correct ones.

In some ways, the Western has simply widened its repertoire of Native American clichés. In the bad old days, we had the crazed warrior lusting after white womanhood, the drunken dupe, noble savage, helpful scout and tortured half-breed. Now we have the Native American as pacifist environmental pioneer, New Age sage and Dalai Lama-like dispenser of spiritual truths. Still, at least they can now speak without adding "um" to every word.

Native American men have fared better than women who, since *Kit Carson* (1903) – in which an Indian maiden helps Kit escape his bloodthirsty Indian captors – have largely featured as "helpful squaws". This oddly persistent motif starts with the resonant story of **Pocahontas**, the Native American princess who married an Englishman but died young. There is real hypocrisy here – a white woman, captured by Native Americans, could expect rape, rejection by whites and death, yet it was perfectly permissible for "civilized" white men to take an Indian "squaw".

Although often presented as easy sexual prey – even a movie as sympathetic as De Toth's *The Indian Fighter* (1955) delights in showing us squaw **Elsa Martinelli** bathing naked in a river – Native

American women in Westerns could be beautiful, noble, smart and self-sacrificing. Delle Bolton's largely mute Swan, the capable Indian wife foisted on Robert Redford in *Jeremiah Johnson* (1972), is mysterious yet convincing, as is Geraldine Keam's loyal, sharp-shooting Indian woman in *The Outlaw Josey Wales* (1976).

🎬 Flaming Star
dir Don Siegel, 1960, US, 101m

A pessimistic, liberal Western with Elvis Presley excelling as the half-breed Pacer, doomed by the racism of Texan frontier life, as whites and Kiowas fight. Some of the Kiowa dialogue is overly poetic, though their grievances against white settlers are eloquently put, but Don Siegel pulls no punches about the escalation of violence and hate. Presley, rejected by the whites, fatally wounded by the Kiowas, rides off to die, leaving his half-brother Steve Forrest among the whites who shunned – and doomed – his family, with slim hope that tolerance might eventually triumph.

Lawmen

"When things get a little rough I go out and kill a few people", says deputy sheriff Stacy Keach in Burt Kennedy's gothic Western *The Killer Inside Me* (1976). The idea that killing prostitutes is good therapy for a deputy suffering from an excessively Freudian childhood is a long way from the reluctant heroism of Fonda's Wyatt Earp in *My Darling Clementine* (1946).

Fonda's Earp was the Hollywood lawman at his most iconic: brave, quietly charismatic, a reluctant do-gooder, yet deadly when necessary. Ford didn't invent this image, but polished and perfected it.

The real Earp was a far cry from this iconic image. **Bill Tilghman**, probably more heroic and less corruptible than his onetime associate – unlike Earp, he was never accused of fraud or of running a brothel – would have made a better model for the celluloid sheriff. But, in a denouement straight out of a revisionist Western, he died in 1924, shot by a drunken probation officer, while Earp went on to cultivate his image in Hollywood.

Until the 1950s, Hollywood Westerns largely glossed over the fact that many lawmen were former outlaws, hired because, in a West where the law was upheld by the gun, they had the necessary expertise. The ultimate study in such ambiguity with a badge is James Coburn's Pat Garrett, who must confront his shady past.

High Noon (1952) provided another pattern for the Western lawman. Cooper's Marshal Kane leaves town, knowing the folk of Hadleyville aren't worth his bravery. His stonefaced self-doubting became a popular motif, inspiring James Stewart's troubled lawman in *Firecreek* (1968).

There was enough criminality in Western law-enforcement to justify the counter-myth to the heroic lawman: the corrupt sheriff whose existence legitimized the heroic gun-fighter, found in films as diverse as *The Far Country*, *A Man Alone*, *One-Eyed Jacks*, *For A Few Dollars More*, *Rio Lobo*, *Silverado*, *Unforgiven* and *Open Range*.

A Man Alone
dir Ray Milland, 1955, US, 96m

A jump ahead of most Westerns of its day, Ray Milland's directorial debut features Ward Bond as a corrupt sheriff, owned by crooked banker Raymond Burr, and Milland as the mysterious and – for the first third of the film – mute gunman blamed by credulous, hysterical townsfolk for a bank robbery Burr himself ordered. Disenchanted, paranoid, claustrophobic, *A Man Alone* is a minor classic.

Mountain men

Mountain men needed a serious makeover to become Western heroes. Real mountain men – like John Johnson, whose life inspired Sydney Pollack's *Jeremiah Johnson* (1972) – were grumpy, smelly misanthropes. Worse, they had beards! When **Clark Gable** trapped beaver in *Across The Wide Missouri* (1951), he did so with the least obtrusive beard possible, while **Burt Lancaster** was anachronistically clean-shaven as the 1820s backwoodsman in *The Kentuckian* (1955).

In the 1960s and 70s, mountain men were briefly fashionable as environmentally conscious proto-hippies. In Pollack's *The Scalphunters* (1968) Lancaster is a model of environmental self-sufficiency, while Jeremiah Johnson was a meat-eating, gun-toting environmentalist. The latter's success inspired such back-to-nature adventures as the TV movie *The Life And Times Of Grizzly Adams* (1974) and *The Mountain Man* (1980), with **Charlton Heston** craggier than Mount Rushmore. In Heston's *Mother Lode* (1982), the mountain man turns psycho-pathic, as if only a lunatic would shun Ronald Reagan's reborn America. Today, the mountain man stereotype is defined as much by images of demented Survivalists as by Grizzly Adams.

Jeremiah Johnson
dir Sydney Pollack, 1972, US, 108m

A strange, meandering, beautiful Western, with Robert Redford unusually cast as the recluse waging a one-man war against the Crow who killed his wife and adopted son. Redford's remoteness, a magnificent cast of supporting eccentrics, a plaintive soundtrack and stunning use of landscape – you shiver in the wintry scenes – create a strangely exhilarating portrait of a lonely life. The real Johnson was called "liver-eating Johnson" – though some argue he didn't routinely eat his victims' livers – a controversy Pollack happily ignores.

Outlaws

Henry King's casting of **Tyrone Power** as Jesse James in 1939 was a pivotal point in the Western's attitude to outlaws. The reforming outlaw was a cliché in William S. Hart's day, but 1939 saw the birth of a full-blown outlaw cult. That year, **James Cagney** was driven to crime by systematic injustice in the gangster Western *The Oklahoma Kid* and King made Jesse a Western Robin Hood – sympathetic, charismatic and gorgeous. A veritable canon of outlaw Westerns recycle or allude to incidents, characters and images from King's movie and the outlaw would seldom again be as one-dimensionally evil.

The great Westerns of Boetticher and Mann built on King's example, portraying hero and villain not as polar opposites but as sides of the same coin. In this, the Western was just recognizing reality. What run-of-the-mill horse operas presented as a simple contest between good and bad, law and violence, was in truth much more complicated. Billy the Kid, Jesse James and Butch Cassidy are easily recast as roguish heroes. They and their gangs mostly robbed banks and railroads, endearing themselves to many poor Westerners who had little time for either institution.

John Wesley Hardin was less easily made over. Despite Bob Dylan's claim that "he was never known to hurt an honest man", Hardin was a racist drunk who shot an Indian in cold blood and liked to kill blacks (who he blamed for the massacre of his uncle's family by Union troops) and has, hence, starred in few Western biopics.

The outlaw hero has been challenged – notably in *The Great Northfield Minnesota Raid* (1972), featuring Robert Duvall's psychotic Jesse – but the critiques have had less influence than Leone's stylishly amoral "heroes", Redford and Newman's

Butch and Sundance and Peckinpah's groovy, martyred, Billy the Kid.

The Lawless Breed
dir Raoul Walsh, 1953, US, 83m

This biopic is officially based on the life of John Wesley Hardin. But little of that desperado's complex story reaches the screen in this well-made, well-acted outlaw yarn. Rock Hudson, as Hardin, recalls his wayward past, hoping it will help his son keep his nose clean, even though he was largely led from unrighteousness by gorgeous Julie Adams.

Sheep

Until *Brokeback Mountain* (2005), sheep have been bit-part players in the Western, lacking the macho, mythological dimension of cattle. Despite their placid public image, sheep have an obstinacy directors have found trying. The 700 sheep on the *Brokeback* set behaved like prima donnas, flatly refusing to drink from a stream for a whole day.

Introduced to North America by the Spanish, sheep were often herded by Native Americans. That may explain the contempt with which the species – and sheep farmers – were regarded by ranchers, even though, by the end of the nineteenth century, sheep were as important, economically, to the West as cattle. The derision greeting **Glenn Ford**'s sheep farmer in *The Sheepman* (1958) is a comic echo of a deadlier dispute. In 1887, cattle barons claiming sheep were destroying the grasslands started a war in Arizona. Ironically, the land was being destroyed – by overstocking of cattle – and only sheep could thrive on the weedy grass that remained.

The Ballad Of Josie
dir Andrew McLaglen, 1967, US, 102m

An unusual Doris Day movie, in which she looks prettily worn out as the frontier widow who, having accidentally killed her violent, alcoholic husband, enrages local cattle barons by deciding to herd sheep – something, she is told, "any idiot with a dog and a Winchester" can do. Hovering uneasily between comedy and realism, with some boring male characters, this intriguing, uneven movie has some fine moments.

Singing cowboys

Although cowboys did sing ballads like "The Colorado Trail" on cattle drives, the singing cowboy – wielding a slightly anachronistic guitar, more often than a gun – is one of the weirder Western archetypes.

When **Gene Autry**'s "That Silver-Haired Daddy Of Mine" sold over a million copies in 1931, B studios noted that most sales were in the American heartland where the Western prospered. The success of Autry's *Phantom Empire* movie serial proved there was gold in them thaar hills. Soon Tex Ritter, Jimmy Wakely, Roy Rogers, Rex Allen and Smith Ballew (who dubbed for John Wayne in his 1930s singing Westerns) were crooning, knightly cowboys. Cheap to make – Autry's *Tumblin' Tumbleweeds* cost $12,000 – these films could hardly fail, though their habit of freezing the action for songs appalled purists. Television killed the singing B Western – Autry made his last film in 1953 – but gave Autry and Rogers their own shows.

In 1978 **Willie Nelson** wrote two fine cowboy songs for *The Electric Horseman*. The scene where Robert Redford, Nelson et al. launch into "Mama Don't Let Your Babies Grow Up To Be Cowboys" ("they'll never stay home/and they're always alone/even with someone they love") harks back to the singing cowboy and offers a romanticized, affectionately critical study of the cowboy image.

Tarts with a heart

You would never guess from Henry Hathaway's *The Sons Of Katie Elder* (1966) that Elder was really a prostitute. Not every Western was that coy. In *Gunfight At The OK Corral* (1957) Elder, renamed Kate Fisher (Jo Van Fleet), too smart to be fooled by Doc Holliday yet too weak to abandon him, is a fine example of the tart with a heart.

The stereotype dates back to **Mary Magdalene**, Victorian melodrama and William S. Hart. Under Hays Office censorship, tarts became saloon girls. Watching Marlene Dietrich vamp it up as Frenchie in *Destry Rides Again* (1939), it wasn't hard to guess how she made money if takings were slow, a point emphasised by Madeline Kahn's sultry, sexually exhausted saloon girl Lily von Shtupp in *Blazing Saddles* (1974).

As such loose women were often foreign, they could arouse the hero – and male viewers – without sullying American womanhood. Some "dance hall girls", like Dallas in *Stagecoach* (1939), were named after places, as if to signify where they plied their trade. Dallas, a sympathetic saloon girl with the power to redeem herself and the hero, was lucky. The traditional saloon girl, like Linda Darnell's Chihuahua in *My Darling Clementine* (1946) and Dietrich (in *Destry Rides Again* and *Rancho Notorious*), sacrificed herself.

As censorship weakened, filmmakers depicted "good time girls" more frankly. In *Warlock* (1959), Dorothy Malone's wronged saloon girl is called Lily Dollar and explicitly refers to her shady past. In 1968, the prostitute came out, decisively, with **Claudia Cardinale**'s enchanting Jill in *Once Upon A Time In The West*. The range was soon over-populated with prostitutes as male directors indulged their fantasies, the best being

Stella Stevens (*The Ballad Of Cable Hogue*, 1970), Jeanne Moreau (*Monte Walsh*, 1970) and Julie Christie (*McCabe & Mrs Miller*, 1971).

In *McCabe & Mrs Miller*, Altman economically exposes why many Western women sold themselves. When Shelley Duvall, during her husband's funeral, makes eye contact with Christie, we know this is the only way she can now support herself.

The most memorable prostitutes in recent Western memory work in the brothel in Eastwood's *Unforgiven* (1992). Writer David Webb Peoples had originally entitled his story "The Cut-Whore Killings". When Eastwood finally kills the sheriff it is a significant victory: for once in a Western, a prostitute's grievance is heeded.

Having invented the stereotype of the tart with a heart in *Destry Rides Again*, Marlene Dietrich perfected it in *Rancho Notorious*.

Rancho Notorious
dir Fritz Lang, 1952, US, 89m

Fritz Lang brings his trademark obsessions – hate, murder, revenge, deceit – to this fatalistic tale of a very mild hero (Arthur Kennedy) seeking revenge for the rape and murder of his girl. He falls for mob diva Marlene Dietrich – who, unusually for a Western, manipulates the men rather than vice versa – and turns as dark as the villains he is pursuing. Despite fake studio backdrops and wooden acting, *Rancho Notorious* is a strong, original Western which is, for the time, oddly licentious: the rape isn't merely alluded to, the doctor informing us, "she wasn't spared anything".

Trusty steeds

The horse is so crucial to the Western that many acquired their own names. The fashion started with **William S. Hart** who called his steed Fritz but we have since had Tony, Champion, Trigger, Topper, White Flash, Silver, Cyclone, Midnight, Mutt and Coco. No wonder Westerns are also called horse operas.

In this, the Western is true to its historical roots. Stealing a horse was unforgivable in the real West – since it often amounted to sentencing the victim to death. In 1882–3 a group of cowboys, incensed by horse stealing in Montana, launched the most violent vigilante campaign in Western history, killing over a hundred bandits. Horses became less prized after 1900, as the range closed. Two million mustangs roamed and ranchers slaughtered them wholesale.

How a Westerner treats his horse says a lot about his character. The hero is master of his steed, which is why you can find horse-taming scenes in Westerns from *Western Union* (1941) to *The Unforgiven* (1959) and *The Electric Horseman*

(1979). Indians are often superhumanly skilful horse-riders, even though their four-legged friends were only introduced to North America in the fifteenth century by the Spanish. Only the criminal, the unreliable, or the stupid neglect their horses. In *The Searchers* (1956) Wayne accuses the Apaches of riding their horses to death and eating them. In *Major Dundee* (1964) Peckinpah highlights the inadequacy of Dundee's troops just by showing us how they mount their horses.

Yet in Delmer Daves' *Cowboy* (1958), **Glenn Ford**'s grizzled rancher complains that the "horse has a brain the size of a walnut". At the other extreme, in Fernando Baldi's spaghetti Western *Blindman* (1971), the blind hero's horse does everything but type. In *Son Of Paleface* (1952), Roy Rogers prefers his horse to the West's tight-waisted, winky-eyed flirts. After all, he croons, the four-legged friend with two honest eyes will ask no questions and tell no lies.

Wagons roll!

It's almost impossible to contemplate the Western without the wagon train – and not just because *Wagon Train* was such a durable Western TV series. The canvas-covered wagon, known as the Prairie Schooner, is as iconic as the sheriff's badge.

The real journeys – the trail to the Pacific could take five months, braving disease, accidents, rivers and Indians – were heroic enough not to need Hollywood hyperbole. But the opening titles of **James Cruze**'s *The Covered Wagon* (1923) still remind us: "The blood of America is the blood of the pioneers. The blood of lion-hearted men and women who carved a splendid civilization out of an uncharted wilderness."

In wagon train movies, directors could always chuck in a set-piece – an Indian attack, a river crossing that almost goes wrong, baddies trying to hitch a ride West – if things got dull. By dwelling on the community seeking a brave new world, they could weave many sub-plots, including a crowd-pleasing romance, pioneering the "ship of fools" movie which explores the overlapping lives of a group confined by space or peril.

The railway Western – perfected by Ford with *The Iron Horse* in 1924 – is a direct descendant of the wagon train movie. Ford would, in 1950, surpass Cruze with *Wagon Master*, a leisurely, romantic evocation of the pioneer spirit that is probably the best wagon train movie although *The Oregon Trail* (1959) has real historical significance, containing, as it does, almost every wagon train cliché known to man.

Yet wagon train movies rarely did big box-office business. The TV series inspired **Gene Roddenberry** to write *Star Trek*; his *Wagon Train* in space epics, as a movie franchise, made more money than the Westerns they sprang from.

Westward The Women
dir William Wellman, 1951, US, 118m, b/w

In this unique, rootin'-tootin' women's ensemble Western a gutsy band of gals do the whipcracking, fighting off Indians, bonding, crying, dying and traversing scorching desert (with one in labour!). Sardonic, misogynist trail guide Robert Taylor, tamed by Denise Darcel's feisty minx, acquires respect for feminine true grit.

Wagon Master is the ultimate wagon train Western and is a genuine rarity as a film that has Mormon heroes.

Western women

Hookers and schoolmarms: the Western contains both kinds of women but, critics insist, no others. Boetticher famously defined a woman's job in a Western as making the hero react: "In herself she has no significance whatsoever."

Yet for a genre portraying a society where women were outnumbered by as much as seven to one, the Western gets in touch with its feminine side surprisingly often. As Anthony Mann noted: "Without a woman the Western wouldn't work." It's hard to imagine *Stagecoach* (1939) without **Claire Trevor**'s Dallas or *Red River* (1948) without **Joanne Dru**, the perfect spirited Hawksian heroine.

Even a director as misogynist as Peckinpah gives us, in *Ride The High Country* (1962), **Mariette Hartley**'s Elsa, a woman whose romantic dreams are crushed by sordid frontier reality. Married in a brothel, Elsa is more convincing than Arthur Penn's women in *Little Big Man* (1970) or *The Missouri Breaks* (1976).

It is rare – though not unknown – for the hero of a Western to be a heroine. In the silent Western *The Wind* (1928), **Lillian Gish** excels as a delicate Virginia girl driven mad by Texan frontier life. After the cross-dressing fest of Calamity Jane (1953), the novelty of Western heroines appealed to directors. So in the 1950s we got *Apache Woman*, *Cattle Queen Of Montana*, *Forty Guns*, *Johnny Guitar* (in which both the hero and lead villain were female), *Two-Gun Lady*, *Westward The Women* and *Woman They Almost Lynched*, to name only a representative sample. At the same time, **Maureen O'Hara**'s mother in *Rio Grande*, Lee Remick's lovestruck prostitute in *These Thousand Hills*, **Julie London**'s Army wife in *The Wonderful Country* and Felicia Farr's barmaid in *3.10 To Yuma* surpassed the old stereotypes.

Sergio Leone deliberately made Claudia Cardinale's Jill the pivotal character in *Once Upon A Time In The West*.

The partial liberation of women coincided with the traditional Western's collapse in the 1960s. In that decade alone, Jane Fonda, Racquel Welch, Claudia Cardinale and Doris Day all played heroines who did more than provoke reactions. True, women were still getting humiliated in diehard Westerns by Hawks, Wayne and their emulators, but the wind of change had blown down too many dusty streets for that to last. In *True Grit* (1969), even the Duke was bossed by a girl, **Kim Darby's** fantastically spirited Mattie.

Women's roles in the 1970s were not as varied; they were often prey in Eastwood Westerns. Recent Westerns haven't empowered women in the Erin Brockovich style, though *The Ballad Of Little Jo* (1993) was a genuine departure and *Lone Star* (1995) was full of believable female characters. Eastwood made some amends for past sins with the spirited, vindicated prostitutes in *Unforgiven* (1992).

Many Rivers To Cross
dir Roy Rowland, 1955, US, 94m

Kentucky trapper Robert Taylor is wed at gunpoint to Eleanor Parker's amorous pioneer woman and spends this raucous frontier comedy romance trying to lose her. Spunky and dogged, she's impossible to shake, repeatedly saving his bacon – her manner of seeing off a Shawnee war party is priceless – before he surrenders to the inevitable.

The Ballad Of Little Jo
dir Maggie Greenwald, 1993, US, 121m

To accept that Suzy Amis could pass as a male farmer – to escape the abuse and bondage that plagued her as a Western woman – is a big ask. But it's worth it. Slow, but appealing, this compound of real stories dares to have a heroine who has a relationship with a Chinaman. What the film lacks in plot, and flair, it makes up for with its grasp of milieu and character, and the sense that the West is really seen from the woman's perspective.

Western Country: iconic locations

The Western in general – and John Ford's masterpieces in particular – are unimaginable without the
natural grandeur of Monument Valley.

Western Country:
iconic locations

"The real star of the Western has always been the land." John Ford

It's no coincidence that the Western is the only major movie genre named after a geographical entity. The American West is many things to many people: a home, a metaphor, a dream, a utopia, a place where America is distilled to its essence. This iconic setting is more than just a spectacular backdrop for the Western: its meaning lies at the heart of the genre.

The landscape of a region whose borders shifted constantly in the nineteenth century – Tennessean Andrew Jackson, President from 1829 to 1837, called himself a Westerner – has become instantly recognizable. Yet, through the combined efforts of filmmakers like **John Ford** and **Anthony Mann**, our image of the West has been so distorted that it is about as accurate as our reflections in a fun-house mirror.

The West was – and just about still is – the big country: a charismatic, glamorous, fabled land of deserts, canyons, gulches, rivers, creeks, cactus and mountains. Filmmakers

bereft of imagination could name their work after a town (Abilene, Dodge City, Laramie, Tombstone, Wichita), state (every Western state has a major Western named after it except Washington), river (Rio Grande/Rio Bravo – the American and Mexican names for the same river) or geographical feature (High Sierra). Or they could just stick West or Western in the title – a device used in 44 major Hollywood A and B Westerns.

Yet the whole West wasn't spun in the Western. Anthony Mann complained: "I have never understood why people make almost all

Westerns in desert country. John Ford adores Monument Valley but Monument Valley is not the whole of the West." Mann was literally right but Monument Valley, as popularized in seven epic Ford Westerns, defined what we thought the West should look like and became a symbol of America.

Monument Valley stands on the border of Arizona and Utah and its dominance of the cinematic Western landscape is a metaphor for how those two states shaped our image of the West. So *The Searchers* (1956), set in Texas, is largely shot in Monument Valley, as is, perversely, the minor Western *Laramie* (1949), "officially" set in the Wyoming town it is named after.

The topographical accuracy of the landscape matters less than its symbolic power. As **Sergio Leone** said, the epic quality of the setting turned Westerns from "little edifying tales" to "grand parables". After 1910, directors routinely shot Westerns in the west, not back east. The setting gave Hollywood a competitive edge as it fought European films at the box office. In the hands of different filmmakers, the landscape could: be a metaphor for the wilderness that threatened civilization out West; parallel a character's inner struggle; convey, by its magnificence, the heroic scale of a pioneer's conquest; or bring a sacred spiritual dimension to the human story.

Leone made the inevitable pilgrimage to Monument Valley in *Once Upon A Time In The West* (1968), but he usually preferred to create a dream-like variation on the traditional Western landscape, rather than trying for mere replication. He saw, beneath the romance and poetic imagery of Ford's Westerns, "baking wooden towns in an intense, astonishing kind of light", and the sun was often more baking and dehydrating than life-nourishing in his films.

Sam Peckinpah largely ignored Monument Valley. Yet he paid ironic tribute to the power of the Fordian landscape in *Pat Garrett And Billy The Kid* (1973). After breaking out of jail, the Kid pauses, on his horse, to create a mirror image of an iconic scene from Ford's *Rio Grande* (1950). In Ford's Western, horse and rider pose heroically in front of one of Monument Valley's most iconic rocks. In *Pat Garrett*, we see the rider reflected in – symbolically dead in? – the water, while the iconic rock is replaced by a small tree. The camera broods on the scene, even after the Kid is gone, asking us to contemplate/mourn the passing of an era.

The American West is big enough to justify a travel guide of its own – Greg Ward's *Rough Guide To Southwest USA* being one of the best available – so what follows is merely an introduction to the most significant Western locations.

The Alamo, Texas

With 2.5 million people a year visiting the 4.2 acres officially known as the Alamo, you don't have to be 'a mathematical genius to work out that you might be pressed for space visiting the most famous church in America.

The Alamo is San Antonio's *raison d'être*, not just attracting tourists but defining its social calendar. When visiting the Alamo, the trick is not to restrict yourself to the obvious, the old church which may, on first sight, seem disappointingly smaller than you imagined. Even when busy, the church has a serenity that obscures the fact that it was once the scene of fierce fighting.

John Wayne's epic movie makes the church more central to the battle than it really was.

To too many viewers, the thirteen days of glory in John Wayne's *The Alamo* seemed to take thirteen days to arrive.

This reflects the prickly priorities of local preservationists who actually demolished the second storey of the Long Barracks, which existed in 1836, to make the church look more impressive.

The other traces of the old Alamo are harder to spot yet worth the look. Much of the fighting occurred in Alamo Plaza, where you can, roughly, discern the outline of the old mission and fort. A plaque marks the spot where **Jim Bowie**'s Low Barracks stood. The palisade, that part of the defences manned by **Davy Crockett** and his volunteers, is marked by paving stones on the plaza. Less romantically, the spot where commander William B. Travis died for the cause is under a post office building.

Wayne didn't shoot his epic here. After being deterred from shooting in Mexico by howls of protest from prominent Texans, he had the Alamo compound rebuilt a hundred miles southwest of San Antonio on the Shahan ranch in Bracketville. The switch was financed by rich patriotic Texans who, to Wayne's disgust, took to flying over the set to see how shooting was going. (The obvious answer, with scenes disturbed by the unhistorical sound of private planes flying overhead, being "Not very well".) Wayne's Alamo village still stands today, and is open to tourists, offering comedy gunfighters, mariachi bands and a John Wayne museum (see www.homestead.com/thealamo-village/alamovillage.html). But none of the sideshows match the thrill of walking through the village, subsequently used as a backdrop for Westerns as diverse as *Two Rode Together* and *Lonesome Dove*.

For more info: www.thealamo.org

🎞 The Alamo
dir John Wayne, 1960, US, 203m (director's cut)

A lumbering, flawed, epic Western in which the final heroics are stirring (Wayne ignores stories that some defenders, led by his character Davy Crockett, surrendered only to be shot), but too delayed. The best thing in the movie is the triangular tension between Crockett, Bowie and Travis, but there is too much piety to the Alamo myth for their confrontations to catch fire. A pity, because Laurence Harvey, often wooden, is passionate and charismatic enough to make Travis a very sympathetic martinet. John Lee Hancock's weighty 2004 reinterpretation, also called *The Alamo*, is intriguing but overlong and a bit half-hearted.

Deadwood, South Dakota

Deadwood, a national historic landmark, has run out of gold – the incentive for 6000 prospectors to flock here in 1876 – but gambling, in rustic saloons and flashy casinos, has brought the old boom town ambience back to this notorious Western town. Gone, thankfully, are the days when, as the tourist board quips, you were gambling just walking into a saloon.

The TV series' portrait of Deadwood in its lawless, gold-crazed heyday is, though exaggerated for dramatic purposes, not too far from reality. **Ian McShane**'s brutal, foul-mouthed entrepreneur Al Swearengen is close to the truth. In the 1890s, his theatre could, through boxing and prostitution, rake in the equivalent of $170,000 a night in today's money.

Stuck in a gulch high up in the mountains, Deadwood offers plenty of corny gunfights, cut-price buffets and a few points of genuine interest to the Western buff. Mount Moriag Cemetery, where **Wild Bill Hickok** and **Calamity Jane** are buried next to each other (at her request), is a short, blustery hike from town. Returning to the centre, drop into Saloon #10 (657 Main Street) where, above the door, is the chair in which Hickok sat when he was shot dead in the back.

A Russian import

Forever being blown down dusty Western streets, skeletal tumbleweeds actually hail from the Ural mountains – they're also known as "Russian thistle" – and didn't reach the West until 1877 when, it is thought, they were transported in flax imported from the Ukraine. The plant soon spread across the West and the Western, providing the title for William S. Hart's farewell film, inspiring the song "Tumbling Tumbleweeds" and becoming instant shorthand for directors who wanted to suggest desolation or imminent spookiness or, as in *The Wonderful Country* (1959), just scare a horse.

In June, Deadwood runs Wild Bill Hickok Days featuring concerts, re-enactments and gun-spinning. They attract some 50,000 visitors to a town with a population of 2000, so you'll either be delighted to join the throng or want to give it a wide berth.

For more info: www.deadwood.org

The White Buffalo
dir J. Lee Thompson, 1977, US, 97m

An acquired taste that takes some acquiring, *The White Buffalo* stars Charles Bronson as the ageing, syphilitic Hickok, losing his sight as he embarks on a weird quest for a huge albino buffalo in a plot so clearly derived from *Moby Dick* that producer Dino De Laurentis must have checked Melville's novel was out of copyright. Thompson and Bronson's hopes of creating an arty Western aren't helped by shots showing the white buffalo's mechanical track. It's not good, but it's not dull.

Dodge City, Kansas

The official website for this legendary city may major on romantic silhouettes of cowboys but news that the council provides free large bins at the public works shop suggests this once lawless city is thoroughly tamed.

The city is content to replay its image, as perfected in films like *Dodge City* (1939), in the Boot Hill Museum on Wyatt Earp Boulevard. The museum's centrepiece is a single-sided Historic Front Street which dates all the way back to 1958. Stagecoach rides, a smithy, a railroad station and the Long Branch Saloon, complete with variety show and can-can dancers, are a reminder of the bad old days when the city had a population of 700, of whom 47 were prostitutes. The Dodge City Gang, which included two of the most famous lawmen in the West, **Bat Masterson** and **Wyatt Earp**, ran many of these prostitutes, controlling the saloons and local politics in the late 1870s and early 1880s. The gang – with Earp's friend **Doc Holliday** – even went to "war" to defend their ill-gotten gains, although the war ended before anyone got killed.

Boot Hill, the most famous cemetery in the West, is disappointing: a sorry patch of grass with some jokey wooden crosses erected above reinterred graves doesn't live up to the myth.

For more info: www.visitdodgecity.org

Dodge City
dir Michael Curtiz, 1939, US, 105m

Not as great as *My Darling Clementine*, *Dodge City* is still the archetypal town-taming Western. This fast-moving tale, shot in sumptuous Technicolor, is a fine vehicle for likeable all-action hero Errol Flynn. There are few moral complexities – in Dodge City not even children on a Sunday outing are safe – and Flynn does the decent thing with aplomb, even realizing that, job done, he must leave. Virginia City calls, a place so bad it's worse than Dodge City was before he arrived. Flynn did star in the Western *Virginia City* a year later.

Cowboy language

The linguistic trade out West was three-way: the settlers took many English words with them, adopted a few Spanish ones that suited and invented many of their own. The landscape they explored led them to create words like "mesa" and to give "bluff" another meaning as they named features they had never seen before. They also invented a slew of words and terms – rambunctious, hornswoggle, bodacious, liquored up (used by Davy Crockett in a letter in 1836) – that typified their attitude to life out West. Here are a few of the more interesting innovations.

Bronco How bronco came to describe a wild or unruly horse is a mystery. A derivation from "bruncus", Latin for a knot in a tree, has been suggested. But being bronco has often, notably in the comedy Western *Bronco Billy* (1980), been portrayed as a virtue by filmmakers.

Bury the hatchet The concept of peacefully burying a hatchet was immortalized in Henry Wadsworth Longfellow's *Hiawatha* in 1855.

Cowboy The word's derivation seems obvious – boys who worked with cows – but it is a literal translation of the Spanish word *vaquero* and, oddly, was used in the War of Independence as an epithet to condemn Tory loyalists in New York State who were notorious for harshly treating opponents.

Hold-up A term for a delay now used to describe the armed robbing of a bank, in the manner perfected by the likes of Jesse James.

Maverick The word for someone of inconveniently independent mind didn't start with the James Garner TV series. It originally applied to unbranded calves that had become separated from their herd, and has been traced back to one Samuel Augustus Maverick, a nineteenth-century Texan cattleman who didn't brand his cows.

Outlaw This all-purpose term for villains in the Wild West has its roots in the old Norse word *utlagi*, literally "ut" for out and "lagi" from "log" for law. The term, signifying someone who could be killed without recrimination because of their criminal acts, became "outlaw" in middle English and became ubiquitous out West. In the 1850s, people living out West were dubbed "border ruffians", a close linguistic cousin of outlaw.

Rodeo Buffalo Bill popularized contests in which cowboys tried to prove how good they were with a lasso, riding steers or unruly horses. But the word comes from the Spanish word *rodear*, which means to go around.

Round up This term for the gathering of cattle is now used by the police – as in *Casablanca* (1942), in which Claude Reins' French police chief orders his men to "round up the usual suspects".

Stetson John B. Stetson's large-brimmed hat – also dubbed the "ten-gallon hat", in allusion to its capacity – became synonymous with the West and was first sold in Central City, Colorado, in 1865. A flat-brimmed version was used by Canadian soldiers in the Boer War, and became the official hat of the Royal Canadian Mounted Police.

Vaquero The first cowboys were *vaqueros* – a Spanish word derived from *vaca*, cow. In southwest and central Texas, this came to mean a ranch-hand, a cowboy who usually hired himself out to different outfits. In California, *vaquero* was Anglicized to become "buckaroo", and applied, usually, to cowboys who stayed on the ranch they grew up on or bought their own family ranch.

Fort Apache, Arizona

The best way to enjoy Fort Apache – and the reservation that surrounds it – is to watch the John Ford Western after you've been. Ford's geographical sleight of hand – shifting the action from this part of eastern Arizona to his beloved Monument Valley, Goosenecks State Park in

Utah and a ranch in California's Simi Valley – means there is no point trailing around here with images of Henry Fonda and the Duke in your mind.

The reservation's headquarters is Whiteriver, cupped in a mile-high valley twenty miles south of Pinetop, the nearest town. A few miles further southwest you will find, as the north and east forks of the White River converge, the real Fort Apache. The US Army outpost was founded in 1870 to support the campaigns of **General Crook**, who was officially allied with the local White Mountain Apache but wanted to make sure he knew what they were up to. Several buildings survive in decent condition, including General Crook's cabin, which now serves as the Apache Office of Tourism, and the commanding officer's old quarters. Sadly, the last remaining wooden barracks burned down in 1985.

The war here was more complicated than in Ford's film. The US Army were aided in their fight against Geronimo by the White Mountain Apache, especially chiefs Alchise and Diable who acted as army scouts. But a walk around the real fort – with twenty or so buildings in the fort, a military cemetery and a reconstructed Apache village – does give you a real sense of the small, isolated communities that lived and fought in places like this across the West.

For more info: www.wmonline.com/attract/ftapache.htm

Fort Apache
dir John Ford, 1948, US, 127m, b/w

Brilliantly cast against type, Henry Fonda is the disappointed disciplinarian who sees his posting out West as a banishment. He mishandles his men, his negotiations with the Indians and his daughter's love affair while second-in-command John Wayne tries damage limitation. Inspired by Custer's catastrophic leadership of the real 7th Cavalry, the film glorifies misplaced heroism and military life in a series of beautifully composed images, from the post ball and the troop's women shoulder to shoulder on the fort ramparts to the inevitable, avoidable massacre.

Lincoln, New Mexico

You can find many ghost towns in today's American West but it's hard to imagine a Wild West town more perfectly preserved than Lincoln, New Mexico. Here on 28 April 1881 – largely as shown in Peckinpah's *Pat Garrett And Billy The Kid* (1973) – **Billy the Kid** took advantage of a trip to the outhouse to shoot his way out of the courthouse and escape the noose.

You can walk into that same courthouse, even mustier now than it was in the 1880s, and stand in the upstairs window from which Billy shot the sheriff. The Lincoln County Historical Center, towards the east end of town, gives an exhaustive account of the Kid's life and times, right down to the coroner's report on the two lawmen he killed in his breakout.

Near the courthouse is the Wortley Hotel, once owned by Pat Garrett, where marshal **Bob Olinger** was lunching when he heard Billy's shots. The hotel has been reconstructed to match its original appearance and is worth visiting – if only to see where the marshal raced onto the street and into the path of Billy's bullet.

Lincoln's other attractions include the Tunstall Store, which gives you as good a feel for a nineteenth-century Western store as you can get, and the Torréon, a circular tower built in the 1850s as a refuge against Apache raids.

Walking the streets – the whole town is now a state monument – it's easy to envisage the conflict here not as a simple combat between good and evil, but as a small civil war in which morality mattered less than adherence to a faction. The corporatist cause, personified by **John Chisum** and supported by Republican capitalists, the Federal government and cattle conglomerates, won, while the smaller ranchers, Democrats, cowboys and small businessmen – including Billy the Kid and store owner John Tunstall – lost, paying for defeat with their lives.

Lincoln is such a time capsule that it is absurd to think that Peckinpah, for cost reasons, had to shoot his story in Durango, Mexico.

For more info: www.newmexico.org

Little Bighorn, Montana

On a grassy hillside above Interstate 90, an hour's drive from Billings, **General George Armstrong Custer** came to a brave, bad, pointless end. The best way to understand the tragedy is to pick up an official map and a Reno-Benteen Entrenchment Trail Guide, drive east to where Major Reno and Captain Benteen survived and then start slowly back to Last Stand Hill.

That way you follow Custer's path, notice how restricted his views were and get some idea of his battle plan. What no tour or biography can explain is why Custer ignored his scouts' warnings that the force he was "pursuing" consisted of several thousand Lakota, Sioux, Cheyenne and Blackfoot. Yet you see, as you tour the area by car and, finally, on foot, that his plan was not without logic and that he couldn't have seen, conclusively, that the scouts were right, until it was too late.

Evan S. Connell's excellent book *Son Of The Morning Star* suggests the notion of a last

The heroic myth of Errol Flynn's *They Died With Their Boots On* doesn't square with the story told by the battlefield itself.

stand is romantic gloss. The battle may not even have lasted an hour: the 210 or so men Custer led died quickly, though not mercifully. The scattered white markers identifying where men died are horribly poignant. As you stand there, it's impossible not to be chilled by the horror

The Sand Creek controversy

On 29 November 1864, **Colonel John M. Chivington** led 700 volunteer soldiers into a camp of 500 Cheyenne and Arapaho people in Sand Creek, south-eastern Colorado, and killed 150 of them, mainly women, children and old men. This became known as the Sand Creek massacre – and was, in 1970, horrifyingly portrayed as such in *Soldier Blue*.

One revisionist historian, however, has called it a battle. Gregory Michno, in his book *Battle At Sand Creek* (2004), challenged the findings of a Congressional investigation that labelled the event a massacre, saying that the areas around Denver were in a panic after Indian attacks and that the Cheyenne fought valiantly. It's hard, though, to reconcile normal concepts of a battle with eyewitness accounts – from Chivington's own officers – of "children on their knees, begging for their lives, having their brains beaten out".

The National Park Service plans to turn the area into a historic park but, so far, has only acquired 920 acres of private land and can't open the park to the public. Sand Creek may remain America's guilty secret for a while yet.

For more info: www.nps.gov/sand

Soldier Blue
dir Ralph Nelson, 1970, US, 114m

For a pro-Indian movie – that draws parallels between the savagery at Sand Creek and the massacre by US troops of villagers in My Lai in Vietnam – *Soldier Blue* doesn't give its Indian characters much screen time or humanity. They are simply slaughtered in graphic scenes that confront the viewer with the ugly reality of the war in the West while tapping into a fashion, in the early 1970s, for onscreen violence. Ralph Nelson seems more interested in his two white survivors, Candice Bergen and Peter Strauss. Shocking, powerful, disjointed, this isn't the best movie Nelson ever made, but it may be the one for which he'll be remembered.

and terror of the 7th Cavalry's last moments. Little Bighorn has, though it's an over-used phrase, a terrible beauty; to visit is to glimpse the savagery and horror of a conflict between civilizations that has, in movies, too often been traduced into a school playground game of cowboys and Indians.

For more info: www.nps.gov/libi

Son Of The Morning Star
dir Mike Robe, 1991, US TV, 187m

Multi-Emmy-award-winning TV version of the life and times of the US Cavalry's most controversial officer. Based fairly closely on Evan S. Connell's book, this portrays Custer (Gary Cole) not as a deranged Indian hater or self-sacrificing hero but as a man who rose too quickly to a level where he proved fatally incompetent. The attempt to add Crazy Horse's point of view – not included in the book – doesn't work.

Mini-Hollywood, Almeria

Offering "wonderful shows every day except Mondays…" at high noon and the less melodramatic time of 5pm, Mini-Hollywood, near the town of Tabernas in Almeria, southern Spain, is a Wild West theme park where over a hundred titles – including Leone's Dollars trilogy, *Django* and many of *Django*'s endless sequels – were shot.

Carlo Simi, Leone's brilliant designer, built the place in 1966 to shoot *For A Few Dollars More*. Despite the owners' grim determination to appeal to all the family by adding a poky zoo, the buildings almost all date from the movie-making days. There's a pleasureable shock of recognition as you turn the corner and see the bank robbed in *For A Few Dollars More*, and you can have a drink in the saloon where Lee Van Cleef and Klaus Kinski rubbed each other up the wrong way.

Texas Hollywood, a couple of miles away, has the abandoned feel of a Western ghost town, even down to the fact that you'll have to drive right up until you're convinced it's open. Between Tabernas and Granada, on a side road off the main highway, Rancho Leone is another Simi creation. The setting for the showdown between **Charles Bronson** and **Henry Fonda** in *Once Upon A Time In The West*, this was obviously built to last and still looks more sturdily impressive than its newer neighbours, the cowboy town and Indian village.

Some Leone fans have crisscrossed the region, armed with books by Christopher Frayling and repeated re-viewings of the movies, trying to locate exactly where such and such a shot was taken. They are often disappointed. But just driving around this part of Andalucía, soaking up the lunar landscape that first attracted Leone, is enough to have you humming the theme to *The Good, The Bad And The Ugly*.

Les pétroleuses (The Legend of Frenchie King)
dir Christian-Jaque, 1971, Fr/It/Sp/UK, 96m

Brigitte Bardot and Claudia Cardinale are the sexy dames feuding over an oil lease in a small Western town – in reality, Mini-Hollywood – founded by the French for their own amusement. The sheriff (Michael J. Pollard) can't woo either Bardot or Cardinale unless he learns French. What this lacks in logic, it makes up for in Russ Meyer-style gusto.

Monument Valley, Arizona/ Utah

"Monument Valley" is a misnomer. The place lacks the permanent stream and higher ground on either side which, in geography textbooks, define a valley. Just east of Highway 163, **John Ford**'s favourite movie location – he even has a point named after him – remains miraculously unspoilt. The familiarity of this iconic combination of red sands, sandstone buttes and pinnacles poking into the sky has enhanced the place's power, not dimmed it. This may be as close as you can get to feeling like you've gatecrashed the set of a classic John Wayne/John Ford Western.

In Navajo, this "valley" is called Tsé Bii' Ndzisgaii (it means "there is a treeless area amid the rocks"). Given the usual fate of Indians (often played by Navajo) in Ford's Westerns, it is pretty ironic that Monument Valley is such a stronghold of Navajo culture and, what's more, is preserved as Ford saw it (he called it "the most complete, beautiful, and peaceful place on earth") because of that.

You can drive around the park yourself, for a small fee. But on a guided tour you get to see more – such as the Sun's Eye arch, with petroglyphs of bighorn sheep – have the freedom to walk up closer to some of the sights and gain some insight into Navajo culture.

You might, if you've got the time, want to take in a sunset or sunrise. If you're lucky, the colours are more vivid than in any Western. You might also make the thirty-mile detour to the Valley of the Gods, which is almost as magnificent.

Most visitors, like Ford, come to Monument Valley feeling they've got so much beauty to see and not enough time to see it. The longer you

The most famous valley since the Valley of the Kings made *Stagecoach* seem of monumental significance.

stay, the more you appreciate the range of landscape – rivers, mountains, plains, desert – that made Ford loath to shoot anywhere else.

He filmed *Stagecoach* (in which the coach crosses the valley three times), *My Darling Clementine*, *Fort Apache*, *She Wore A Yellow Ribbon*, *Wagon Master*, *Rio Grande*, *The Searchers*, *Sergeant Rutledge* and *Cheyenne Autumn* here, but he didn't discover the valley as a movie location. It was first used as a setting in *The Vanishing American* (1925), an adaptation of the Zane Grey novel. After Ford monopolized it, Western directors had a choice:

either pay homage as Leone did in *Once Upon A Time In The West* (1968), or ignore it, as most chose to do, for fear of seeming to copy Ford.

The only accommodation within twenty miles is Goulding's Monument Valley Lodge, where you can watch a library of Westerns, see the cabin the Duke used in *She Wore A Yellow Ribbon* and, if you're lucky, buy some John Wayne toilet paper (motto: "It's rough, it's tough and it doesn't take any crap"). Harry Goulding, who started the lodge, liked to take tourists around the area and, fortunately for the Western, introduced Ford to the place.

The Vanishing American
dir George B. Seitz, 1925, US, 110m, b/w

The Western that discovered Monument Valley is even more important as a rare sympathetic treatment of the issues afflicting the Native American. Richard Dix is the Navajo who returns from service in World War I to find his way of life threatened by corruption, unjust laws and his love for a white schoolteacher. The quality of the performances, landscape photography and Zane Grey's story are undermined by a strange prologue which presents the Indians' disappearance in fascist terms as historical/scientific progress in which the weak give way to the strong.

Paramount Ranch, California

A Western town created for the movies, Paramount Ranch is a miraculous place where log walls are made of fibreglass, fireplaces are made of foam and a dusty wind really does, most days, blow down the main street. If you find the sense of *déjà vu* overwhelming, don't worry. Since the 1920s, the ranch has pretended to be Dodge City, Laredo, Tombstone and Colorado Springs, the mining town in the TV series *Dr Quinn, Medicine Woman*.

The prickly icon

As surely as settlers colonized the West, the imaginary West has been colonized by the saguaro cactus, also known as the **organ pipe cactus**. Immortalized in the 1907 photograph "Saguaro Gatherers" by Edward S. Curtis, it has appeared so often in Westerns, especially those made by Ford, that it has come to symbolize the genre. Ironically, this particular cactus does not roam across the Western US, flourishing only in the Sonora desert, a finger of which reaches into southern Arizona. In a typical lifespan of 200 years, they can grow up to 50 feet. Although filmmakers have dwelt, lovingly, on their iconic prickly exteriors, the Tohono 'O'odham Indians prize them for their delicious crimson fruit.

Paramount Ranch lies northwest of Los Angeles in the Agoura Hills, surrounded by the considerable grandeur of the Santa Monica mountains. In 1927 Paramount bought the 2400-acre Rancho Las Virgenes for use as a movie ranch. The locale was versatile enough to provide the backdrop for colonial Massachusetts, ancient China and the Wild West – there's even a lot called the Backdrop Trail because it has no telephone poles or distinguishing features whatsoever. The ranch became synonymous with Westerns when **William Hertz**, a fan of the genre, bought the southeast part of the ranch in 1953 and built a Western town, using Paramount's old prop storage sheds. That fake Western everytown, complete with a main street of storefronts, including a sheriff's office, a saloon, a post office and a Wells Fargo office, is the main attraction for tourists visiting what is now a national park.

With the likes of John Wayne, Henry Fonda, Roy Rogers, Gary Cooper, Kirk Douglas and

Barbara Stanwyck all having starred here, the Paramount Ranch is the ultimate place to stage your very own fake gunfight.

For more info: www.nps.gov/samo/maps/para.htm

Tombstone, Arizona

The most famous town in the Wild West, a town that boasts it's too tough to die, Tombstone was named by the first prospector **Edward Schieffelin** who, exploring the area in 1877, was told by cavalry stationed nearby that he'd find nothing there but his own tombstone.

Fortunately for the Western, Schieffelin proved them wrong.

Today Tombstone is a slightly corny tourist trap, full of snarling gunfighters (they'll stage a gunfight for cash), but don't let that deter you. Surprisingly little has changed here. You can pace down the wooden sidewalk, glance over the dusty street and then push through the swinging saloon doors as if you were Wyatt Earp.

The buildings in Tombstone's central grid of streets mainly date back to the 1880s, and signs point out the scenes of the most famous shoot-outs. The major attraction is the OK Corral, where you can see the hearse used to take the

The OK Corral awaits its famous gunfight, memorably, if inaccurately, staged by John Sturges.

victims away, and, in a courtyard strewn with crude dummies, see the positions of the shooters. Sadly, the figures' locations are as much at odds with contemporary accounts as John Ford's staging in *My Darling Clementine* (1946). You can also see the room from which Doc Holliday's girlfriend **Big Nose Kate** watched the gunfight.

There are other sights worth your time in Tombstone. The Bird Cage Theater on Allen Street shows seven bird cages, said to have been used by prostitutes and frequented by the Earps and the Clantons, hanging in the main hall. It

would be remiss not to complete the story of the OK Corral by going half a mile north on US-80 to Boothill Graveyard, which shut in 1884, having already been filled by 284 burials. You can see where the OK Corral's victims rest, their peace disturbed by the strains of country music.

For more info: www.cityoftombstone.com

Gunfight At The OK Corral
dir John Sturges, 1957, US, 122m

Proficient and pleasing on the eye in bright Technicolor, this retelling of the famous gunfight is curiously flat. Even the

---

Cowboy couture

Some blame it on the fact there's a Texan in the White House, others point to *Brokeback Mountain* or **Kate Moss** and her cowboy boots. Whoever's to blame, stylists agree cowboy chic is back.

The West's greatest single contribution to fashion is denim, though it became popular among prospectors before cowboys wore it. The cowboy style at its simplest consists of a basic wardrobe of boot-length jeans, Western shirts, plaid jackets and denim vests with the sleeves torn out. Classic accessories include cowboy boots, hats, rodeo-style buckles, bandanas, neckerchiefs and, if you want camp rather than campfire, winged chaps.

Functional cowboy garb was transformed for **Buffalo Bill**'s Wild West shows. In came those winged chaps (not especially popular on the real range but they looked good in the arena), fringed jackets, fringed cuffed gloves and pearl-buttoned plaid shirts with piping and embroidery. The cleaned-up, denatured cowboy style was perfected by **Tom Mix** and is seen in countless B Westerns.

In the 1930s, jeans were seen on some screen cowboys – **Gary Cooper** is said to be the first celebrity to

have stonewashed his jeans – and at dude ranches where gullible easterners grew to associate them with a romantic ideal of the West: freedom, rugged individualism, and a life that, being spent largely outdoors, was deemed more authentic.

In the 1950s, the Western's golden decade, even **James Dean** adopted the cowboy look. When advertising genius Leo Burnett was looking to reposition Marlboro cigarettes as a man's smoke, he asked colleagues: "What's the most masculine symbol you can think of?" One of his writers replied, "a cowboy", and the Marlboro Man was born.

Filmmakers had begun to experiment with the basic look. Alan Ladd looked almost as good in buckskin in *Shane (1953)* as Doris Day did in the same year's *Calamity Jane*, while, in the 1960s, Clint's Man With No Name wore a hippy-style poncho – and fought villains with flared trousers. A frock coat adapted from the Civil War medical coat was worn, dirtied up, in *The Wild Bunch* and Leone's Dollars trilogy.

By 1969, the classic cowboy style was iconic enough to be spoofed in *Midnight Cowboy*, with urban cowboy John Voight angrily rejecting aspersions about his sexuality with the shout: "John Wayne ain't no faggot!" The scene proved prescient as gay America final five-minute shoot-out which took just 44 minutes to film is merely good, not spectacular. The movie is saved by the actors – Burt Lancaster and Kirk Douglas as Earp and Doc Holliday and Jo Van Fleet as Doc's burned out former girlfriend – and introduces a latent homosexual sub-text into the film's central relationship.

Shrines and museums

In addition to thousands of Westerns, the West has inspired hundreds of museums and quite a few shrines to its great and (not so) good. Some of these have been touched upon already. Here are six of the most fascinating.

Billy The Kid Museum, Fort Sumner

www.billythekidmuseumfortsumner.com

Don't be deterred by the corny sign: the Billy The Kid Museum in Fort Sumner has 60,000 – count 'em! – relics of the Kid's era, including the original wanted poster, his rifle, chaps and spurs and some locks of his hair. There's another museum across the way, which covers similar ground. But then Billy, shot here by Pat Garrett in 1881, is the biggest thing to have happened to the place.

adopted the jeans/chaps/plaid shirts/moustache look and, come the mid-1980s, decided not to wear jeans under the chaps. **Vivienne Westwood** even designed a T-shirt showing two trouserless cowboys getting very well acquainted, which Sid Vicious wore in concert.

But cowboy fashion wasn't all Village People. Ralph Lauren perfected a citified rugged Western fashion worn, today, by **Robert Redford**, and launched a nice line in Navajo throws. Then **Madonna** turned cowgirl, courtesy of Dolce & Gabbana, for her 2001 album *Music*, convincing many style mavens that "if Madge is wearing it, it must be fashion".

Soon Sienna Miller and Kate Moss were stepping out in cowboy boots (Madonna having reputedly worn a diamond-studded pair at her wedding). Italian shoe designer Salvatore Ferragamo must have been happy: he learnt his trade in a cowboy boot factory. Miller and **Victoria Beckham** even embraced the prairie skirt, last seen to dubious effect in the TV Western *Little House On The Prairie*, but revived by Jean-Paul Gaultier and Anna Sui. The one style that hasn't really caught on – possibly because you have to be Cher to get away with it – is the Native American look.

After *Brokeback Mountain*, the classic cowboy look is back. The vogue is for rough and rugged with a certain naive innocence, although other designers say the full-blown "rhinestone cowboy" look – merging bling and the open range – is the way ahead. Cowboy fashion, in all its guises, has never really gone away.

Buffalo Bill Historical Center, Cody, Wyoming

www.bbhc.org

With the possible exception of John Ford, nobody mythologized the American West quite like Buffalo Bill. So somehow it's fitting that his historical center in Cody, Wyoming, should offer – in the kind of deal you'd expect from Bill's travelling show – five museums in one! The highlights are the museum devoted to Buffalo Bill himself, the Whitney Gallery of Western Art and the Plains Indian Museum.

The James Farm, Kearney, Missouri

www.legendsofamerica.com/we-jessejames9.html

It's no great shock that the Missouri farm where Jesse and Frank James grew up – where Jesse was whipped by Union soldiers as a teenager and their brother Archie was killed by Pinkerton detectives – is said to be haunted. The house – where Jesse is buried – is now run by the Friends of the James Farm, restored from near ruin. Staff say that on foggy mornings you can hear mumbled voices and the clatter of horses' hooves. This is more a shrine than a museum. You can even see the feather duster Jesse was holding when he was shot. It's also worth visiting two other Missouri sites: the Jesse James Bank Museum in Liberty (the real-life equivalent of the bank Tyrone Power robs in the movie) and the Jesse James Home in St Joseph, where he was shot in the back – you can see the bullet hole, now a foot wide thanks to tourists chipping away.

The Museum of the American West, Los Angeles

www.autrynationalcenter.org

Actually, through the generosity of the Gene Autry family, you get three museums: the Southwest Museum of the American Indian, the Museum of the American West and the Institute for the Study of the American West.

There are some intriguing real exhibits from the Wild West, such as pistols used by Belle Starr, Annie Oakley and Butch Cassidy, but the celebration of the Western movie is even more striking, with gunbelts and costumes from epic Westerns, a replica Western movie set and a collection devoted to singing cowboys which even includes music by John Wayne (as Singing Sandy Sanders).

National Cowboy Museum, Oklahoma City

www.nationalcowboymuseum.org

The National Cowboy Museum has it all: arguably the greatest collection of Western art (from greats like Frederic Remington and Charles B. Russell to the present day); a massive array of artefacts from cowboy life; some fine sculpture; and a collection of artwork, personal belongings and memorabilia from John Wayne.

William S. Hart Park, Newhall, California

www.hartmuseum.org

An hour's drive from Los Angeles, in Newhall, California, the former home of William S. Hart contains original furnishings, an array of classic Western art (from the likes of Frederic Remington and Charles B. Russell), Native American artefacts and props from the silent movie star's career.

Festivals

Festival Of The West

Phoenix, Arizona, March, www.festivalofthewest.com

For sixteen years the Festival of the West has celebrated the best in Western music, square dancing and movies. Normally a minor stalwart of Western cinema is on hand to host the Western movie festival.

High Noon Western Americana

Phoenix, Arizona, January, www.highnoon.com
An annual auction of Western artefacts – everything from lots connected to Hollywood cowboys to chaps and saddles – from 230 dealers.

Roy Rogers and Dale Evans Film Festival

US, February, www.happytrails.org/events/film-festival
/ff1.html
This celebration of Roy and his other half has been running for nine years – though in 2006 it moved to Apple Valley, California – and offers fans such treats as an optional visit to Roy's old ranch, the chance to watch some rare Rogers films and an awards dinner.

Tombstone Film Festival

Tombstone, July
It seems paradoxical that Tombstone has struggled to hold a regular festival in honour of the Western. The Tombstone Film Festival returned in 2006, after a year's absence, but given its uncertain history (it was even moved to Willcox in 2003) it's hard to be confident about its future.

Way Out West:
Westerns around the world

The Chinese Western *Warriors Of Heaven And Earth* (2003) replaces the Wild West frontier with the clash of cultures on the Silk Road in Asia.

Way Out West:
Westerns around the world

There may be only one Monument Valley – in America – but that hasn't stopped filmmakers across the world making Westerns. The international menu includes Westerns associated with almost every clichéd dish: spaghetti, sauerkraut, chop suey and, yup, kangaroo.

Australia

In 2005, *The Proposition*, scripted by rock star **Nick Cave**, was billed as "the first Australian Western". Even by the movie industry's forgetful standards this was some claim, ignoring both *Kangaroo* (1952), Lewis Milestone's outback Western with Maureen O'Hara, and Tony Richardson's unsatisfactory Aussie outlaw tale *Ned Kelly* (1970). The first Australian filmmaker to blaze this particular trail was Jack Lee with his so-so *Robbery Under Arms* (1957), a movie chiefly notable as a historical curio and for Peter Finch's impressive turn as a bushranger (Australian for outlaw).

Although there are obvious similarities between Australia and America – climate, epic landscape, outlaw mythology, guilt over the treatment of an indigenous population – Aussie directors have not consistently been drawn to the Western. Some movies, notably *The Chant*

Tom Selleck left his *Magnum PI* floral shirts behind to play a hired gun with scruples in *Quigley Down Under*.

Of *Jimmy Blacksmith* (1978), have drawn on the genre, and in the mid-1970s there was a flurry of "kangaroo Westerns". The stand-out was Russell Hagg's *Raw Deal* (1977), in which the federal government hires gunfighters to quell a rebellion. **Simon Wincer** made *The Man From Snowy River* in 1982 and, eight years later, the more accomplished *Quigley Down Under*. Steve Jodrell's *Shame* (1987) crossed social realism and the Western in a powerful tale of rape and law in an outback town.

Rolf de Heer's *The Tracker* (2002) – in which an aboriginal Australian is accused of murdering a white woman – and **John Hillcoat's** *The Proposition* both use the Western to reflect on Australian history, suggesting a renewed appreciation of the genre.

Quigley Down Under
dir Simon Wincer, 1990, Aus/US, 119m

The plot isn't subtle: rifleman Tom Selleck, hired by nasty Alan Rickman to hunt aborigines, throws Rickman through a window and helps the natives. But the Northern Territories offer a magnificent backdrop, the principal players (including Laura San Giacomo as Selleck's crazed love interest) act well and the gunfights, chases and ambushes are well done.

🎬 The Proposition
dir John Hillcoat, 2005, Aus, 104m

A nihilistic, bleak, "mud-and-rags" Western, punctuated by graphic violence, *The Proposition* is in the same corral as HBO's *Deadwood*. Nick Cave and John Hillcoat have obviously learned from Leone and, though their work is rich in allegory, the premise is disarmingly simple: Guy Pearce must kill his outlaw brother to stop their 14-year-old sibling being strung up by lawman Ray Winstone. *The Proposition* touches on the genre's familiar themes – the clash between wilderness and "civilization" and family loyalty versus survival – to capture a very savage frontier.

Britain

For obvious reasons – lack of landscape, the pointlessness of competing with the Americans in a genre they invented, lack of British actors who looked good in the saddle – Britain's contribution to the Western has been on a par with Switzerland's contribution to naval warfare.

Some Westerns were made in the very early days of the British film industry. One has survived: in Theo Frenkel's *Fate* (1911), said to be the first Western shot in colour, an Englishman becomes the leader of a tribe of renegade Indians. But Britain's impact on the genre has largely come through actors, directors and writers. Out West, the Englishman is usually a figure of fun, like the comically bowler-hatted **Charles Laughton** in *Ruggles Of Red Gap* (1935) or **Kenneth More**'s "I say old chap" turn in *Sheriff Of Fractured Jaw* (1958). **Stewart Granger** had a decent career in Westerns, for a British actor, co-starring in Richard Brooks' grim *The Last Hunt* (1956) and making German Westerns in the 1960s. Among directors, Edgar Wright's *Fistful Of Fingers* (1994) is a genuinely funny parody that almost lives up to its slogan: "The greatest Western ever made … in

Somerset". In the 1970s, though Michael Winner flirted with the genre with two so-so efforts – *Lawman* and *Chato's Land* – Britain's biggest gift to the Western was Alan Sharp, the Scottish writer who penned *The Hired Hand* (1971) and *Ulzana's Raid* (1972).

The most conspicuous Westerns made in Britain are two comedies – *Ramsbottom Rides Again* (1956), starring Arthur Askey, and *Carry On Cowboy* (1965) – and, more seriously, *The Singer Not The Song* (1961). Even British Westerns set in Canada are scarce, with the Hammond Innes adaptation *Campbell's Kingdom* (1957), starring Dirk Bogarde, the pick of the bunch.

🎬 The Singer Not The Song
dir Roy Ward Baker, 1961, UK, 132m

A truly bizarre Western that proves how odd moviemaking can get if you adapt a Western novel set in Mexico by a writer (Audrey Erskine Lindsop) who's never been west of Torquay in a vain bid to keep your star, Dirk Bogarde, at your studio, let him wear fetishistically tight leather trousers and cast John Mills as the handsome priest for whom he has a repressed passion. The homoerotic undertones are so loud they become overtones, but this still works. Just.

Canada

In the Western, Canada is represented by one and a half clichés: the Royal Canadian Mounted Police (Nelson Eddy warbling "When I'm calling you") and gold prospecting, the latter cliché only half Canadian because directors can be hazy about where Canada's Klondike ends and Alaska's goldfields begin.

Canada produced its own Mountie Westerns as far back as 1938 with *Death Goes North*. The best of this genre is probably Dan Candy's *Law* (1973), in which **Donald Sutherland**'s obsessive policeman and the stunning landscape mask deficiencies in the plot. Only a few Westerns made in Canada have engaged with the Canadian experience, the best being *The Drylanders* (1962), Peter Pearson's wistful *Paperback Hero* (1973) and *The Grey Fox* (1982).

The Grey Fox
dir Phillip Borsos, 1982, Can, 110m

Richard Farnsworth is unstudied, graceful, natural and charming as the gentleman bandit who, after 33 years in jail, goes back to robbing people because robbing people is what he does best. Phillip Borsos cannily obscures his lack of budget with a pseudo-documentary style that suits the fact that the bandit's story is pseudo-true.

China

China – or, to be precise, Hong Kong, until its reunification in 1997 – has two dishes on the Western's international menu: the chop suey Western (Hong Kong-produced kung fu Westerns) and the noodle Western (a Western in a Chinese setting – though confusingly the makers of the 1985 Japanese comedy *Tampopo* called that a noodle Western). Though the image of the TV series *Kung Fu* overshadows the Chinese Western, not every Western from China represents such an obvious meld of East and West.

Warriors Of Heaven And Earth: proof that not every Chinese Western is kung fu crazed.

In 1960 James Clavell introduced the Chinese gunfighter, played by Hawaiian actor James Shigeta, in *Walk Like A Dragon*. That movie, spaghetti Westerns and martial arts inspired Eastern filmmakers, leading to *Kung Fu Brothers In The Wild West* (1973), less formulaic than it sounds, and Antonio Margheriti's *Blood Money* (1974), in which gunfighter Lee Van Cleef and kung fu genius Lo Lieh must decipher tattoos on women's buttocks to find a fortune. These, in turn, inspired American martial arts Westerns like Tom Laughlin's *The Master Gunfighter* (1975) and the Italian martial arts/spaghetti Western *Shanghai Joe* (1972).

There was a minor resurgence in the mainstream meld of East and Western with *The Peace Hotel* (1995), starring **Chow Yun Fat**, followed, in 2000, by the **Jackie Chan** action/comedy Western *Shanghai Noon*.

Ping He personifies a more serious Western tradition, calling his *Warriors Of Heaven And Earth* (2003) a Chinese Western. For Ping He, "The American West is about taming the frontier, the Chinese Western is about cultures meeting on the Silk Road." Familiar Western themes – bandits harassing a village, a hero in disguise, a mysterious stranger – run through his *Swordsman In Double Flag* (1991) and *Sun Valley* (1995).

Warriors Of Heaven And Earth
dir Ping He, 2003, Ch, 114m

A moustache-twirling villain (Wang Xueqi), Chinese soldiers battling on camelback and eye-catching scenery beautifully captured by Zhao Fei's camera are the highlights of Ping He's Chinese Western set in the seventh century on the Silk Road. Army officer Jiang Wen and Japanese emissary Nakai Kiichi unite to protect a young monk returning from India. The action scenes will disappoint those expecting *Crouching Tiger, Hidden Dragon*-style thrills but this is super-sized, accessible entertainment.

Eastern Europe

In Communist Poland, *Shane* packed cinemas as *The Man From Nowhere*. The Poles warmed to buckskinned **Alan Ladd**, fighting the territorial ambitions of cattle baron Stryker who, like the Russians, insisted that he was only reclaiming what was rightfully his.

The Western's popularity in Communist Eastern Europe would have appalled Karl Marx. No Communist regime there completely resisted the Western's charms. Even in 1949, when Eastern Europe was at its most ideologically correct, Czech puppet animator Jiri Trnka made *Home On The Prairie*, a 23-minute musical comedy Western sending up classics like *Stagecoach*. Yugoslavia and the German Democratic Republic led the Eastern Bloc in sheer volume. In 1966 the success of *The Sons Of The Great Mother Bear* led DEFA, the East German state film studio, to produce a cycle of movies in which the cowboys were villains and the heroes were Indians. So popular was the Wild West that **Dean Reed**, the American singer who defected to become "Red Elvis", starred in the GDR's own singing cowboy fest, *Sing Cowboy Sing!* (1981). In Yugoslavia, directors such as Hajrudin Krvavac and Aleksandr Djordevic popularized partisan films – movies that revisited World War II Western-style (Nazis bad, partisans good) – in the 1970s. Czech Westerns weren't churned out as regularly but a few – notably *Lemonade Joe* (1964) – were truly original.

Even after the fall of Communism, the genre didn't lose its appeal. Vladimir Michalek's *Sekal Has To Die* (1998) is a fine Moravian Western. In Romania, folk myths and the Western had blended back in 1929 in *Haiducii*, while Transylvania was the setting for a series of 1980s Romanian Westerns. Some Westerns were Eastern Bloc co-productions.

Vladimir Vajnshtok's *Armed And Dangerous: Time And Heroes Of Bret Harte* (1977) was a Russian/Romanian/Czech collaboration that, inspired by an American Western novel, had cowboys with American names speaking Russian yet adhered to the principles of Marxist-Leninism.

It would be simplistic, but not entirely wrong, to suggest that Westerns endured here because they suggested that some eternal truths transcended ideology, that a Shane would one day ride to the rescue. In 1989 Poland's Solidarity party printed a poster of **Gary Cooper**, characterizing the country's first free elections in decades as a national high noon. Leader **Lech Walesa** said: "Cowboys in Western clothes were a powerful symbol for Poles. Cowboys fight for justice, against evil, and for freedom, physical and spiritual." Coop triumphed in his last battle – Solidarity won the election.

Lemonade Joe (Limonádový Joe)
dir Oldrich Lipský, 1964, Cz, 99m, b/w

In Stetson City, sharp-shooting Joe fights black-hatted villain Hogo Fogo for the right to sell lemonade and the heart of virginal Winifred Goodman, while distracted by temptress Tornado Lou. Lemonade Joe starred in Czech magazines in the 1940s, inspired by singing cowboys, so every character has a key song: Tornado Lou sings "When The Smoke Thickens In The Bar Do You See My Moist Lips?" Naïve, charming, and one of the best comedy Westerns of the 1960s.

The Sons Of The Great Mother Bear (Die Söhne der großen Bärin)
dir Josef Mach, 1966, GDR, 92m

DEFA's first Western inverted the Hollywood Western's mythos by making heroes of Indians, seasoned the ideological correctness with a revenge plot and sold eight million tickets in the GDR alone. Serbian sports teacher Gokko Mitic became a star as the heroic Dakota chief. The political certainties aren't completely crude – Mitic seeks vengeance against a renegade Indian who murdered his

father – but the tribe's suffering is sparked by white settlers deranged by rumours of gold in the Black Hills.

The Oil, The Baby And The Transylvanians (Pruncul, petrolul si Ardelenii)
dir Dan Pita, 1981, Rom, 108m

The famous Romanian Red Western – last in a trilogy that started with *The Prophet, The Gold And The Transylvanians* (1977) – tells of three Transylvanian brothers adjusting to frontier life. While the youngest brother awaits a new baby, the fast-drawing middle brother becomes sheriff and big brother finds oil. Dan Pita's curious, parodic film exploits the incongruity of Romanian peasants out West, casting top Romanian actors, speaking dialogue – in English – that sounds borrowed from a 1940s Hollywood Western.

France

French critics have had a long, passionate love affair with the Western. In the 1950s the interest of French intellectuals like **André Bazin** in this most American of genres puzzled many who were unaware that France had begun making Westerns almost as early as America.

Some early American Westerns made more money in France than in the US. Between 1909 and 1911, **Gaston Méliès**, brother of the great cinema pioneer Georges Méliès, made one-reeler Westerns in Chicago and Texas. **Joë Hamman**, a ranch hand who had met Buffalo Bill, starred, usually as Arizona Bill – a homage to his idol? – in 25 Westerns from 1907 to 1912, filmed in Paris and the Camargue region near Marseille. The Camargue offered a good enough facsimile of the American West to be the backdrop for Westerns until the 1970s. The sets weren't quite as credible: in a still from Hamman's *Pendaison à Jefferson City* (*Hanging At*

Jefferson City, 1910) the saloon looks very much like a Parisian café.

World War I effectively killed the early French Western. In 1936, **Jean Renoir** lovingly genuflected to Arizona Bill with the character Arizona Jim in *Le crime de Monsieur Lange*. In the 1950s, critics like Bazin and filmmakers like François Truffaut began extolling the virtues of Ford and Hawks and of films like *Johnny Guitar* (1954).

With Germany and Italy proving, in the 1960s, that the Euro-Western could make money, such enthusiasm inevitably turned into movies. Yet France never found a successful formula or industrial base for Westerns, making them sporadically in the 1960s and 70s, often in collaboration with Italy. Some, like Robert Hossein's *Cemetery Without Crosses* (1969), were French spaghettis; others, like *Les pétroleuses* (*The Petroleum Girls*, 1971), re-created the West for laughs. A few, like Luc Moullet's 1971 take on the Billy the Kid legend, were too bizarre to be categorized. *Soleil rouge* (1971), the most famous French Western from this period – if only for its multinational cast (Ursula Andress, Charles Bronson and Toshiro Mifune!) – may be the worst. A few set trends: Louis Malle's comedy Western *Viva María!* (1965) anticipated the Zapata Westerns of the 1970s.

As the Euro-Western waned, French interest lapsed. But the release of *Blueberry* (2004), an incoherent, intriguing Western loosely derived from a series of French graphic novels, shows the genre has not completely lost its appeal.

The neglect of France's contribution to the Western is surpassed only by the genre's neglect of the role of the French in the West's history. The stereotypical French character in a Western, often called Frenchie, is a prostitute. Despite this, French critics were among the first to take the Western seriously, forcing the rest of the world to re-evaluate the genre.

Viva María!
dir Louis Malle, 1965, Fr/It, 120m

The comedy Western that made Jeanne Moreau a star, *Viva María!* looks back to *Heller In Pink Tights* (1960) and forward to the politicized spaghettis. Moreau and Brigitte Bardot are stars of the circus – with a song-and-dance routine that flirts with striptease – but the gorgeous duo become so indignant at the peasants' plight that they become revolutionaries. Touching on the IRA (Bardot's dad was a member) and the Mexican revolution, this film is an unlikely source for Leone's *Duck, You Sucker* (1971).

Cemetery Without Crosses (Une corde, un Colt)
dir Robert Hossein, 1969, Fr/It, 90m

Robert Hossein directs and stars as the reluctant gunfighter, living alone in a Daliesque ghost town, recalled to arms by his old flame Michèle Mercier to avenge the murder of her husband. The standard spaghetti vengeance plot – complete with hostages – is given a classy treatment in a strong, sinister Western, co-written by Dario Argento, future master of the bloodthirsty *giallo* thrillers.

A Girl Is A Gun (Une aventure de Billy le Kid)
dir Luc Moullet, 1971, Fr, 100m

Stick-thin, in striped pants, with floppy page-boy hair, *nouvelle vague* icon Jean-Pierre Léaud doesn't look like Randolph Scott, but his booming voice makes lines like "I wondered how they found my trail so fast. Now I know, they got a dog" sound both funny ha-ha and funny peculiar. Léaud's gunslinger is aided – or not – by Rachel Kesterber's tanned, blue-eye-shadowed vixen. Moullet called this a marriage of *Duel In The Sun* and Robert Bresson's *Les dames du Bois de Boulogne*. That's stretching it, but this is pleasingly odd.

Germany

There is no more emphatic proof that, as early as the late nineteenth century, the myth of the West was doing strange things to the European imagination than the literary oeuvre of **Karl May**.

Born in poverty in 1842, jailed for fraud, May started writing fiction in prison, eventually penning some twenty adventure novels set in an American West he had never visited though, confusingly, he insisted his stories were based on experience. Books like *Old Surehand* (1894-96), starring Winnetou, an Apache warrior, and Shatterhand, his fair-haired German companion – a more educated version of James Fenimore Cooper's prototypical hero – influenced a generation of Germans, including **Adolf Hitler**. In 1943, with the Russian front going badly, the Führer ordered his generals to read the Winnetou novels, believing it would boost their morale.

Germany's Western movie tradition dates back to the 1930s. In 1932 August Kern made *Der goldene Gletscher*, a Western gold-rush drama; Luis Trenker's *Der Kaiser von Kalifornien* (*The Emperor From California*, 1936) was in the same vein. The German actor Hans Albers starred in two significant 1930s Westerns: the parody *Sergeant Berry* (1938) and *Wasser für Canitoga* (*Water For Canitoga*, 1939), which aspired to Fordian epicness, with Albers as the martyred hero trying to pipe water to a Canadian mining community.

After the war, demand for Westerns was so great that Hollywood films like *The Big Trail* (1930) were re-released, often dubbed and partly reshot with German actors. The real boom in German Westerns started in 1962, when Harald Reinl directed May's *The Treasure Of Silver Lake*, with former Tarzan Lex Barker as Shatterhand and French actor Pierre Brice as his Apache chum. The film was such a hit that a kitsch tongue-in-cheek formula was born with a motley crew of actors – Herbert Lom, Stewart Granger and Charles Aznavour – playing Winnetou or obvious derivatives thereof. These films made such an impact that, in 2002, Michael Herbig's comedy/Western *Manitou's Shoe*, made $28 million at the German box office, despite some sniffy reviews.

Without these "sauerkraut" Westerns (Granger estimates they made $2 million profit just in central Europe and Scandinavia), the Italian studio Cinecittà might never have made Westerns. When the sauerkraut formula turned stale in the late 1960s, some directors mixed sauerkraut and spaghetti in such movies as *Potato Fritz* (1976), a Western that united Hardy Krüger, Stephen Boyd and Paul Breitner, the multi-millionaire Maoist German international footballer.

🎬 Winnetou The Warrior (Winnetou – 1. Teil)
dir Harald Reinl, 1963, W. Ger/Fr/Yug, 91m

The second – and best – of the Winnetou series, with Lex Barker and Pierre Brice on fine form as Karl May's hero and noble savage, though the Croatian landscape is even better. Fans of Peckinpah-style revisionism may find some scenes – notably Barker repelling a horde of bad guys in Tom Mix outfits – hard to take.

India

The term "curry Western" was invented to describe *Sholay* (1975), a tale of hired crooks, gangsters and revenge deliberately patterned on the Western – especially the films of Leone and Peckinpah – and Kurosawa's samurai movies. *Sholay* was so successful at the box office, it made curry Westerns briefly fashionable in the mid-1970s. Feroz Khan, a singing action hero, made a few: *Khotte Sikkey* (1974), *Kala Sona* (1975) and *Kabeela* (1976). Mukul Anand's *Khuda Gawah* (*God Is My Witness*), a tale of revenge, banditry

More violent than many spaghetti Westerns, *Bandit Queen* is a brutal, compelling Indian variation on the outlaw Western.

and love, released in 1992, and Asif Kapadia's *The Warrior* (2001), a spaghetti-meets-*Sholay* affair in which a mercenary renounces his old boss and is hunted through the Himalayas, proved Leone's influence on Indian filmmakers has endured.

Sholay
dir Ramesh Sippy, 1975, Ind, 204m

A milestone in Indian cinema, *Sholay* is an exhilarating mix of strong narrative, cult dialogue and sublime soundtrack. Sanjeev Kumar enlists two crooks (Amitabh Bachchan and Dharmendra) to wreak vengeance on a gangster (Amjad Khan) who has killed most of his family. The crooks are more minded to help when they fall for Kumar's daughter-in-law (Jaya Bhaduri) and local girl Hema Malini. The classic Bollywood conflict of good and evil is played out in stylish comedy, music and dance – including a famous sequence in which Malini dances on glass to save Dharmendra.

Bandit Queen
dir Shekhar Kapur, 1994, Ind/UK, 121m

Initially banned in India for its violence and sexual content – including a harrowing scene in which Phoolan Devi (Seema Biswas), the bandit queen of the title, is gang-raped – this is a bitter indictment of sexism, the caste system and Indian society (the line "she's a woman – and low caste" becomes a recurring motif). The real Devi, a low-caste woman driven to lead her own gang (becoming an outlaw was, for her, a step up in society), was as famous in India as Jesse James was in America. This fine movie's grim, unflinching realism makes this uncomfortable, if compelling, viewing.

Italy

Italy made many fistfuls of dollars from Westerns. In 1968, the peak year for spaghetti Westerns, Italian film exports were worth $50 million, $35 million more than a decade earlier. But Italy's love affair with Westerns dates back to, at least, **Puccini**'s opera *La fanciulla del West* (*The Girl Of The Golden West*, 1911). The first feature-length Italian Western, Carl Koch's *Una signora dell'Ouest*, was made in 1942, while, in the 1950s, violent Wild Bill Hickok B Westerns were popular.

After falling profits from pepla – fake Hollywood epics – the Cinecittà studio was looking for a new formula in the early 1960s when Germany's Winnetou films made a mint. Although **Sergio Leone** hogged most of the glory, he was merely the most talented of a string of Italian Western directors that included Sergio Corbucci, Sergio Sollima, Duccio Tessari, Damiano Damiani, Giuliano Carmineo, Tonino Cervi, Enzio Barboni, Enzo Castellari and Gianfranco Parolini. Although Carlo Lizzani made only two spaghetti Westerns, they bear the imprint of his bandit films, suggesting Italy had its own "wildness" that gave the Wild West mythos greater resonance here than elsewhere.

To Italian filmmakers, mercenaries, gunfighters and bounty hunters were much more interesting than cavalry officers, Indians or sheriffs, as many Italians, certainly on the left, saw their own state as every bit as corrupt, enfeebled and enslaved – either to big business or the CIA – as the stereotypically ineffective spaghetti sheriff.

Critics initially defined these films by their violence. When Burt Kennedy told an incredulous John Ford the Italians were making Westerns, he described them as "No stories, just killing". But Leone Corbucci and Sollima reinvented the Western, changing the genre's rhythms, humour and iconography.

From 1963 to 1969, Italy made Westerns at such a rate that they manufactured the formula to death. In 1968, when Leone effectively bade farewell to the genre with *Once Upon A Time In The West*, critic Andrew Sarris dubbed the Italian Western a violent self-parody, with characters riding around like "portable ammunition dumps".

In the early 1970s, Italian studios desperately invented derivatives – the comedy-spaghetti (the *Trinity* series), the kung-fu spaghetti (*The Stranger And The Gunfighter*, 1974), horror Westerns and spy Westerns. Nothing helped. By the end of the decade, the Italian Western was as moribund as the American Western.

For A Few Dollars More (Per qualche dollari in piu)
dir Sergio Leone, 1965, It, 130m

In the most complex, atmospheric *Dollars* Western – with a clever structure, shorter script and longer pauses – Clint's well-travelled stranger is uneasily teamed with Lee Van Cleef's mysterious major in a search for Gian Maria Volontè's malevolent desperado Indio. Intriguing flashbacks reveal the major's motive for revenge, and Morricone's eeriest theme tinkles recurringly from a pocket watch. Drawing on almost every Western cliché, this brings Leone's themes of the family's civilizing influence and clerical hypocrisy richly into focus.

A Pistol For Ringo (Una pistola per Ringo)
dir Duccio Tessari, 1965, It, 98m

"I warn you, if you kill me while I'm lying here … I'll slit your throat." A few cracking lines, an unusual plot and strong central performances – from Fernando Sancho as the bank robber and Giulano Gemma as anti-hero Ringo – lift this. Ringo infiltrates a gang of bank robbers who have taken hostages on a farm, but can't intervene when the gang start killing them. Ennio Morricone provides an intriguing soundtrack; the sequel, *Il ritorno di Ringo* (1965), contains one of Morricone's finest scores.

Django
dir Sergio Corbucci, 1966, It/Sp, 95m

Mudfighting whores, a coffin-dragging hero, a violin-playing dwarf bartender, a Ku Klux Klan priest forced to eat his own severed ear: Sergio Corbucci's blood-spattered Pop Art spaghetti Western has all these and more. Franco Nero is Django, the mysterious black-coated hero notable for fingerless gloves, a coffin and an anachronistic machine gun. *Django* has inspired many filmmakers – one obvious homage being the ear cutting in *Reservoir Dogs* (1991).

Django was the hero of at least fifty European Westerns, of wildly varying quality, in the 1960s and early 1970s.

Face To Face (Faccia a faccia)
dir Sergio Sollima, 1967, It/Sp, 108m

Proof that not all spaghetti Westerns were cynical style exercises. This is the second, and most thoughtful, of Sollima's Western trilogy – after *The Big Gundown* and before *Run, Man, Run* – that dwelt on anti-Fascist, anti-capitalist themes. Gian Maria Volontè, a depressed history professor seeking rejuvenation out West, rescues outlaw leader Tomas Milian and is seduced by violence. There is a final three-way shoot-out – and Morricone wrote the score – but this is a very different Italian Western.

Kill And Pray (Recquiescant)
dir Carlo Lizzani, 1967, It, 102m

Directed by Carlo Lizzani under the parodic pseudonym Lee Beaver, *Kill And Pray* is a violently entertaining Western with a Marxist message slipped in among the shoot-outs and showdowns. Capitalists order a massacre of townsfolk but young Lou Castel survives in a West peopled by Pier Paolo Pasolini, a revolutionary priest, and Mark Damon, hamming it up as a decadent dandy in a Dracula cloak.

Ace High (I quattro dell'Ave Maria)
dir Giuseppe Colizzi, 1968, It, 132m

Comedy Westerns finally suffocated the Italian Western in about 1976 but this is an entertaining spaghetti spoof. Eli Wallach is essentially Tuco from *The Good, The Bad And The Ugly* (1966), only this time he's licensed to chew scenery. He robs Bud Spencer and Terence Hill of their ill-gotten loot, yet persuades them to help him kill an old enemy. The highlight is the stunning final shoot-out around a roulette wheel.

Death Rides A Horse (Da uomo a uomo)
dir Giulio Petroni, 1968, It, 120m

This starts like a horror movie – with mass murder on a dark, stormy night – and becomes a strange buddy movie, with John Philip Law's traumatized young gunslinger and Lee Van Cleef's veteran pursuing the same criminals. Ennio Morricone's score, full of choral chanting and kettle drums, is superb. With baroque tortures, acid flashbacks and Martian desert landscapes, this is an odd treat.

Keoma
dir Enzo Castellari, 1976, It, 105m

A late classic in a genre ruined by industrialized plagiarism, *Keoma* stars Franco Nero as a half-breed Indian who returns home to find his old town infected by a plague and turned into a veritable concentration camp by landowner Donald O'Brien. The score, by the De Angelis brothers, is shocking. But that's the only flaw in a bloody, entertaining Western that fuses mysticism, *King Lear* and Peckinpah.

Japan

Japan's passion and reverence for the American Western runs deeper than **Akira Kurosawa**'s admiration for **John Ford**. Japan even had its own singing cowboy, Akira Kobayashi, who, in *Rider With A Guitar On The Plains* (1961), saved the Ainu, the indigenous people in Japan who often "stand in" as Native Americans in such movies.

Some directors have been more imaginative. **Kihachi Okamoto**, a Ford fan, used the genre's basic scenarios in his samurai movies and, most especially, his *Desperado* series of war films, where the lone army troop on patrol is attacked by Chinese/Injuns, the Imperial Army is the cavalry and Yuzo Kayama is John Wayne. But when Okamoto went all out for Western thrills in *East Meets West* (1995), the movie never quite took off. Kurosawa's strategy of eschewing outright imitation has been more fruitful.

Kurosawa invented the modern samurai movie with *Seven Samurai* (1954). Although these warriors had been part of Japanese society for 1000 years, they had stayed largely offscreen until Kurosawa's film made a fortune in Japan and was remade, very closely, by John Sturges in *The Magnificent Seven* (1960).

Influenced by *Shane* and *High Noon*, Akira Kurosawa's *Yojimbo* inspired, in turn, *A Fistful Of Dollars*.

Kurosawa admitted *Yojimbo* (1961) had been inspired by *High Noon* (1952) and *Shane* (1953). It, in turn, inspired *A Fistful Of Dollars* (1964), although Leone's homage shades into plagiarism. This cross-fertilization marked the point at which the Japanese Western was most influential – at home and abroad. Japanese filmgoers flocked to see the spaghetti Westerns (or "macaroni Westerns" as they called them)

but their popularity didn't immediately benefit Kurosawa, whose work had inspired them.

Yojimbo
dir Akira Kurosawa, 1961, Jap, 110m, b/w

When Toshiro Mifune's titular hero springs to the aid of harassed villagers, he could be acting heroically, like Shane, or could just be bored. The ambiguity is part of what gives Kurosawa's masterpiece its depth. He had always praised the Western's grammar and, with *Yojimbo*, he proved just how much it influenced him, creating a dusty frontier town that could as easily have been in Utah as Japan.

Mexico

If you imagined Mexico entirely from what you saw in Westerns, you would picture a sweaty country in revolutionary turmoil, populated by sneering villains, red-hot señoritas, gullible cardboard heroes like the **Cisco Kid** and fat men who, between fiestas and enchiladas, might fling a hat in the air and shout "Caramba!" Occasionally, if things weren't spicy enough, **Pancho Villa** would ride into town, fire madly into the air and ride out again, or Zorro would carve a Z into a tree, wall or forehead.

Despite such lazy, racist stereotyping, Mexico has warmed to the Western, only partly because many American Westerns, from the 1950s on, were shot there to save money. In the late 1960s/early 1970s, in an odd piece of cultural appropriation, Italian directors like **Sergio Corbucci** made Mexico's revolution a metaphor for an Italian nation they saw as beguiled, corrupted and dominated by Yankee imperialism. Bizarrely, even in the American Western, Pancho Villa and his fellow Mexican revolutionaries were usually glorified in such films as *Viva Villa!* (1934, with Wallace Beery as Villa), *Juarez* (1939, with Paul Muni as Benito Juarez), *Viva Zapata!* (1952, with Brando as Emiliano Zapata) and *Villa Rides* (1968).

As you might expect, Mexican cinema has been obsessed by the country's 1911 revolution

Zapata Westerns

Italian Westerns were routinely scathing about authority figures and the Church, America's traditional allies in Italian society, and in movies that Corbucci called "Zapata Westerns" – after the Mexican revolutionary leader Emiliano Zapata – directors used the Mexican revolution as an allegory of Yankee imperialism past and present.

 ### A Bullet For The General (¿Quién sabe?)
dir Damiano Damiani, 1966, It, 135m

In Damiano Damiani's politicized spaghetti Western, American involvement in the Mexican revolution is analogous to CIA interference in Latin America. Lou Castel is the gringo ostensibly helping Mexican bandit El Chuncho (Gian Maria Volontè) but secretly betraying the revolution. Klaus Kinski thoroughly enjoys himself as a deranged priest/bandit.

 ### Companeros
dir Sergio Corbucci, 1970, It, 118m

In Sergio Corbucci's tale of arms dealing in the Mexican revolution, Jack Palace stars as a villain with a wooden hand and a carnation who feeds his Mexican victims to his falcon – a none too subtle metaphor for American imperialism. But Corbucci keeps the action coming, with a late, intense battle scene. Evil as Palance – and by extension America – is, the other characters are almost as flawed.

 ### Duck, You Sucker (Giù la testa)
dir Sergio Leone, 1971, It, 157m (restored version)

Once you get over Rod Steiger's over-acting as a cigar-chomping peasant, *Duck, You Sucker* is an entertaining romp, enlivened by James Coburn's fine turn as the IRA terrorist fleeing his past in Mexico. Eccentric, parodic, left-wing, revisionist – is the contest between federales and revolutionaries a replay of Nazis vs. Italian partisans? – with a self-satirizing score by Ennio Morricone, Leone's Zapata Western was badly cut on release.

– contemporaneous with the birth of movies in Mexico – and the 1867 revolutionary prequel, in which Emperor Maximilian was overthrown and executed. Less predictable is the industry's discovery of that artificial Hollywood stereotype, the singing cowboy. Fernando de Fuentes' *Allá en el rancho grande* (*Out On The Big Ranch*, 1936) made a star of Tito Guizar, inspired countless imitations and defined a new genre, the "charro" Western, in which the stereotypes weren't any more realistic – golden-hearted bandits and gorgeous señoritas – but were home made.

From the 1940s, Mexico churned out Westerns, dominating the Spanish-speaking market, and developing its own Clint Eastwood, **Rodolfo de Anda**, star of the *El Texano* films of the 1960s and 70s. But the Mexican Western didn't attract much

El Mariachi, Robert Rodriguez's debut feature, is a quirky Mexican spin on the mistaken identity Western.

critical attention until 1971 when Chilean mov-iemaker **Alejandro Jodorowsky** made *El Topo* (see p.134), probably one of the most remarkable Westerns ever made, in Mexico with Mexican money. In 1972, de Anda made his directorial debut with *Indio*, starring Emilio Fernandez, probably the most famous Mexican movie star.

The next Mexican director to earn international acclaim for a Western was **Robert Rodriguez**, who started his Leone-style trilogy with *El Mariachi* in 1992. The first two instalments – *El Mariachi* and *Desperado* (1995), with Antonio Banderas as Mariachi – impressed, but the third, *Once Upon A Time In Mexico* (2003), was more mainstream and less inventive.

Allá en el rancho grande (Out On The Big Ranch)
dir Fernando de Fuentes, 1936, Mex, 95m, b/w

Fernando de Fuentes' escapist singing cowboy movie, starring Tito Guizar, is a fine example of the *comedia ranchera* (ranch comedy). Blending Cinderella and cockfighting, this was the first Mexican movie to sell overseas and inspired many clones. Fuentes remade it in 1948 with Jorge Negrete as the likeable ranch hand.

El Mariachi
dir Robert Rodriguez, 1992, Mex/US, 81m

The only Mexican Western to help reduce cholesterol – director Robert Rodriguez was so desperate to raise funds for his debut he earned $3000 as a human lab rat for a cholesterol-reducing drug – *El Mariachi* is a bold, expressive, independent Western. Two men in black arrive in a small town – one with guns, the other with a guitar – in an inventive spin on the mistaken identity Western.

Russia

Joseph Stalin, according to his protégé and successor Nikita Khruschev, "liked cowboy movies.

He used to curse them and give them their proper ideological evaluation but then immediately order new ones."

The real mystery is that Stalin didn't have more homegrown Soviet Westerns to admire. Apart from Canada, Russia is the only major filmmaking nation to have an American-style frontier, with native tribes hunting reindeer and living in a local variant of the tepee (the yurt), and an epic, wild, landscape. It's just that in Russia's case, that frontier, Siberia, has been too cold to provide a suitable backdrop for a breed of Soviet Western.

In the 1920s, when Lenin permitted small private business in the New Economic Policy, American movies became briefly fashionable. Cowboys appeared in a few Soviet films, notably *The Extraordinary Adventures Of Mr West In The Land Of the Bolsheviks* (1924). In the late 1920s, the great **Sergei Eisenstein** wrote a script from Blaise Cendrars' gold rush novel *L'Or*, and tried, in a disastrous sojourn in Hollywood, to film it. However, by 1929, with Lenin dead, the Soviet film industry was being ordered to end the "cult of Americanism".

But the Western's simple division of good and evil appealed to Stalin and his apparat-chiks. Many directors drew on the Russian Civil War to make Western-style movies set on the steppes or in Soviet Asia (where Bolshevik troops had fought Islamic rebels). With the Volga standing in for the Rio Grande and the Urals a less iconic Monument Valley, these films (now called Osterns, or Red Westerns) celebrated ideological pioneers taming a wild frontier. The most successful was *White Sun Of The Desert* (1970), though Nikita Mikhalkov's *At Home Among Strangers* (1974), a Civil War action story with a buddy movie feel and stunts recalling *Butch Cassidy And The Sundance Kid*, was a smash. In similar vein, Samvel Gasparov reworked *The Searchers* with *Hatred* (1975) and the town–taming Western with *The Sixth One* (1981), while Ali Khamraev's *The Bodyguard* (1979) paid homage to Anthony Mann, with

its tale of a grizzled trapper escorting a prisoner set against fierce landscapes.

The collapse of Communism gave spaghetti director Enzo Castellari the chance to make an intriguing Russian spaghetti called *Jonathan Of*

Westerns ho!

Even in countries that haven't consistently produced Westerns, the genre has intrigued filmmakers. The spaghetti Western inspired Turkish aficionados to create *Vur* (1972), a violent, action-packed Western featuring bounty hunters, a sexy female gunslinger and a boss who won't stay dead. Here are five intriguing Westerns from remote parts of the globe.

Cacique Bandeira (The Dead Man)
dir Héctor Olivera, 1975, Argentina/Sp, 104m

Any doubt that Leone influenced this movie, adapted from a story by Jorge Luis Borges, is blown away in the swirling, operatic finale. But Héctor Olivera is subtler as he recalls the Uruguayan civil war of the late nineteenth century and its outlaw hero Benjamin Ortalora before that full-blown Latin American spaghetti showdown.

O cangaceiro (The Bandit)
dir Lima Barreto, 1953, Brazil, 105m, b/w

An intriguing Cannes-prize-winning Brazilian Western in which bandit leader Alberto Ruschel falls for Marisa Prado, the schoolteacher his gang has kidnapped, and helps her escape. The film is mostly a prolonged chase but it's beautifully shot by H.E. Fowley, and Barreto pays homage to Ford and Kurosawa, while drawing on Brazil's mythos about the bandits of the *sertao*, the arid plains in the northeast of the country.

Tears Of The Black Tiger (Fah talai jone)
dir Wisit Sasanatieng, 2000, Thai, 110m

"Paint your dragon, cowboy": Philip French's review

of this kitsch Thai Western sums it up in four words. Wisit Sasanatieng certainly knows his Westerns, paying homage to Peckinpah, Leone and Sam Raimi's *The Quick And The Dead* (1995) in his tale of a bandit, Black Tiger, his estranged girlfriend and a lovestruck policeman who wants to whisk her away in his MG. *Tears Of The Black Tiger* is a truly bizarre blend of acid Western, postmodern irony, campy melodrama and romantic tearjerker.

Utu
dir Geoff Murphy, 1983, NZ, 104m

With its tale of a Maori scout (Anzac Wallace) in the British Army's service who seeks revenge on his employers after discovering a village the colonial troops have massacred, *Utu* – the word roughly means revenge or retribution – is a Kiwi *Ulzana's Raid*. Wallace goes from hero to killer, attacking a remote farm – and murdering a woman – provoking homesteader Williamson (Bruno Lawrence) to seek revenge. Sometimes let down by a flawed script, *Utu* is redeemed by its dramatic power and by its inspiring anti-hero Wallace, a reformed armed robber in real life.

Utvandrarna (The Emigrants)
dir Jan Troell, 1971, Swe, 151m

Max von Sydow and Liv Ullmann are magnificent as the Swedish peasants who, tired of poor land and scarce crops, emigrate to Minnesota. Jan Troell's film is a powerful reminder of how hype and hope were qualified by the reality of frontier life and of the emigrant/immigrant experience, a part of the West's history too often overlooked. The sequel, *Nybyggarna* (1972), is good, but not as powerful.

The Bears (1994). But economic crises killed the Red Western – and revisionist versions thereof – as Russian film production plummeted to a tenth of pre-*glasnost* levels.

📽 White Sun Of The Desert (Beloe solntse pustyni)
dir Vladimir Motyl, 1970, Rus, 85m

This unusual blend of comedy, action, music and drama is consciously modelled on Italian Westerns. Anatoly Kuznetsov is the lone hero of the Revolution who, travelling home through the central Asian deserts, inherits a harem abandoned by a renegade Muslim leader. He tries to protect them and instruct them in the ways of women's liberation, with predictably amusing consequences. The film was so popular that some lines – notably "The East is a subtle matter" – became folk sayings.

📽 A Man From Boulevard Des Capuchines (Chelovek s bulvara Kaputsinov)
dir Alla Surikova, 1987, Rus, 99m

Ukrainian film director Alla Surikova acquired an international reputation with this entertaining, daringly postmodern Western parody. Andrei Mironov enthrals a sleepy Wild West town with his Chaplinesque film shows, civilizing the townsfolk and intriguing the Comanche so much that they go to war just to gain admission.

Spain

Spain's greatest gift to the genre is not the paella Western but Almeria, where Leone and other directors re-created and redefined the American West. Hotel owners did better out of the spaghetti Western boom than Spain's filmmakers.

Ironically, the most obvious precursor of the spaghetti Western, *Gunfight At Red Sands* (1963), was directed by a Spaniard, **Ricardo Blasco**. Shot in a town that Leone would use, by Massimo Dallamano, director of photography on the *Dollars* movies, it starred Richard Harrison, later to play spaghetti hero Ringo, and featured an Ennio Morricone score. The film provided the blueprint for the revolution ahead; its obscurity typifies the general critical neglect of Spanish Westerns.

The neglect was not entirely undeserved. Many Spanish Westerns tried to obscure a lack of budget with novelty. Eugenio Martin's *The Ugly Ones* (1966) merely proves that, as a spectacle, old ladies getting dragged behind horses pales after a while. Rising from the mire are Julio Buchs' *A Bullet For Sandoval* (aka *Desperate Men*, 1969), an atmospheric tale of inter-generational conflict starring Ernest Borgnine, and *Trinity Sees Red* (1970), a rare Western from the versatile Mario Camus. Alex de la Iglesia's comedy Western *800 Bullets* (2002) affectionately recalls this era, with Sancho Gracia as a stuntman who once wore Clint's poncho now reduced to falling off roofs for tourists.

Some Spanish cineastes insist Leone was influenced by **Joaquín Luis Romero Marchent**. The Spanish director started making Westerns in the 1950s but is chiefly famous for the bloody abandon of *Cut Throats Nine* (1973), so violent it makes *The Wild Bunch* (1969) look genteel.

📽 Gunfight At Red Sands (Duello nel Texas)
dir Ricardo Blasco, 1963, Sp, 95m

Blasco's only major Western that didn't feature Zorro, *Gunfight At Red Sands* is a decently made European Western worth watching as a historical curio. Blasco had all the ingredients – an American actor (Richard Harrison), a spaghetti plot (Harrison seeks vengeance on the gang that murdered his family), a Morricone score, the setting – but didn't cook them as well as Leone.

Over The Horizon: the wider picture

HBO's compelling, foul-mouthed drama *Deadwood* has single-handedly revived the TV Western.

Over The Horizon:
the wider picture

There's more to Westerns than movies: the genre has graced the small screen, inspired some seriously underrated fiction and music, and prompted a slew of intriguing websites...

TV series

Mention of the TV Western conjures up a few clichéd images: Leif Erickson standing straight-backed on his porch in *The High Chaparral*, Michael Landon weeping in *Little House On The Prairie*, Ian McShane swearing in *Deadwood*.

Yet the TV Western has been more varied than these memories might suggest. The series range from famous, predictable but quality oaters like *Wagon Train* to more challenging programmes (like *Deadwood*), and *Howdy Doody*, starring a cowboy puppet with 48 freckles – which, in 1954, was one for every state in the union! Ethnic minorities got a look in (with *The Cisco Kid*), as did women (with *Annie Oakley*), in what can only be described, in a terrible pun, as a bonanza for fans of the genre.

The first TV Westerns, like *Hopalong Cassidy*, were straight B-movie transplants. But from the mid-1950s, the TV Western grew more adult, a trend that peaked with *Have Gun, Will Travel*, in which Richard Boone's pseudonymous do-gooding hero Paladin quoted Socrates, Shelley and Shakespeare. Later producers sought to ring the changes, introducing such novelty series as *Kung Fu* and *Dr Quinn, Medicine Woman*. David Milch's *Deadwood*, a critical and commercial hit in 2004, has signalled a mini-revival on the range.

Here's a selection of the best, most significant, or unusual TV Westerns. Sadly, *Howdy Doody* doesn't make the cut. *Hopalong Cassidy*'s star William Boyd is profiled on p.152.

Bonanza
1959–73

In Barry Levinson's *Tin Men* (1987), comedian Jackie Gayle is obsessed with *Bonanza*, its lack of realism and the fact that none of the four central male characters ever talk about women. Such sacrilegious thoughts seldom occurred to anyone at the time. Ben Cartwright (**Lorne Greene**) had lost three wives to childbirth, Indians and horses so he might have had reservations about a fourth. Son Adam (**Pernell Roberts**) would have been quite a catch, for all his truculence. Little Joe (**Michael Landon**) did marry but his wife immediately died. As for Hoss (**Dan Blocker**), if his name really was Norwegian for "good luck", it was a shame that good fortune never transformed his love life.

After Greene chewed out the producers so that the Cartwrights didn't take aim at every stranger on the horizon, *Bonanza* became a well-made, bland, self-satisfied, comforting series for viewers who found *Gunsmoke* too gritty and didn't mind that, for such a likeable bunch, the Cartwrights were strangely prone to being wrongly charged with murder.

Not all of their adventures were predictable. Lucky Hoss saw a fake leprechaun, Ben tended Vera Miles, who'd been bitten by a rabid wolf, and Little Joe turned hippie briefly. There have been one-off prequels and sequels but, for a series about a 40-year-old dad and three 30-year-old sons, *Bonanza* had quite a run.

In *Deadwood*, Ian McShane pleads for some dialogue that doesn't rhyme with trucker.

Deadwood
2004–

Even by the salty standards of HBO (*The Sopranos, Sex And The City*), the sensational, sepia-toned Western series devised by *NYPD Blue*'s David Milch is notorious for the highest rate of political incorrectness and profanity in serial drama yet. (Apparently, the f-word alone is heard on average 91.6 times per episode.) Happily it is also wildly acclaimed for reinvigorating the genre. Set in the Black Hills of Dakota from 1876, and meticulously researched, *Deadwood* collects a dizzying ensemble of historical and fictitious outlaws and opportunists in the squalid mining camp swollen on gold fever, liquor and licentiousness.

The nominal good guy in a huge, terrific cast is **Timothy Olyphant**'s shopkeeper sheriff Seth Bullock, whose moral dilemmas are routinely manipulated by **Ian McShane**'s vile, fascinating villain Al Swearengen, who presides over the Gem saloon-brothel and most of the power struggles, swindles and murderous activities. Robin Weigert's filthy, foul-mouthed Calamity Jane is a mean drunk with an impulsively tender heart. Characters die with electrifying unpredictability (the historically inevitable but sudden loss of **Keith Carradine**'s Wild Bill Hickok shocked audiences as much as it did townsfolk), and in its high-calibre writing and direction, its poetic turns of phrase, its dramatic confrontations, *Deadwood* exudes power, passion, greed, corruption and human frailties on a Shakespearean scale.

Gunsmoke
1955–75

Is *Gunsmoke* the best TV Western ever? It was certainly the longest running. John Wayne introduced the first episode and *Gunsmoke* usually had the moral certainty of a formula John Wayne Western although, as the Duke pointed out, it was "honest, adult, realistic".

Marshal Matt Dillon (played by **James Arness**, recommended by Wayne, who probably turned down the part) was the show's good-humoured, capable, law-abiding hero, saving the day, winning

The quartet at the heart of *Gunsmoke*: a marshal (Matt Dillon), a saloon girl (Amanda Blake), a sidekick (Ken Curtis) and the doc (Milburn Stone).

showdowns and helping troubled wayfarers. His motto, whenever trouble brewed, was "If you're gonna use that gun, you better start on me."

Like Wayne in his later movies, Dillon had a surrogate family: saloon proprietor Miss Kitty (Amanda Blake), no-nonsense Doc Adams (Milburn Stone), excitable limping deputy Chester B. Goode (Dennis Weaver) and Festus, a Gabby Hayes-style comic deputy played by Ken Curtis.

John Meston, who had helped produce the radio show *Gunsmoke*, oversaw the series' first five years on TV. For some aficionados, this was the golden era, when the show had a real flavour of the Old West. Dillon opened early episodes with a sermon from Boot Hill on killing and being killed and Miss Kitty, later respectable, was a prostitute who dallied with the marshal. In the early years, the show, calling on writers like **Sam Peckinpah**, touched on child abuse, rape, slavery, prostitution and murderers who killed for thrills. Ironically, in the 1970s Blake complained the show had less room to comment on social issues in Nixon's America than in Eisenhower's day.

By creating America's favourite surrogate family – before the Waltons – *Gunsmoke* could explore the community life of an outpost of civilization. Typically the arrival of a stranger would raise issues, threaten the peace or pose questions which could be dealt with through compassion or, reluctantly, the gun. Often the show offered no easy answers, its ambiguous endings something of a risk for a show chasing Nielsen ratings.

Gunsmoke was finally cancelled – a false alarm in 1967 had led to questions in Congress – in 1975, not because its ratings had dipped, but because its audience was too old to appeal to advertisers. Dillon had been the last Western lawman standing on the small screen. His retirement sounded the death knell for the TV Western.

Have Gun, Will Travel
1957–63

CBS originally wanted laconic icon Randolph Scott to play the part of Paladin, the gunslinging knight-errant with a high IQ, a fondness for dropping literary references into conversation and a mission: to leave his lavish San Francisco hotel suite and seek justice on behalf of anyone that paid him $1000.

But Scott was too busy so **Richard Boone** relished the chance to play a completely different kind of Western hero. His trademark ruffled shirt and expensive brandy were replaced, in each episode, by an unusual – for a Western – do-gooding outfit of black, with silver conches on his hat and a silver knight motif on his holster. Apart from Boone, the only other regular character was a Chinese minion called Hey Boy (Kam Tong) who, when the actor was busy, was replaced by a girl called Hey Girl (Lisa Lu).

Probably the only Western where you could see a gunfight and improve your classical education (how many other heroes had names inspired by Charlemagne's court?), *Have Gun, Will Travel* was unusual and sophisticated enough to attract a relatively large female audience. Paladin often rode to the aid of minorities, giving the justice system a kick up the pants when necessary. He hung up his spurs in 1963 – Boone felt he had been to the same well too often. But he had created an existentialist Western that was an obvious inspiration for **Clint Eastwood**'s vigilante cop thriller *Magnum Force* (1973).

The High Chaparral
1967–71

The High Chaparral was *Bonanza* for liberals. Rancher John Cannon (**Leif Erickson**) was as honest as a day on the range was long, his

Ishi: The Last Of His Tribe

Today, when every TV movie contains at least one of the original Charlie's Angels, it's hard to believe the format was once used to tell stories that couldn't be cut up into thirty-minute chunks. Sadly, gems like *Ishi: The Last Of His Tribe* (1978) are rarely rerun even as late-night schedule fillers.

Scripted by **Dalton Trumbo** and then, after his death, by his son Christopher, this 150-minute TV movie beautifully tells the true story of how the last surviving member of the Yahi tribe was discovered by an anthropologist (played by **Dennis Weaver**) in California in 1911. The tribe's decline is told in flashback as Weaver befriends the last Yahi, learns the Ishi language (much of the film is sub-titled) and confronts a personal and historical tragedy. It's easy to see why *The Washington Post* called this "one of the best ten TV movies ever made".

The same story was told again, less compellingly, in a big-budget cable TV movie *The Last Of His Tribe* (1992), with Jon Voight as the anthropologist and Native Canadian actor Graham Greene as the last of his tribe.

Mexican wife Victoria (Linda Cristal) was beautiful and dignified, his brother Nuck (Cameron Mitchell) and brother-in-law Manolito (Henry Darrow) were essentially loveable rogues, while son Blue (Mark Slade) was eye candy.

The High Chaparral broke several boundaries. It was the first prime-time Western to give two lead roles to Hispanic actors (Cristal and Darrow) and was much more even-handed in its portrayal of the Apaches, acknowledging the legitimacy of their grievances over the loss of land. The series was shot on the range and had a grimy reality that rivals never had. The show widened its range of dramatic possibilities by admitting that, deep down, several of its strong, varied, cast of characters couldn't stand each other. Erickson is usually seen as the patriarchal paragon of virtue but his marriage to Victoria was, initially, one of convenience, saving him from going flat broke.

The series lost something when gormless Blue was replaced by a character with the plain daft name of Wind. Aficionados insist that, as the series wore on, Cristal became fixated with plucking her eyebrows, an obsession which signalled a decline in the show's quality.

Kung Fu
1972–75

There has been nothing quite like *Kung Fu* on television before or since. An Eastern Western, starring **David Carradine** as a warrior monk with a lethal brand of pacifism, it is still remembered, celebrated, parodied today.

Inevitably, given the series' combination of martial-arts action, Taoist mysticism and the American West, **Quentin Tarantino** was a big fan, showing episodes at a revenge movie marathon in Austin, Texas, before casting Carradine as Bill in his *Kill Bill* films.

Kung Fu was brilliantly timed. It was just ahead of the public's discovery of martial arts, a year after Japanese actor Toshiro Mifune had starred as a samurai in the French/Italian Western *Soleil rouge*, and able to capitalize on foreign interest in Bruce Lee's kung fu movies.

Sometimes, the scripts simply served to suggest why east and west should never meet. But the slow-motion sequences, Jim Helms' eerie score, lush cinematography (by TV standards) and Carradine's nuanced, underplayed hero helped give *Kung Fu* a flavour of its own. As Kwai Chang Caine (aka Grasshopper), Carradine spoke very slowly – possibly to lighten the burden for script-writers instructed by network censors to strictly ration out the ass-kicking sequences – in a low-key style that minimized the embarrassment of lines like "The eagle flies high, yet the mouse scuffles fearfully". He quit, killing the series, in 1975, by which time comedians had reduced the "when you can take this pebble from my hand, grasshopper…" shtick to a million punchlines.

The Lazarus Man
1996

All previous cases of morning-after-the-night-before syndrome pale beside that suffered by **Robert Ulrich**, who awakes in a grave with no idea who he is, several stab wounds, a vague rec-ollection of a gorgeous brunette and a nagging feeling that he was recently beaten over the head in the theatre where Abraham Lincoln was shot. Calling himself Lazarus, he tries to secure his future by unlocking the mystery of his past.

That was the startling premise for one of the most original Westerns ever to grace the small screen. Producer Dick Beebe called it "*The Fugitive* meets *The X Files* meets *Bonanza*". Though the storyline – and the vibe – harked back to the left-for-dead amnesiac in the 1960s Western series *A Man Called Shenandoah*, this is steeped in the kind of melancholy you find in certain late 1960s/early 1970s movie Westerns, a mood accentuated by the soundtrack, built entirely around a single plaintive note.

Sadly, Ulrich's announcement that he had cancer prompted the network to cancel the show, so though we learned that he was one of Lincoln's bodyguards – and that the conspiracy to assassinate Lincoln was masterminded by a sinister major – we never found out much more. Ulrich died in 2002.

The Lone Ranger
1949–75

Let's clear one thing up straightaway: "Kemo sabe", as Tonto calls the Lone Ranger, does not mean "horse's ass". That idea may have origi-nated in a jokey suggestion in a Gary Larson cartoon. If anything, "kemo sabe" means "scout". Which does confuse things rather, as Tonto's horse is called Scout.

The partnership between the Lone Ranger (usually **Clayton Moore**, but **John Hart** had the role for a season) and Tonto (**Jay Silverheels**) is more equal than that between Batman and Robin, Holmes and Watson or the Cisco Kid and Pancho. Tonto may speak broken English but he's not stupid, helping his wounded buddy, tracking miscreants and unearthing vital information.

Moore and Silverheels are good enough to obscure the series' serious flaws – acting that sinks below B-movie standards, phoney outdoor sets, and plots so repetitive that the pistol shots rang out at the same time each episode. But the Lone Ranger had a superhero costume and morality, a great theme – courtesy of Rossini's *William Tell* – and always defeated the bad guy.

The heroic duo rode onto the big screen in *The Lone Ranger* (1956), followed by *The Lone Ranger And The Lost City Of Gold* (1958). The utter failure of a 1981 remake, *The Legend Of The Lone Ranger*, was hailed as karmic pay-off for the producers who had sued Moore to stop him wearing the black mask at personal appearances.

Tonto shows the Lone Ranger how to track a villain.
Silver looks distinctly unimpressed.

Lonesome Dove
1989

This beloved adaptation of **Larry McMurtry**'s weighty novel single-handedly revived the Western. Winning seven Emmys (a record for a mini-series) and, unusually for a Western, drawing a larger number of female viewers than male, *Lonesome Dove* was the TV event of 1989.

Robert Duvall makes the most of his all-time favourite role as rascally adventurer Augustus McCrae, buddy of terse, tyrannical Woodrow Call (Tommy Lee Jones), a spiritual descendant of some of John Wayne's darker loners. (Indeed, McMurtry had originally written the story in 1971 as a movie script, hoping Wayne would play Call alongside James Stewart as McCrae.) Former Texas Rangers, bored with the peaceful life, they embark on an epic cattle trail to Montana, encountering formidable rancher Anjelica Huston and traumatized saloon whore Diane Lane. The multiple sub-plots include hardship, horse-stealing, hanging and heroism. But finally Call returns, chastened, realizing that behind his dream of a cattleman's paradise lies, to play off his parting words of disillusionment, a vision of hell.

Maverick
1957–62

This comedy adventure Western launched **James Garner** on his career as, in Kim Newman's words, "the undisputed master of the light Western". As dandy, unflappable Bret Maverick, Garner was a charming, relaxed chancer, whose worst intentions were let down by the fact that he was, secretly, quite decent, and who always had a quote from "pappy" to justify anything he did. The persona served him well on the big screen and as chivalrous private eye Jim Rockford.

The show perfectly suited Garner's gifts – the episodes which dwelt solely on his brother Burt (Jack Kelly) or even his cousin Beauregard (Roger Moore) were never quite as entertaining – but *Maverick* was more than a star turn. Episodes were directed by André De Toth, Budd Boetticher and Gordon Douglas, while Robert Altman was one of the writers.

Maverick had a confident feel for Western clichés and liked to spoof them, notably in *Bolt From The Blue*, Altman's inspired send-up of the anti-lynching classic *The Ox-Bow Incident* (1943). Forced to concede there ought to be a trial before they hang Moore (wrongly) for horse stealing, the locals are cock-a-hoop when the judge dispenses with witnesses, cross-examinations and juries to find Moore guilty.

The show ended in 1962, still in reasonable nick, perhaps because the writers had finally decided they couldn't come up with any more dialogue beginning "My pappy used to say…".

Rawhide
1959–66

There's more to *Rawhide* than Frankie Laine's "rollin', rollin', rollin'…" theme and the discovery of **Clint Eastwood** as an actor. For a start, most fans agree that trail boss Gil Favor (**Eric Fleming**) was the show's focal point and, although Clint became a bona fide Western legend, the continual cattle trail wasn't as compelling when Eastwood's trailhand Rowdy Yates took charge.

Rawhide prided itself on its gritty realism but that didn't stop the producers importing a slew of celebrity guest stars (including Dean Martin, Barbara Stanwyck, Lon Chaney Jr and Frankie Avalon) and, for the most part, making effective use of them. In the episode *The Captain's Wife*, Stanwyck is a Western Lady Macbeth, endangering the fort, herself and her husband's career with her insane ambition. The series wasn't afraid to exploit the wriggle room created by pro-Native-American Westerns like *Broken Arrow* (1950), exposing, in *Incident Of Iron Bull*, the bloodlust and racism among some cavalry and settlers.

Rawhide may have essentially been *Red River* without the oedipal undertones (or the budget – Favor's herd never seemed large enough for him to make a good living) but it was hugely popular. When Ronald Reagan was elected president, his secret service codename was Rawhide.

Wagon Train
1957–65

The quintessential Western from the genre's golden age on the small screen, *Wagon Train* made grumpy **Ward Bond** – as the wagon master perennially heading West in the 1870s – into a Western icon. For a show fondly remembered as fine family entertainment, *Wagon Train* featured a surprising amount of torture and often seemed to be looking for an excuse for its male stars to bare their chests. The show was never quite as good after Bond died (in 1960) and his scout Robert Horton left the series (in 1962), but it was so well regarded that stars of the calibre of Bette Davis and Ernest Borgnine were happy to guest.

As the series was inspired by **John Ford's** *Wagon Master*, it was only fitting he should direct an episode – *The Colter Craven Story*, broadcast in 1960. John Wayne starred as General Sherman, John Carradine, another Ford regular, had a guest role, and Ford's son-in-law Ken Curtis was given a small part. The episode, which dwelt on

In *Rawhide*, the cattle herd was too small to keep Clint Eastwood and Eric Fleming busy, so they took up defeating villains as a hobby.

cowardice, so pleased the producers that they thought about running Ford's original 72-minute cut as two episodes. Tamer heads prevailed and the network cut 15 minutes.

Books

Movie books

The BFI Companion To The Western
ed. Edward Buscombe (BFI, 1988)

Essential reference guide to the Western and the West, offering insightful commentary on movies, TV series, personnel and, crucially, the West itself.

The Crowded Prairie
Michael Coyne (I.B. Tauris, 1997)

A witty, incisive, informed read that uses the Western as a barometer of American values, illuminating both the nation's politics and the movies he explores. Coyne offers an unusual explanation for the death of the Western – it was the Vietnam War that did it.

The Encyclopedia Of Westerns
Herb Fagen (Checkmark, 2003)

A generous, authoritative, reasonably comprehensive directory of Westerns, with the occasional review enlightened by the author's own interviews. Would be better still if it treated spaghetti Westerns more seriously.

Gunfighter Nation
Richard Slotkin (University of Oklahoma Press, 1992)

Like Coyne's *The Crowded Prairie*, this uses the Western as part of a wider inquiry into America's self-image in which JFK is a pivotal reference point. This might sound dry but, on the way, such Western icons as the Virginian, William S. Hart and Shane are entertainingly deconstructed.

Horizons West
Jim Kitses (BFI, 2004)

Academic, but thought-provoking, study of the genre's greatest directors. The appreciation of Budd Boetticher's canon is worth the cover price alone.

The Six-Gun Mystique
John G. Cawelti (Bowling Green Press, 1971)

A scholarly, thoughtful, dense critique of the Western which moved one reader to ask on Amazon: "Now that Jacques Derrida's dead can't we stop reading stuff like this?" That's a tad harsh but this isn't a book to be read late at night when you're feeling drowsy.

Spaghetti Westerns
Christopher Frayling (I.B. Tauris, 1998)

This expanded second edition of Frayling's essential guide is the definitive book on what is, critically, still a neglected part of the genre. Not always that easy to read, though.

Western Film
Brian Garfield (Da Capo, 1982)

Thorough, terribly opinionated, sometimes predictably wrong-headed, often unpredictably radical, this is a good read, marred by a dismissive attitude to the Italian Western.

The Western Reader
ed. Jim Kitson, Gregg Rickman (Limelight, 1998)

An intriguing anthology. Among some fine scholarly interpretation are reasonably enlightening interviews with the likes of Anthony Mann and Clint Eastwood.

Westerns
Philip French (Carcanet Film, 2005)

A classic critical guide when first published in 1973, this suffers from the accumulation – not integration – of too many subsequent developments and movies. It's still one of a handful of books that are indispensable to any aficionado.

Wild West Movies
Kim Newman (Bloomsbury, 1990)

A funny, sharp tour of the major Western themes and some of the genre's stranger detours, infused by Newman's enthusiasm, knowledge and knack for finding intriguing parallels. Priceless.

Biographies

The New Biographical Dictionary Of Film
David Thomson (Little, Brown, 2004)

An inspiring, witty primer – although you'll violently disagree with him at times.

Clint: The Life And Legend
Patrick McGilligan (HarperCollins, 1999)

Not for starry-eyed Clint fans, this exposes the star as, in the words of *The Daily Mail*, "a violent, compulsive sexual predator who cheated on his wife for 25 years and forced Sondra Locke to have abortions". Presenting Clint as a real anti-hero, it offers an entertaining, if poisonous, insight into the man and his movies.

Gary Cooper: American Hero
Jeffrey Myers (Aurum, 2005)

Entertaining, detailed biography of the genre's most enigmatic hero. Myers doesn't miss much – the affairs, the politics, the movies are all in here – yet he doesn't make you feel you're much closer to understanding Coop.

James Stewart
Donald Dewey (Time Warner, 1997)

An intelligent, well-researched, sympathetic – but not uncritical – biography, with its fair share of revelations, this is particularly good on the films, which are given separate treatment at the appropriate point in his life rather than, as so often, condensed into the life story.

John Wayne: The Politics Of Celebrity
Garry Wills (Faber, 1997)

A provocative, critical, yet appreciative biography of the Western's greatest icon. Not a conventional "and then he did this…" biography, yet all the better for it as Wills destroys quite a few myths about Wayne and the Western.

Last Of The Cowboy Heroes
Robert Nott (McFarland, 2000)

An insightful appreciation of three of the genre's underrated heroes – Audie Murphy, Randolph Scott and Joel McCrea – that dwells, in detail, on the final Westerns they made in the 1950s, often for Budd Boetticher who writes the foreword.

Robert Mitchum: Baby, I Don't Care
Lee Server (St Martins Press, 2001)

A beautifully written, entertaining biography. Server is helped by the fact that Mitchum's life is more interesting than most but he makes the most of his material in chapters with such fine headings as "The Ferret-Faced Kid" and "Our Horseshit Salesman". A classic.

Sam Peckinpah: "If They Move … Kill 'Em"
David Weddle (Faber, 1994)

A gung-ho biography of the Western's most turbulent genius, packed with great quotes, incidents and perceptive comment. Indispensable.

Searching For John Ford
Joseph McBride (Faber, 2003)

The definitive biography of the Western's great sentimental sadist. McBride met Ford and the experience – along with 125 interviews – gives his portrait conviction and authority. For Fordians there are plenty of treats here: the hysterically funny list of "improved" titles for *The Quiet Man* that the studio tried to foist on him; an illuminating look at most of the films and a considered re-evaluation of the director's "heroic" conduct during the Hollywood blacklist era.

Sergio Leone: Something To Do With Death
Christopher Frayling (Faber, 2000)

Historian Christopher Frayling seems to have annexed Sergio Leone as a literary product, devoting much of his career to books that share Leone's obsessive concern for detail. Frayling has insight, access and objectivity, scrupulously balancing the director's obvious genius with evidence of his cruelty, jealousy and insecurity.

Fiction

Few literary genres are taken less seriously than Western fiction. Yet the genre does not entirely deserve the disdain.

The novel that probably invented the genre is **James Fenimore Cooper**'s *The Last Of The Mohicans* (1826). Although Cooper's Natty Bumppo was the prototype Western hero, **Owen Wister**'s *The Virginian* (1902) was probably the first quality novel to define the cowboy as a heroic stereotype. Influential as that novel has been, Wister's style isn't sufficiently interesting to make this a must-read for the general reader today. In many ways, **Mark Twain**'s *Roughing It* (1872), a semi-fictional account of his travels in the Wild West, is a better read although not as central to the Western genre.

The bestselling Western novelists of the twentieth century, **Zane Grey** and **Louis L'Amour**, are as badly underrated as the genre as a whole. Grey's best work – and his personal favourite – is *The Vanishing American*, while L'Amour's finest, *Hondo*, was described by John Wayne (who starred in the movie) as "the best Western novel I have ever read".

Here is a selection of Western novels – some classic, some contemporary – that you might enjoy reading.

The Big Sky
A.B. Guthrie (William Sloane Associates, 1947)

The novel *The Big Sky* may come as a shock to those familiar with Howard Hawks's movie. The director was attracted, as so often, by the theme of professional men doing whatever was necessary, and the book's darker moments of massacre were too much for him. But Guthrie was a gifted historical novelist and his tale of frontiersman Boone Caudill brilliantly captures the texture of north-west America before the cowboys and settlers rode in. Like many Western heroes, Caudill is soon obsolete, dreaming of the days when the mountains stood "all purty in the sun" with "not a man track on her save Injun".

The Chivalry Of Crime
Desmond Barry (Little, Brown, 2000)

In this gritty, epic reimagining of one of the great Western myths, the legend of Jesse James inspires a boy to become an outlaw. Harris's novel blows away the gloss of Hollywood and the cobwebs of myth to create a portrait of the outlaw gang – and the West they lived in – that feels new, fresh and horribly real. (Intriguingly, Barry said he was inspired partly by the crime on his doorstep in the Welsh town of Merthyr.)

Close Range
Annie Proulx (Scribners, 1999)

This collection of Wyoming tales is now chiefly famous as the source of *Brokeback Mountain* but, when it was published, it was the stark, near perfect "The Half-Skinned Steer" which astonished critics, with John Updike selecting it as one of the best American short stories of the twentieth century. Many of these tales share a fatalism which some have found crushing, though Proulx's fierce love for Wyoming and its people shines through. Tales like "A Lonely Coast", portraying the solitude and random violence afflicting waitresses, have real power. A second collection set in Wyoming, *Bad Dirt*, is less bleak, yet less compelling.

Comanche Moon
Larry McMurtry (Simon & Schuster, 1997)

The most vigorous novel in the *Lonesome Dove* series, dwelling on the last Indian-fighting years of Texas Rangers Augustus McCrae and Woodrow Call. McMurtry goes beyond romanticism to capture the boredom, suffering and occasional bursts of violence which typified Western life. *Lonesome Dove* aficionados were troubled by inconsistencies between this and the more famous novel. Taken on its own merits, *Comanche Moon* is a fine novel, distinguished by a subtler presentation of Indian characters than in much of McMurtry's fiction, and succeeding not as a minutely detailed work of historical fiction, but as a gripping psychological adventure.

The Complete Western Stories Of Elmore Leonard
(William Morrow, 2004)

Before Elmore Leonard became the world's coolest writer, he earned his living writing Western stories, often for pulp magazines. Still too little known, these stories, in their economical, terse style, offer an intriguing contrast to the flowing flamboyance of works like *Get Shorty*. Leonard's Western fiction is no hack work. The films *Hombre* and *Valdez Is Coming* were based on his novels. And two of the finest stories in this anthology were spun into movies: "The Captive" became *The Tall T*, and "3.10 To Yuma" was expanded into the classic Glenn Ford Western. The dry, remote, forbidding landscape of Arizona's Apache Country is an ominous presence in many stories.

Crazy Horse: The Strange Man Of The Oglalas
Mari Sandoz (Alfred A. Knopf, 1942)

Mari Sandoz is most famous for her novel *Cheyenne Autumn* – adapted by Ford – but this remarkable history-as-novel is a magnificent portrait of a life driven and eventually ended by forces beyond the Lakota chief's control. To research it, Sandoz slept on the open prairie, lived on the Pine Ridge reservation, and interviewed many Lakota who had known Crazy Horse. A Nebraska homesteader, Sandoz creates a biography of Crazy Horse which – in contrast, say, to Dee Brown's *Bury My Heart At Wounded Knee*

– feels not like a white person's empathetic history but like a story told from the Native American viewpoint.

The Day The Cowboys Quit
Elmer Kelton (Doubleday, 1971)

Drawing on a real incident – a strike by Texas cowboys in 1883 – Elmer Kelton's novel, unusually for Western fiction, touches on themes of class struggle. The strike – sparked by the cattle barons' diktat that cowboys should not own their own cattle – is over before the book finishes but the dispute reverberates as central hero Hitch is torn between admiration for the rancher he works for and loyalty to the cowboys he manages. Kelton's passing-of-an-age novel is full of telling, often grim, detail – the cowboy wetting himself as he is hanged, the painful recovery from a pistol whipping – that brings this little-known saga to life.

Hondo
Louis L'Amour (Fawcett World Library, 1953)

Often pigeonholed as a Western writer, Louis L'Amour once said that, while he didn't resent the claim, he preferred to think of himself as a writer of the frontier – wherever that frontier might be. In *Hondo*, his debut novel, L'Amour blithely and economically captures the brutal unpredictability of frontier life in nineteenth-century Arizona as his titular hero rides through Apache country with a dog named Sam to save a woman and her son from the ravages of war. This fast-moving tale has sold over two million copies and is probably L'Amour's best Western novel.

The Last Of the Mohicans
James Fenimore Cooper (Carey and Lea, 1826)

The most famous in a series of novels chronicling the adventures of a Daniel Boone-like hero called Natty Bumppo (aka Hawkeye or Leatherstocking) and his faithful Indian companion Chingachgook, the multi-million-selling *The Last Of The Mohicans* tells of massacres, kidnappings and romance in New York province during the French–Indian war of 1754–63. With this tale Cooper coined some of Western fiction's most enduring clichés and archetypes, including the courageous, independent pioneer in tune with nature; the white man and faithful Indian servant combo;

Comic cuts

Desperate Dan

With a stetson the size of Texas and a pain threshold so high that he could shave with a blowtorch, Desperate Dan is one of the all-time Western heroes. First appearing in *The Dandy* in 1937, Dan was originally a baddie, a desperado – hence the name – but soon realized the error of his ways. In 1997 Dan struck oil, became rich and left Cactusville and *The Dandy*, only to return by popular demand. He may be nearing his 70s, but he can still lift a cow with one hand.

Lucky Luke

Bearing some resemblance to Woody in *Toy Story*, Lucky Luke is a cowboy from Belgium who, after Asterix and Tin Tin, is the third-largest-selling comic-book character in continental Europe. He has crossed Billy the Kid, helped build the West's first transcontinental telegraph and, in 1983, earned plaudits from the World Health Organization when he gave up cigarettes to chew straw. Unfortunately, as he's fictional, he doesn't count in the name-a-famous-Belgian game.

and the idea of the Native American as a noble savage – brave and cunning in war, generous, vengeful, superstitious and modest in peace. His style can seem romantic, fanciful and absurd, but for all that, Cooper's story is intriguing enough to hold your attention.

Little Big Man
Thomas Berger (Little, Brown, 1964)

Thomas Berger's unreliable memoirs of Jack Crabb, a white man raised by the Cheyenne, sparked a renaissance in the Western novel, had Henry Miller comparing him to Mark Twain and inspired one of the great revisionist Western movies. Crabb's recollections are both funny and apposite – for example, he says of Wild Bill Hickock, "He was never himself a braggart. He didn't need to be. Others did it for him." Few novels give you as good a feel for how characters in the Old West talked, walked and smelled. The movie, good as it is in parts, doesn't quite do the novel justice; the tall tales work better on the printed page. The sequel, *The Return Of The Little Big Man*, is nearly as good.

Montana 1948
Larry Watson (Milkweed, 1993)

Much as Schaefer used a child's-eye view to burnish the heroism of Shane, Larry Watson uses his child narrator

David to expose the hollowness behind the impressive façade of his war-hero uncle. David suspects his uncle of murder, watches as his dad, the sheriff, has to arrest him and realizes that he has been molesting Indian women all his life, the victims too afraid to protest because his family are so powerful in the community. This is a page-turning thriller, a gripping psychological tale of a family falling apart, and an exquisitely observed, morally horrifying portrait of a Western community. It may be more satisfying, if less charismatic, than Cormac McCarthy's coming-of-age novel *All The Pretty Horses*.

Monte Walsh
Jack Schaefer (Houghton Mifflin, 1963)

Shane may be the most famous Western novel after *Lonesome Dove*, but many consider *Monte Walsh* the greater literary achievement. Thriller writer George Pelecanos said "This is the kind of cult novel that is carried around in back packs and passed on to heirs. Men have named their sons Chet and Monte after reading it." Jack Schaefer's slow, rhythmic character study is less plot-driven than the movie adaptation, telling the story of Walsh's life, from the age of 16 until his death, in loose episodic fashion. The themes are simple – the joy of work, the difficulty of living by a code, the subtleties of male friendship – but this novel is as well crafted and durable as a really good saddle.

Nobody's Angel
Thomas McGuane (Random House, 1981)

Nobody's Angel was written as the novelist grappled with his sister's death. Witty, precise and tender-hearted, this was the novel which revealed that Montana was to become McGuane's mythic place of discovery, like Faulkner's Deep South or Chandler's California. There is so much going on in the life of ex-soldier, cowboy and whiskey addict Patrick Fitzpatrick – his sister wants to burn the house down, his grandfather wants to abscond to be in movies, his stallion seems determined to kill him – that it's easy, at first, to overlook the fact that Fitzpatrick himself is spinning out of control. *Nobody's Angel* is a resonant portrait of a family out West oppressed by "sadness-for-no-reason".

Roughing It
Mark Twain (American Publishing Company, 1872)

Mark Twain's semi-fictional, semi-autobiographical account of a six-year odyssey out West touring Nevada, San Francisco and the Sandwich Islands was hailed as a masterpiece of "wild, preposterous invention and sublime exaggeration" on publication. With this book, Twain didn't just perfect the Western tradition of tall tales, he gave Western fiction its very own vernacular and unforgettably portrayed the West as a humorous, amorally violent, rapacious and racist land of opportunity. The book is best appreciated as Twain would have envisaged it, in the University of California's scholarly 2002 edition.

True Grit
Charles Portis (Simon & Schuster, 1968)

In one of the funniest post-war Western novels, Mattie, a 14-year-old Arkansas girl in the 1880s out to avenge her father's blood calls on a Texas Ranger turned bounty hunter and Rooster Cogburn, a lawman full of grit and whiskey. The book is about Mattie, the movie is about John Wayne, and many who might have enjoyed the novel, but disliked the Duke's politics, never discovered it. But Cogburn and Mattie are two of the Western novel's immortal characters. *True Grit* has a big theme – the quest for justice – lightly treated and draws a convincing portrait of frontier life but the novel's most remarkable element is its narrator. Mattie's monologues – especially her diatribe on pigs with evil intent in their hearts – are worth the cover price alone.

Websites

General movie/TV sites

B Westerns
www.surfnetinc.com/chuck/trio.htm
The only problem with moseying down to The Old Corral site to mull over B Westerns is that you'll never want to leave. They're all here: heroes, heroines, second leads, saddle-pals, henchies, drivers, singers, kids and villains.

Classic Film And Television
http://members.aol.com/mg4273/film.htm
Thoughtful site which has useful essays on Ford, Hawks, Mann etc.

Dennis Schwartz
www.sover.net/~ozus/cinema.htm
Opinionated movie reviews, many of them of obscure Westerns, and a dodgy photograph of Dennis.

eBay
www.ebay.co.uk
Where else would you find John Wayne collectable knives, or a cheap DVD of the John Wayne/Marlene Dietrich/Randolph Scott gold rush Western *The Spoilers*?

Euro-Westerns
www.nostalgiacent.com/eurowest.htm
If you remember a Euro-Western where Stella Stevens

travels around with a coffin but can't remember the title, go here. (It's *A Town Called Bastard*, by the way.) Loads of essential and inessential info.

Images Journal

www.imagesjournal.com/issue10/infocus
A celebration of thirty great Westerns, with snappy, intelligent essays about the movies and a good overview of the genre.

Jump The Shark

www.jumptheshark.com
If you want heated discussion about the unlucky fate of Eric Fleming (Gil Favor in *Rawhide*) or the hippy episodes of *Bonanza*, go here.

Senses Of Cinema

www.sensesofcinema.com
Serious, eclectic site for cinema buffs with good essays on directors like Boetticher, Ford and Peckinpah.

Spaghetti Westerns

www.wildeast.net/spaghettiwestern.htm
A great spaghetti Western site, where, among other things, you can buy a DVD of 35 spaghetti Western trailers.

Western Films

www.filmsite.org/westernfilms.html
A good overview of the genre, with detailed analysis of some Western classics.

People

These days, if you're looking up a particular actor or director, wikipedia (http://en.wikipedia.org/wiki) is a good place to start.

Gene Autry

www.autry.com
Nice official site for the late singing cowboy.

Tremont Blackman

www.gailycolouredplasticbag.co.uk/index.php/2005/09/27/mule-trainnnnnnn-thwack/
Tremont is an "entertainer" who sings "Mule Train" and hits

himself with a tea tray. He's made a career out of it on British television and you can find scattered traces of his fame on the Internet. This site is a good place to start your quest.

Hopalong Cassidy

www.hopalong.com
Git along now – if you're a fan, you'll spend many hoppy hours here.

Gary Cooper

www.garycooper.com
Official shrine to Coop, thankfully not as laconic as he was.

Clint Eastwood

www.clinteastwood.net
A cybertemple of Clintness, full of amusing stuff, from info on his films to the story of his album of cowboy favourites – yup, Clint was singing even before *Paint Your Wagon*.

Fistful Of Leone

www.fistful-of-leone.com
The starting point in cyberspace for any Leone fan.

Sam Peckinpah

www.geocities.com/Hollywood/Academy/1912
A cracking fan site, with opinions on all of his films, and a great series of links to the best Peckinpah info on the net.

Sam Peckinpah relaxes on set.

Western soundtracks

A Western wouldn't be complete if we weren't being stirred, moved, exhilarated or amused by the score. *High Noon* wouldn't be *High Noon* without Dimitri Tiomkin's ominous soundtrack, reminding us of reckonings to come.

In the traditional Western, as Elmer Bernstein says, "music will inevitably be tied to the scenery, not the characters". His own *The Magnificent Seven* and Jerome Moross's score for *The Big Country* are fine examples of this tradition. But in the 1960s, Sergio Leone's collaboration with Ennio Morricone produced music that seemed to emerge from "within the scene", playing as much to the characters as to the landscape. They called on instruments – a wooden flute, whips, a 1961 electric Fender Stratocaster guitar – and sounds – the whistle, everyday noises that, in context, struck the audience as unusual – not often used in a Western. And, as Morricone says, "For some scenes, he [Leone] left the music alone and gave it time to express itself."

The boom in movie soundtracks came after the Western had been pronounced dead. So some of the classic scores – by the likes of Victor Young and Dimitri Tiomkin – are still unavailable. Below is a selection of the best Western soundtracks currently available, which will have you restlessly tapping your feet, or wanting to sit on a porch like Fonda in *My Darling Clementine* and contemplate life, the West and your chances in a gunfight.

John Ford's musical pioneers

The Sons of the Pioneers were one of the most successful and durable country and western vocal groups, whose biggest gift to the Western was probably a singer called Leonard Slye, better known as **Roy Rogers**. But they made a significant, none too widely known, contribution to John Ford's Westerns.

Ford liked to use folk songs in his Westerns; they are more closely associated with his work than any single composer. In *Stagecoach* (1939), for example, songs like "Shall We Gather At The River?" and "Rosa Lee" are symbols of community. He often hired **Stan Jones**, famous as the writer of "Ghost Riders In The Sky", to pen ballads for his Westerns, giving him the odd minor acting role.

With this approach, it was inevitable that he would call on the Pioneers and he cast them as the regimental musicians in his 1950 Western *Rio Grande*. For most, their songs enhance the film; for a minority, they slow the narrative down. But their rendition of "I'll Take You Home Again, Kathleen" emphasizes the cavalry's great Fordian virtue: a lot of them are Irish. That same year they sang four songs in Ford's *Wagon Master*, and in *The Searchers* (1956) they sang Jones's "What Makes A Man To Wander?" over the credits, defining the theme of the film.

Ford didn't, as is often said, give the Pioneers a new career in the movies – they'd been churning out B Westerns for decades – but he did give them long-overdue exposure to a wider audience. However, as his vision darkened, there was less scope for them in his films. Folk songs are notably absent from *Cheyenne Autumn* (1964), perhaps because they alluded to a sense of community that Ford had come to question.

Plenty of albums offer a greatest-hits-style introduction to the genre. *True Grit: Music From The Classic Films Of John Wayne* (Silva), played by the City of Prague Orchestra, celebrates some of the best work of Victor Young and Max Steiner. Also on Silva are two good anthology CDs: *The Wild West: The Essential Western Film Music 1* and *2*. When scores are re-released, check out online reviews as sound quality can vary horribly.

If it's classical music inspired by the West you're after, it's hard to beat Aaron Copland's *Billy The Kid* and *Rodeo*, not least because his music inspired so many Western soundtrack composers to come.

The Big Country
Jerome Moross (Silva)

This complete original score is one of the best in Western history, with an energy, ambition and sweep to match the film.

A Fistful Of Sounds
Ennio Morricone (Camden Deluxe)

The complete soundtracks to *A Fistful Of Dollars*, *For A Few Dollars More* and *Once Upon A Time In The West* on two CDs. A haunting, surprising, satisfying experience.

The Western playlist

There's more to Western music than twangy guitars, yodels around the campfire and songs about horses. The celluloid singing cowboy may have been popularized by Hollywood in the 1930s but cowboy ballads, sung on the first cattle drives, were a kind of folk music. Here is a playlist of some intriguing, yodel-free Western songs.

AMERICA, WHY I LOVE HER
John Wayne from *America, Why I Love Her*
In 1973 Wayne felt America was getting down on itself and recorded an album of patriotic verses, spoken to a stirring musical background. It's kitsch, compelling and sincere – much like the Duke himself.

BLUE PRAIRIE
Sons Of The Pioneers from *Empty Saddles*
Though "Tumblin' Tumbleweeds" is more famous, "Blue Prairie" is the darkest, most beautiful song from a group renowned for superb harmonies and brilliant arrangements.

BONANZA
Lorne Greene from *On The Ponderosa: Lorne Greene And His Western Classics*
Lorne's booming, unpredictable baritone makes his version of the *Bonanza* theme unforgettably unintentionally hilarious.

COWBOY
Harry Nilsson from *All-Time Greatest Hits*
Arguably the only singer who sang Randy Newman songs better than Randy, Nilsson's rendition of a cowboy's lament for his disappearing world is simply beautiful.

DESPERADO
The Eagles from *Desperado*
Marvellously mournful anthem for a doomed hero whose senses have been dulled riding too many fences.

DON'T TAKE YOUR GUNS TO TOWN
Johnny Cash from *The Best Of Johnny Cash*
Nobody did foreboding quite like Johnny Cash and this masterful tale of a mother's despairing warning to her son is sublime.

FRANK AND JESSE JAMES
Warren Zevon from *Warren Zevon*
Arty LA singer/songwriter Warren Zevon gives his affectionate, funny, commanding take on one of the Western legends.

GHOST RIDERS IN THE SKY
The Outlaws from *Playin To Win/Ghost Riders*
Stan Jones' classic has been covered by everyone from Peggy Lee to Walter Brennan and Finnish death metal freaks Impaled Nazarene, but the Outlaws' awesome rendition stays true to the original vibe, while rocking it up with electric guitars.

The Horse Whisperer
Thomas Newman (Hollywood)

If the landscape was the real star of Robert Redford's Western, Newman's score – sweeping, epic, sad, uplifting, syrupy yet with a strange harsh beauty – ran it pretty close.

The Long Riders
Ry Cooder (Wea)

The old ballads and Civil War tunes fit snugly alongside Cooder's own compositions to produce a soundtrack album more genuinely memorable than Walter Hill's movie.

The Magnificent Seven
Elmer Bernstein (Ryko)

Occasionally imperfect sound can't hide the quality of a truly timeless score, written by Elmer Bernstein aided, as he admits, by Aaron Copland.

The Missouri Breaks
John Williams (Rykodisc)

A quirky score for a very quirky Western. Not easy listening, but compelling, with a beautifully bittersweet love theme.

HIGH NOON
Tex Ritter from *Tex Ritter, American Legend*
Though Frankie Laine had the hit with this classic theme, Ritter's version – heard in the film – has more genuine desperation about it.

I'M AN OLD COWHAND
Dan Hicks and his Licks from *Striking It Rich*
Johnny Mercer's ditty – arguably the wittiest cowboy spoof ever – is beautifully rendered by Hicks, whose forte is funny, sad, drivin' violin bluegrass.

JESSE JAMES
Woody Guthrie from *This Land Is Your Land*
Folk legend Woody Guthrie wrote many songs about outlaws, feeling "they were wrong alright but not half as dirty and sneakin' as some of our higher-ups". He was inspired by Henry King's biopic to adapt Jesse's old ballad.

MAMA DON'T LET YOUR BABIES GROW UP TO BE COWBOYS
Willie Nelson from *Simply The Best*
The most iconic of the songs Willie Nelson wrote for *The Electric Horseman*, an unforgettable evocation of the glamour and pathos of the cowboy life.

RAWHIDE
Frankie Laine from *Greatest Hits*
Frankie Laine's über-histrionics give this cattle-drive song exactly the right rollin', rollin' momentum. The Blues Brothers' version matches Laine's for manic energy.

THE STREETS OF LAREDO
Eddy Arnold from *Cattle Call*
Originally an Irish folk ballad about a man dying of a sexually transmitted disease, this was remade into a classic ballad about a dying cowboy, never heard better than in Eddy Arnold's measured, melodic rendition.

THEY'RE HANGING ME TONIGHT
Marty Robbins from *Gunfighter Ballads And Trail Songs*
A true Westerner, Marty Robbins was the king of the cowboy ballad. The plaintive melancholy of this tale of love turned murderous suits his voice, which has a touching frailty about it as if he's always choking back a sob.

WHERE HAVE ALL THE COWBOYS GONE?
Paula Cole from *The Fire*
Sparky pop hit in which Paula Cole, liberated from backing Peter Gabriel, laments the lack of John Wayne, prairie songs, happy endings and cowboys. Despite her offers to wash dishes and do the laundry for a man who drinks beer and pays the bills, she's still alone as the song ends.

YELLOW ROSE OF TEXAS
Stan Freberg from *The Very Best Of Stan Freberg*
Mitch Miller's pompous hit version is thoroughly deconstructed by the professional musical assassin Stan Freberg in a version which deteriorates into an argument with his "smart alec Yankee drummer".

Pat Garrett And Billy The Kid
Bob Dylan (Sony)

The best way not to get upset by Bob Dylan's distracting, pointless presence in Peckinpah's movie is to remind yourself he's there for the soundtrack. And he does a fine job: this is haunting, tragic – with the occasional foot stompin' interlude – and more focused than the movie.

Red River
Dimitri Tiomkin (Naxos)

Entire scores from the great Wayne Westerns are still too rare so we should be grateful to John Morgan, who restored the score, conductor William Stromberg and the Moscow Symphony Orchestra for recapturing the epic thrill of one of Tiomkin's finest soundtracks.

Unforgiven
Lennie Niehaus (Varese)

Brief, beautiful, understated, Lennie Niehaus's score for Eastwood's farewell masterpiece is poetic, harsh and not at all clichéd. Clint wrote the soaring "Claudia's Theme" himself – if he weren't genuinely gifted he'd be insufferable.

Wigwam Vol. 2
Karl Ernst Sasse, Wilhelm Neef, Wolfgang Meier (Cinesoundz/Allmedia)

An intriguing compilation of soundtrack music from eight East German Westerns, giving an entertaining insight into how Germans, under Soviet occupation, were influenced by the Wild West and the epic Western score. All the better for the odd clippety-clopp of horses' hooves.

Picture Credits

The Publishers have made every effort to identify correctly the rights holders and/or production companies in respect of the images featured in this book. If despite these efforts any attribution is incorrect, the Publishers will correct this error once it has been brought to their attention on a subsequent reprint.

Cover credits

James Stewart in *Winchester '73* © Universal.

Illustrations

CORBIS Bettmann/CORBIS (8) Christie's Images/CORBIS (16) Kobal 20th Century Fox (31) 20th Century Fox (32) Malpaso (43) Crossbow Productions Warner Bros Creative Design (55) 20th Century Fox (79) Republic Pictures (81) Proteus Films (123) Kay-Bee Pictures New York Motion Picture Corporation (165) Columbia Pictures (183) Ford-Smith Productions Warner Bros (191) Warner Bros Seven Arts Productions (202) Argosy Pictures Universal Studios Home Video (203) Argosy Pictures Universal Studios Home Video (207) Paramount Pictures Rafran Cinematografica San Marco Production (217) Batjac Productions The Alamo Company MGM/UA Home Entertainment (223) Paramount Pictures (233) Columbia Pictures Film Production Asia Huayi Brothers Taihe Film Investment Xi'an Film Studio China Film Co-Production Columbia Tristar Home Entertainment (244) HBO Roscoe Productions (262) Arness Productions CBS Television Filmaster Productions (263) Moviestore 20th Century Fox (26) RKO Radio Pictures (29) Pandora Filmproduktion JVC Entertainment Networks Newmarket Capital Group 12 Gauge Productions (45) 20th Century Fox Campanile Productions (57) Arturo Gonzalez Producctiones Cinematograficas Constantin Film Produktion Produzioni Europee Associati MGM Home Entertainment (67) Paramount Pictures (72) Paramount Pictures Salem-Dover Productions (77) Cinema Center 100 Productions Stockbridge-Hiller Productions Paramount Home Video (83) Castle Rock Entertainment Columbia Pictures Rio Dulce Warner Home Video (85) Alpha Productions Mirisch Corporation MGM Home Entertainment (89) Paramount Pictures (90) John Ford Productions Paramount Pictures (93) 20th Century Fox (98) Charles K. Feldman Group Monterey Productions MGM/UA Home Entertainment (112) C.V. Whitney Pictures Warner Bros (115) Paramount Pictures (117) Walter Wanger Productions Warner Home Video (128) Paramount Pictures (137) Malpaso Warner Bros (138) Warner Bros Seven Arts Productions (145) Walter Wanger Productions Warner Home Video (154) Arturo Gonzalez Producctiones Cinematograficas Constantin Film Produktion Produzioni Europee Associati MGM Home Entertainment (159) United States Pictures (174) Paramount Pictures (204) Warner Bros (228) Pathe Entertainment (242) Columbia Pictures Los Hooligans Productions (255) Wrather Productions Apex Film Corporation WEA Video (267) CBS Television (269)

PICTURE CREDITS

Index

Page references to films discussed in the Canon chapter and people described in the Icons chapter are indicated in bold.

INDEX

INDEX

INDEX

Y

Z

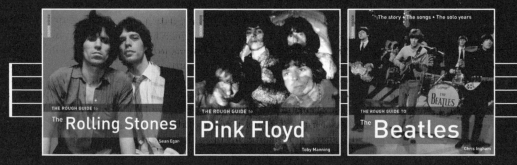
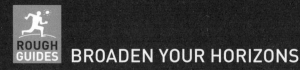

Rough Guides presents...

BROADEN YOUR HORIZONS

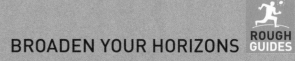

UK & Ireland
Britain
Devon & Cornwall
Dublin **D**
Edinburgh **D**
England
Ireland
The Lake District
London
London **D**
London Mini Guide
Scotland
Scottish Highlands & Islands
Wales

Europe
Algarve **D**
Amsterdam
Amsterdam **D**
Andalucía
Athens **D**
Austria
The Baltic States
Barcelona
Barcelona **D**
Belgium & Luxembourg
Berlin
Brittany & Normandy
Bruges **D**
Brussels
Budapest
Bulgaria
Copenhagen
Corfu
Corsica
Costa Brava **D**
Crete
Croatia
Cyprus
Czech & Slovak Republics
Dodecanese & East Aegean
Dordogne & The Lot
Europe
Florence & Siena
Florence **D**
France
Germany
Gran Canaria **D**
Greece
Greek Islands

Hungary
Ibiza & Formentera **D**
Iceland
Ionian Islands
Italy
The Italian Lakes
Languedoc & Roussillon
Lanzarote **D**
Lisbon **D**
The Loire
Madeira **D**
Madrid **D**
Mallorca **D**
Mallorca & Menorca
Malta & Gozo **D**
Menorca
Moscow
The Netherlands
Norway
Paris
Paris **D**
Paris Mini Guide
Poland
Portugal
Prague
Prague **D**
Provence & the Côte D'Azur
Pyrenees
Romania
Rome
Rome **D**
Sardinia
Scandinavia
Sicily
Slovenia
Spain
St Petersburg
Sweden
Switzerland
Tenerife &
    La Gomera **D**
Turkey
Tuscany & Umbria
Venice & The Veneto
Venice **D**
Vienna

Asia
Bali & Lombok
Bangkok

Beijing
Cambodia
China
Goa
Hong Kong & Macau
India
Indonesia
Japan
Laos
Malaysia, Singapore & Brunei
Nepal
The Philippines
Singapore
South India
Southeast Asia
Sri Lanka
Thailand
Thailand's Beaches & Islands
Tokyo
Vietnam

Australasia
Australia
Melbourne
New Zealand
Sydney

North America
Alaska
Baja California
Boston
California
Canada
Chicago
Colorado
Florida
The Grand Canyon
Hawaii
Las Vegas **D**
Los Angeles
Maui **D**
Miami & South Florida
Montréal
New England
New Orleans **D**
New York City
New York City **D**
New York City Mini Guide
Orlando &
    Walt Disney World® **D**

Pacific Northwest
San Francisco
San Francisco **D**
Seattle
Southwest USA
Toronto
USA
Vancouver
Washington DC
Washington DC **D**
Yosemite

Caribbean
& Latin America
Antigua & Barbuda **D**
Argentina
Bahamas
Barbados **D**
Belize
Bolivia
Brazil
Cancùn & Cozumel **D**
Caribbean
Central America
Chile
Costa Rica
Cuba
Dominican Republic
Dominican Republic **D**
Ecuador
Guatemala
Jamaica
Mexico
Peru
St Lucia **D**
South America
Trinidad & Tobago
Yúcatan

Africa & Middle East
Cape Town & the Garden Route
Egypt
The Gambia
Jordan
Kenya
Marrakesh **D**
Morocco
South Africa, Lesotho
    & Swaziland
Syria

Available from all good bookstores